Peasants in the Promised Land

Kty 9

Jaroslav Petryshyn

with
L. Dzubak

Peasants in the Promised Land

Canada and the Ukrainians

1891-1914

James Lorimer & Company

TORONTO 1985

Cover Design: Dreadnaught
Maps: David Hunter
Illustrations are reproduced courtesy of: Public Archives Canada (cover, 1, 2, 6, 9, 10, 12, 13, 18), Saskatchewan Archives Board (3, 5), Glenbow Archives (4, 11, 14, 15, 16), Manitoba Archives (7), Ontario Archives (8), Archbishop's Chancery, Winnipeg (17).

Canadian Cataloguing in Publication Data

Petryshyn, Jaroslav, 1947-
    Peasants in the promised land

ISBN 0-88862-926-5 (bound). — ISBN 0-88862-925-7 (pbk.)

1. Ukrainians — Canada — History. 2. Ukrainians — Government policy — Canada — History. 3. Canada — Emigration and immigration — History. I. Title.

FC106.U5P47 1985   971'.00491791   C85-099400-4
F1035.U5P47 1985

The publication of this book was assisted by Multiculturalism Canada.

James Lorimer & Company, Publishers
Egerton Ryerson Memorial Building
35 Britain Street
Toronto, Ontario   M5A 1R7

6 5 4 3 2 1   85 86 87 88 89 90

CONTENTS

In memory of Ann Petryshyn (Dec. 12, 1926–Oct. 6, 1983)
Dear Mom: We all loved you. And we miss you.

PREFACE

Ethnic minorities in Canada have come of age. Unfortunately, their histories have not. A wide gap remains between the reality of Canada as a multicultural society and the portrayal of Canada in history texts as a bicultural nation. Until recently, historians, preoccupied with constitutional evolution and leading political figures, have given the country's historiography an Anglo-Celtic and/or Francophone perspective. This has left unexplored a critical aspect of Canada's development: the ethnic minorities. What follows, I hope, is a small dose of corrective medicine.

Perspectives

This book details the formative period of Ukrainian immigration and settlement in Canada. It attempts to view these processes from the perspective of both the host society and the immigrants. To understand the relationship between the two, I explore the intellectual and social roots of each community. Just as the Ukrainians came equipped with their own *Weltanschauung* or conception of life, so too did Canadians have their own ideas and perception of themselves. When one group's view ran counter to the other's, a clash was inevitable.

In the late nineteenth century and early twentieth century, Canada was imbued with Imperialist thinking. Nowhere was this more evident than in the image of the North-West. It was argued that new settlers upholding British-Canadian traditions would flood into the great, unpopulated hinterland and, ultimately, enable the Dominion to shed its peripheral existence within the Empire and assume equal partnership with Great Britain. The dream of populating the North-West with the "superior" Anglo-Celtic race, however, received a rude and unexpected check when strangers appeared, unabashedly ignorant of "British institutions and principles of life."

That the Imperialist concept was subverted was the result of the influential roles played by railway and business interests, which set aside social desires for economic needs. The ascendancy of a philosophy that stressed economic utility over cultural desirability struck a fatal blow to the notion of a British-Canadian West. It was within this social and ideological context that the arrival of the Ukrainians evoked a strong response from Canadians.

As East Europeans of various nations kept streaming in, not only to settle the land but to mine its resources, build its transportation system, and stoke the fires of its industries, a debate raged among Canadians on the cultural, social, and political acceptability of these foreigners. What was to be done about the newcomers whose language was incomprehensible, whose religion was "priest-ridden but Godless," and whose education appeared non-existent? How would they fit into the Anglo-Celtic model? Assimilation, with all its varieties and nuances, seemed the solution. The church and the public schools were deemed logical agents. Indeed, a great deal of the history of relations between the host society and the Ukrainians revolved around Anglo-Canadian attempts to "Canadianize" and, concomitantly, to "evangelize" the stubborn, wayward peasants.

From the Anglo-Celtic point of view, the process of assimilation was complicated not only by the immigrants themselves, but by the dualistic nature of Canada. The Roman Catholic Church, supported by a powerful French-speaking hierarchy in the North-West, posed a serious threat to the essentially Protestant "Canadianization" efforts. Seeking to preserve and nurture the French presence in the North-West, Roman Catholics promoted bilingual education and separate schools. They saw the immigrants (most of whom were nominally Catholic) as their allies, albeit unequal ones. The Ukrainians were truly caught in the middle of a struggle between two different views of Canada. Pyrrhic victories were won by both sides until the advent of World War I foreshadowed the ascendancy of Anglo-Celtic conformity. Indicative of the tensions and bitterness was the conflict over the bilingual schools.

But what of the Ukrainians themselves? These peasants from Galicia and Bukovyna came to Canada to escape their native environment. Yet in a sense the old world came with them. In the new land, the essence of their heritage would act as a buttress against the pressures that threatened their established avenues of existence. A part of the immigrant would always remain in the old world, yearning for the import of security it provided. An important aspect in delineating the immigrant experience, then, revolves around the *Weltanschauung* of their homeland at the turn of the century. The old country greatly affected the gestalt of the immigrant community in the new country; it would condition the response of the Ukrainians to the political, social, religious, and economic milieu in which they found themselves.

The lure of free land provided both a great opportunity and a terrible punishment. Isolation and hardships suffered by peasant pioneers in a primitive environment were genuine. No matter how well suited the Ukrainians may have seemed for life on the prairies, to be thrown into a virgin land of immense proportions and climatic extremes was a traumatic experience. How they survived, both physically and mentally, is yet another aspect of their experience which is explored in this book.

Adjustments of the old to the new characterized the development of Ukrainian social and political institutions. The churches, schools, and reading halls of the old world could not be transplanted intact, but the foundations of familiar institutions formed a base on which the appropriate Canadian adaptations could be built.

The process of adaptation, however, was wracked with conflict. Old world attitudes interacting with new world realities led to factionalism within the Ukrainian immigrant community. Inevitably, the divisions were intensified through the immigrant press, where fierce verbal battles raged throughout the period under consideration.

Ultimately, whether individually or collectively, Ukrainians sought to establish a niche which made them an integral part of the Canadian fabric and yet preserved the viable remnants of their past. In the process, they became inextricably intertwined in a society caught up in fundamental and profound change.

Acknowledgements

The research and writing of this study has posed a number of challenges in terms of character and scope. Rather than adopting an encyclopedic approach which attempts to leave no stone unturned, I have treated this study as a synthesis. As such, new research material has been incorporated with existing works, both published and unpublished. An enormous debt is owed to a rising generation of Ukrainian and Ukrainian-Canadian historians, whose handiwork is evident in the pages that follow. Orest Martynowych, Andrij Makuch, and John Paul Himka, through their published and unpublished articles and theses, are but the most obvious contributors.

The volume could not have been completed in its present form without the "Edmonton brain trust." Andrij Makuch, Nestor Makuch, and David Lupul performed their tasks as research assistants diligently and judiciously. Andrij Makuch, especially, went beyond the normal bounds of duty; he responded cheerfully to the demands placed upon him, systematically and meticulously uncovering new source material while compiling lengthy files of published and unpublished works.

Critical to the project was Luba Dzubak. For a year she gave her mind and soul to it, meticulously translating Ukrainian into English, compiling the raw research into manageable form and, in no small way, contributing to parts of the rough draft. Besides moral support, her keen eye and sober judgment were invaluable in weeding out inconsistencies and idiosyncrasies.

Appreciation is also extended to Myron Momryk, who aided in locating a number of photographs. Thanks also go to Lillian Zuzak and Dr. William Zuzak. The former not only typed the manuscript but used her editorial experience much to the enhancement of the volume. The latter read portions of the manuscript and made numerous suggestions and comments. Moreover, both extended the warm glow of friendship through a "time of troubles."

Acknowledgement is in order to colleagues at Grande Prairie Regional College. Many took an interest and the time to enter a smoke-filled, paper-littered office to offer words of encouragement. All exhibited the collegiality necessary to foster scholarly activity in a small college setting. Also, I wish to thank the Grande Prairie Board of Governors who granted the sabbatical which allowed for the completion of the manuscript.

I am indebted to Ted Mumford and Lise Gunby, editors at James Lorimer, for their support, helpful suggestions, and assistance throughout the editing/publishing of this work.

Finally, I am grateful to Multiculturalism Canada, which assisted the publication of this book.

Errors of commission, as well as those of omission, are my responsibility.

J.P.
Oshawa, Ontario, 1985

PART I

SETTING THE STAGE

CHAPTER 1

THE DUAL FRONTIER

The North-West existed as two radically different frontiers during the second half of the nineteenth century. In reality, it was a harsh, prosaic environment, a land of "frost in the foothills, drought on the plains, hail storms in the summer and fire in harvest"[1] where life would be hard and failures all too common. However, to most Canadians in 1867, the North-West stood as a splendid metaphor — an incomprehensible stretch of Eden where the plains met the horizon and where hundreds of millions of acres of "fat black earth" awaited the human touch to yield their treasures of stored fertility. It was envisioned as a huge uniform landscape set at the edge of the new Dominion, warranting occupation and development.

The Imperialist Vision of the North-West

The vastness of the region staggered the imagination, obscuring the variety of its topography. First tangible proof of the country's possibilities was found in the fertile and easily cultivated valley of the Red River. Along the river's sluggish course, land which had once served as a mecca for fur traders and buffalo hunters was, by the 1860s, a "patchwork of grain fields and clusters of farm buildings."[2] The bottom of a post-glacial lake in nature's distant past, the valley contained nearly 7,000 square miles of rich soil where the bulk of Manitoba's population was destined to settle. For those venturing across the formidable Canadian Shield, this valley was the first and lasting impression of the North-West.

Yet toward the west, the land sloped upward and was broken by two escarpments before reaching the foothills of the Rockies. A line from Pembina to the Pasquia Hills could mark the edge of the first escarpment. Encompassing an area of 105,000 square miles — almost the size of the United Kingdom — this land promised agricultural potential, but the great diversity of its soil and rainfall ensured that the future settlers' success would very much depend upon their choice of land and the whims of nature. The same could be said of the second escarpment, which embraced most of the future province of Alberta. An area of nearly 134,000 square miles (between the 49th and 54th degrees of latitude), it too had its own character. From the semi-arid conditions in the south to the outreaches of the Peace River and beyond, this portion of the North-West misled potential agriculturalists as much as it encouraged them. To the would-be Canadian nationalist, however, these subtleties were blurred; the North-West represented, in the poetry of its empty landscape and the glory of its sunsets, infinite potential for success.

The results of the first scientific survey, completed by Captain John Palliser in 1860, had been disheartening. He reported to the British government, which had commissioned the survey, that the large central-southern portion of the area was an extension of the American desert. Appropriately named the Palliser Triangle, the area was subsequently mapped by surveyors who strove to disprove Palliser's interpretation. Professor John Macoun, a botanist, traversed the area on various trips from 1872 to 1881. His optimistic conclusions were summarized in his book, *Manitoba and the Great Northwest,* which maintained that the topography was not as inhospitable as Palliser had suggested. By also asserting that Alberta's climate, "by a freak of nature," was suitable for farming, Macoun upheld the arguments of those anxious to portray a positive image of the west.

Expansionists, promoters, government officials, Canadian Pacific Railway agents, and Canadian Imperialists, captivated by the promise of unlimited potential for development in the North-West, adorned it with magical qualities. In 1884, for example, a government publication described the District of Alberta by quoting Tennyson:

> For I dipt into the future, far as human eye could see
> Saw the vision of the world, and all the wonders that could be
> Saw the heavens fill with commerce argosies of magic soils
> Pilots of the purple twilight, dropping down with costly bales.[3]

A halo of superlatives shrouded the North-West, obscuring the fact that one could not live on imagery alone.

Even before Confederation, the North-West was seen as indispensable to Canada. The *Toronto Globe*, in 1862, solemnly declared:

> The non-occupation of the North-West Territory is a blot upon our character for enterprize. If Canada acquires this territory it will rise in a few years from a position of a small and weak province to be the greatest colony any country has ever possessed, able to take its place among the Empires of the earth. The wealth of four hundred thousand square miles of territory will flow through our waters and be gathered by our merchants, manufacturers and agriculturists. Our sons will occupy the chief places of this vast territory, we will form its institutions, supply its rules, teach its schools, fill its stores, run its mills, navigate its streams. . . .[4]

Such grandeur rested not only on the North-West's resource and agricultural potential, but also on the character of the society that was to develop. As one writer noted, "the destiny of a country depends not on its material resources; it depends on the character of its people."[5] The assumption was that "the institutions and social practices of the East were to be transplanted to the North-West . . . and these in turn would inevitably develop in the North-West to the point of lighting the way to a new and better civilization for all of Canada . . . a place of renewal and improvement of national institutions."[6] Such views, at first promoted by expansionists such as George Brown and William McDougall and nationalists such as Charles Mair and others of the Canada First Movement, developed, in the 1880s and 1890s, into the widespread Imperialist conception of the nation's future.

Imperialism, in the Canadian context, was a sentimental and intellectual movement. Imperialists were those who believed in the inherent superiority of everything British and who fervently desired a "closer union of the British Empire through economic and military cooperation and through political changes which would give the Dominions influence over imperial policy."[7] Their sentiments were aptly expressed in the following verse:

> Shall not we through good or ill
> Cleave to one another still?
> Britain's myriad voices call
> Sons be welded, each and all
> Into an Imperial whole,
> One with Britain, heart and soul
> One life, one flag, one fleet, one throne.[8]

In the last two decades of the nineteenth century, Imperialists were plentiful, filling magazines and newspaper columns with their proselytizing rhetoric. George Denison, George M. Grant, George Parkin, George Wrong, John Willison, Vincent Massey, Arthur J. Glazebrook, Edward Peacock, Sir Edmund Walker, and Sir Joseph Flavelle, a veritable Who's Who of the nation's intellectual, business, and political elite, articulated Imperialist ideas. They were followed by others: Stephen Leacock, Andrew Macphail, and William Grant, who, with their own indelible writing, contributed to the Imperialist concept. Their prose could be read in such prestigious journals as the *Queen's Quarterly, The Round Table, University Magazine,* and the *London Times.*[9]

The Imperialists were a unique breed. Looking backward to the United Empire Loyalists (the centennial of their settlement in Canada was celebrated in 1884) as the historical basis for their contentions, and to the concomitant agrarian way of life as the most principled of enterprises, they loudly proclaimed the superiority of Anglo-Saxondom. Aligning themselves with the Americans and British, they believed that "some of the best blood of the British race flows in our veins; and our system of government, our social organizations and our social habits are of a standard which is scarcely equalled in any country in the world."[10] At a time when theories of racial superiority were popular and accepted, Imperialists sincerely believed that heredity could explain society's misfits: "paupers and criminals are generally such because of inherent defects."[11] Canada's political and social institutions — its preference for law and order and its capacity for self-government — were equated with the genius of the British nationality. They were, the Imperialists believed, a product of the moral, social, and political spirit that emanated from the greatest Empire the world had ever known.

It was only the presence of Quebec that defied the Imperialists' "desire for a sense of Canadian nationality rooted in the same language, identical traditions and similar racial characteristics."[12] Yet the Imperialists considered the French-Canadians of small consequence because the rapid growth of the English-speaking section of the population would, in time, exert total dominance over the Canadian nationality, especially in the North-West.[13] The foundation of a British civilization in the west had already been laid by the Hudson's Bay Company, which quickly taught the native peoples to respect the British and the North-West Mounted Police (founded in 1873), who preserved not only law and order but also British institutions in the North-West.[14]

The emergence of a strong Imperialist movement in a country only a quarter-century old was largely the result of the Dominion's trying economic circumstances in the 1880s and early 1890s. After the economy reached a peak of activity in 1873, expectations were heightened for further growth, but a period of depression began which did not lift until

1896. It was a depression of international proportions. World production by heavy manufacturers had outpaced demand, while the escalating output of foodstuffs and raw materials from the United States, Canada, and other developing countries where Britain had invested capital also depressed prices. Between 1873 and 1878, agricultural prices declined by 26 per cent.[15] In the United States this meant "a sharp contraction in railway and building construction; in Great Britain, a severe contraction of credit and a steep decline in foreign trade."[16] Because of her external dependencies — exports, foreign capital, and immigration — Canada was in a vulnerable position. After 1875, the severity of the depression in Canada was intensified by crop failures. Except for brief spells, the economy did not revive for another two decades. The stagnation in the economy increased anxieties about Canada's prospects.

The Imperialists awaited impatiently the nation's future. Unfortunately, the immediate road to Canada's ultimate destiny seemed blocked. Economic depression, the undermining of agrarian values through rapid industrialization and urbanization, the emergence of *nouveau-riche* entrepreneurs who shunned aristocratic traditions, the increasing emigration from Canada to the United States, and the ever-present danger of annexation by the republic to the south seemed to weaken the very fibre of British Canada. With increasing emphasis, the Imperialists placed their aspirations on Canada's hinterland — the North-West.

As yet sparsely populated, the North-West would surely become the home of large numbers of people. The northern climate would quickly weed out all undesirables, leaving only hardy agriculturalists to perpetuate the way of life considered ideal by the Imperialists. The emigration of Ontarians to the United States could be stemmed by sending them to the North-West. From northern Europe would come those decreed capable of appreciating liberty and democracy. When tempered by the climate, they would quickly adapt to British-Canadian norms. In the context of Imperialist thinking, then, the North-West would ensure the continuation of the best that British traditions had to offer. Indeed, with control over their own unadulterated hinterland, the Imperialists would no longer be provincials or colonials but Empire builders. The conquering of that vast territory by settlers upholding British-Canadian values would enable Canada to shed its peripheral existence within the Empire and assume equal partnership with Great Britain.

The ascendancy of Imperialism during this period cannot be underestimated. Attempts to define the "Canadian nationality" permeated the political and social milieu. Imperialist thought reached its zenith at precisely the time mass emigration to the North-West began. Idealists who desperately wanted to guard the quintessence of the British race in

America were to suffer a traumatic setback when Ukrainians
\the crownlands of Galicia and Bukovyna disembarked on Canada's shores.

The Settlement Imperative

Sir John A. Macdonald, gazing westward from the windows of the new
Dominion's Parliament buildings, thought in terms of Canada's "manifest destiny" when he conceived the notion of adding this territory to
his Confederation. It could not be otherwise. In 1867, Canada consisted
only of Ontario, Quebec, New Brunswick, and Nova Scotia — a fine
foundation for a British nationality upon the North American continent, but a truncated one. From the beginning, the far-reaching goal of
Confederation was the development of a transcontinental nation.
Therein lay the success of Canada. The acquisition and exploitation of
the North-West was indispensable to the rounding out of Confederation.

The consolidation of this huge tract of land within a national
framework did not proceed smoothly. Rupert's Land and the North-
West Territories were acquired from the Hudson's Bay Company in
1870, in exchange for 6,313,900 acres (1/20 of the surveyed lands south
of the North Saskatchewan River)[17] and £300,000. The way for Canada's westward expansion was cleared, but not without a rebellion from
its indigenous population. It took a military expedition and the promise
of a province before the white flag of the Riel republic was supplanted
by the Union Jack. Thereafter, there was still the problem of how to
weld this vast real estate to the Dominion. Transportation and settlement had to be initiated quickly, especially when the greedy, rapacious
Americans were looking on.

Perhaps, it was believed, Canadians could follow the example of the
Americans, who had successfully combined railway construction and
settlement. Success in settling the American west seemed to be based on
two simple factors: free land was made available, and railways, in addition to making the land attractive by supplying a transportation system,
promoted settlement. Business interests had played an important role.
While the American government sat back and looked on, the settlement
of the American west seemed to follow a natural course of events. While
industrial companies brought immigrants into the country who could
supply new industries in the east with cheap labour, the natural expansion of the existing United States population and those immigrants seeking land progressed westward. The benefits were immediately visible.
Had not the movement of people into the Mississippi Valley and be-

yond provided a great stimulus to the development of the United States? Could not the North-West do the same for Canada? Railways into the North-West would make the lands valuable, and a generous homestead policy would attract settlers. Macdonald believed this to be the only logical course. Under his direction, the government launched a transportation and settlement policy.

The first step in this national scheme happened to land on the new province of Manitoba, "the first square upon the chequer board."[18] Under the Manitoba Act of 1870, public lands were withheld from the control of this diminutive province and given to the federal government; further, the act provided that all "ungranted or waste lands" in the entire North-West would be "administered by the government of Canada for the purposes of the Dominion."[19] Ottawa had been rather heavy-handed. Macdonald was now free to pursue a double-edged public lands policy. Its first expression was the Dominion Lands Act of 1872, which entitled settlers to a quarter section (160 acres) free of charge. The second was the awarding of substantial grants of land to railway corporations to induce them to build the necessary transportation system to bring the settlers into the territory. Macdonald felt deep anxiety as he pushed his policy through. The American west was expanding rapidly and threatened to deprive the North-West of prospective immigrants.

Macdonald's first attempt at a government-sponsored railway project, hatched in desperation and the murky world of political intrigue, ended in scandal. Nevertheless, in 1880 a contract was drawn up with Stephen's syndicate of Montreal. The newly formed Canadian Pacific Railway received $25 million and 25-million acres of land as well as tax exemptions and protective privileges in exchange for the promise to construct a transcontinental railway entirely through Canadian territory by 1890. Canada's future was riding on the deal; Macdonald was risking the country's fiscal well-being, pledging its credit to the utmost to rush the C.P.R. across the continent. "Let us not be faint-hearted; let us borrow freely," became Macdonald's national message to the skeptics.

The federal government's policy of western settlement and a railway to the Pacific drew generally favourable reaction from Canadians, although in the case of the railway there was furious debate over the terms, speed, and method of construction. In the years immediately following Confederation, Canada was enjoying a rising prosperity brought about by the reconstruction boom in the United States following the Civil War, and by the Prussian boom in Europe.[20] By 1873, moreover, its territories were assembled — not only had the North-West been snared, but also British Columbia and Prince Edward Island. (Only stubborn Newfoundland remained aloof.) With only 3.5 million inhabitants occupying the Canadian half of the continent, what was needed were people and a transportation-communication network. The Dominion government began its search for citizens. To this end, by 1872, its annual expenditure for the promotion of immigration exceeded half a million dollars.[21]

Macdonald was not in office when the depression settled in, having alienated the electorate in the so-called Pacific Scandal. However, with the economic crisis worsening throughout the latter half of the 1870s and the dull Mackenzie and anemic Liberals unable to stem the tide, Macdonald had his chance for a political comeback. Western settlement and a transcontinental railway were Macdonald's two original planks, but now he added a third: protective tariff. Eastern manufacturers, feeling the pinch of American competition, demanded some form of tariff protection. Macdonald agreed readily. A protective tariff would contribute to his railway and colonization scheme. The North-West, after all, could only be exploited if there was a strong industrial base in the east. And of course the wily Macdonald knew that the tariff would be politically popular. Set in place in 1879, the tariff became the third door to an east-west nation. Canada, despite the depression, could now stabilize its economy internally. With these policies carefully executed, surely the great, empty, forlorn prairies would quickly fill up with bustling humanity, providing the east with raw materials and a market for its manufactured goods.

Great expectations resulted in a land boom in 1882. The construction of the railroad had begun, and regulations allowed colonization companies to purchase lands distant from the railway. The government contracted 26 companies to colonize 2,842,742 acres. Nine were completely unsuccessful at placing settlers; the others put together placed a total of only 1,243 settlers.[22] The enthusiasm of the investors, most of whom were British, cooled when it became evident that settlement would not happen overnight. Many speculators lost their investments through cancelled contracts, or merely became stuck with bad investments.

The National Policy, conceived in a time of optimism but implemented in a time of depression, failed. The C.P.R. had been built by 1885, but the nation had also acquired a huge national debt and the North-West remained virtually empty; by 1891, the population of Manitoba and the North-West Territories barely reached a quarter of a million. Canada's economy stagnated. The brief trade revival of 1879 through 1883 dissipated and the general financial improvement in most countries from 1888 to 1890 was negated in Canada by poor crops and bank failures.[23] With the personal income of Canadians declining vis à vis their American counterparts, Canada witnessed a mass exodus of its population from Ontario and Quebec, mostly to the United States. As

Table 1-1
Population of Canada, 1871-1891

	Decade 1871-1881	Decade 1881-1891
Total population	3,485,761 (1871)	4,324,810 (1881)
Natural increase	923,077	544,670
Immigration	342,675	886,177
Emigration	426,703	922,418

Table 1-1[24] illustrates, between 1871 and 1891 more people left Canada than entered.

The flight of Canadians to the United States particularly incensed the Imperialists. Even more painful to them was Britain's apparent lack of concern over where her emigrants were destined. The United States received the large majority of British emigrants throughout the 1870s and 1880s. In addition, there were movements to annex Canada, at least economically, to the United States, some Canadians claiming that free trade with Americans was the natural manner in which to proceed. To the Imperialists these developments amounted to treason. Why could the Canadian emigration not be diverted to the Canadian west? Why did Britain not send her emigrants to Canada? Why could Canada not develop free-trade relations with Britain? These were questions that perplexed many an Imperialist.

The gloomy situation was further complicated by animosity between the French and English. Attention was drawn to the west by the second Riel rebellion, the hanging of Riel and the negative repercussions in Quebec, and the abolition of French and bilingual schools in 1890 by the Manitoba government. Canada's vulnerable spot, its dual nature, was laid open to exacerbation. With ambitious politicians, such as Honoré Mercier, and reactionary bigots, such as D'Alton McCarthy, fanning the flames, ethnic and religious strife between the "founding races" became the index of the 1880s and 1890s. If the country was economically crippled, it was equally handicapped politically by the counter-productive forces emanating from Quebec and Ontario.

When Macdonald died, 6 June 1891, it appeared that the goals he had set for Canada — settlement of the North-West and a prosperous east-west economic system based on railways and tariffs — was but a bold, imaginative dream. Canada was not a happy country.

CHAPTER 2

CANADIAN IMMIGRATION AND THE NORTH-WEST

Canadian immigration policy until at least the latter half of the 1890s was molded, in large part, by the idea of "manifest destiny." Canada, inevitably, was to evolve within the British Empire. Collaterally, immigrants from the United Kingdom and western Europe were to set the standard. They were to populate Canada's empty interior. Yet for a myriad of reasons such a flow failed to materialize. Detrimental to immigration was the depressed state of the Canadian economy throughout the 1880s and 1890s and the unequal competition from the United States. Until the American hinterland was filled, the Canadian counterpart would remain the "last best west."

The stream of settlers to the north did not begin until the second half of the 1890s. Although land-hungry people did come from the United Kingdom, the United States, and western Europe, there were others trekking from strange parts of the world. Indeed, there was a shift of emigration centres from northwestern to southeastern Europe. In the end, the influential roles of the railway and business interests in the North-West forced greater consideration of economic needs rather than social desires; immigrants thought to be culturally undesirable became, in the scheme of things, acceptable for their economic value.

The policy of accepting large numbers of immigrants who belonged to "marginally desirable races" culminated during Clifford Sifton's term as Minister of the Interior. Under his astute direction, Canada's immigration policy matured from an abstract, unworkable program based on social considerations to a successful, well-administered plan geared to satisfying the economic requirements of the North-West. But as the policy became a success in terms of the number of settlers, it was subjected to strong criticism by those who had hoped for a strong, free, British-Canadian nation.

The Nation Awaits

It was not a lack of ideas that hampered the first immigration efforts. As early as 1872, Thomas White, prior to his appointment as Minister of the Interior in 1873, outlined a detailed plan in the *Canadian Monthly and National Review*. White believed that "the chief reservoir from which emigrants may be drawn to Canada, and the place therefore where the most active exertions should be put forth in the interest of immigration, is the United Kingdom."[1] British emigration to the United States had averaged more than 100,000 per year since 1847, and from 1849 to 1854, more than 200,000 per year. In the period from 1860 to 1865, 719,433 immigrants from Britain settled in the United States.[2] White believed that the success of immigration depended on the government's ability to divert the British exodus to Canada.

White divided governmental responsibilities into two categories: inducements for the British to emigrate to Canada and assurances that the Dominion was a "home worthy of their acceptance."[3] He noted that the government had first to inform the populace of the United Kingdom about Canada through lectures and the mass distribution of printed matter. Booking agents who helped to disseminate information, he added, should therefore be compensated by the Canadian government, in addition to receiving percentage payments from shipping companies on the tickets sold. White also emphasized the reception of immigrants: "it is impossible to over-estimate the importance of this feature of a complete immigration policy. . . . The value of first impressions has passed into a proverb, but with no people are first impressions more influential than with the average emigrant on his arrival in a new country."[4] He recommended that distribution points at Halifax, Hamilton (for immigrants entering Canada via New York), and Point Levis have ample buildings and competent staff. St. John's, Montreal, Toronto, London, Fort William, and Fort Garry (Winnipeg) also had to be equipped with comfortable and convenient immigration depots.[5]

White's formula for the acquisition of desirable immigration seemed reasonable. In fact his outline of the administrative details was used in the early 1890s by the Conservatives and modified by a subsequent Minister of the Interior, Clifford Sifton. But it was simply not profitable to settle immigrants in the North-West during the early 1870s.

The climate in the North-West did not allow for simple methods of agriculture. First and foremost, the western farmer had to contend with the uncontrollable forces of nature. Dust storms, insects, early frosts, droughts, high winds, and heavy rainfall at harvest time destroyed crops. Because of the short growing season, limited precipitation at times, and dry soil, special methods of cultivation and hardy, fast-growing strains of wheat were needed. The North-West had to await technological innovations in agriculture. These were occurring in the United States but needed time to develop. John Deere's steel plough had been introduced in the United States in the 1830s, but Oliver's chilled steel plough, "a milestone in the advance across the prairie," was commonplace only in the mid-1870s.[6] The technique of dry farming, worked out in Utah and California in the 1850s and 1860s by the trial-and-error method, was indispensable to soil conservation, yet its use was little known in Canada. The mechanical grain elevator, which was destined to become "as characteristic a feature of the prairie landscape as the native vegetation," was introduced only in the early 1880s.[7]

The most important of these advancements in agriculture was the discovery of hardier strains of wheat. Although Red Fife Wheat, which matured ten days earlier than any other variety, had been brought into Ontario from eastern Europe in 1842, the number one hard strain still had to be developed. It was not widely used in Manitoba until the 1890s. New strains of wheat played a significant role in advertising the Canadian North-West. They were displayed at various agricultural exhibitions and were frequently awarded high honours. For example, the Manitoba exhibit at the agricultural exhibition in Islington, London (1895) was awarded the gold medal in the world-wide competition.

Yet there were difficulties. The price of wheat was significantly influenced by transportation costs. After the completion of the C.P.R. in 1885, the wheat farmer received the price determined at Fort William, less C.P.R. freight and elevator charges.[8] But only rapid expansion of transportation facilities and an increased volume of wheat reduced transportation costs. The remoteness of the prairie farmer from markets for most of the latter half of the nineteenth century was indeed an economic burden.

The tariff which was part of the National Policy of 1879 was also an economic burden to the wheat grower. Manitoban farmers relied on American manufacturers for their implements, but the tariff was 25 to 35 per cent of the cost.[9] It was only after 1896, when new and powerful western interests demanded lower tariffs, that "considerable decreases were granted, particularly on articles entering into the cost of production of western agriculture, such as farm implements and tools, binder twine, and barbed wire."[10]

The Railway's Stake in Immigration

Following the initial land boom of 1882, railroads and land companies remained in the forefront of immigration work, although the results were discouraging to all. The federal government had granted large tracts of land to railways to alleviate the financial burden of developing the North-West. By orders-in-council of 9 July and 14 October 1879, the odd-numbered sections in surveyed territory were reserved for railways. Lands five miles wide on each side of the railway were withdrawn from homestead, or preemption entry, and placed on sale. Until 1889, the lands in the North-West were classified according to their proximity to the railway and were priced accordingly.[11]

The government exempted C.P.R. land from taxation for 20 years after the first patent for land was issued, withdrawing the exemption only if the land was bought or sold. The railway naturally delayed patenting lands, which caused large financial losses to municipalities. The *Free Press* severely criticized this exemption, and the Manitoba Legislature responded with a resolution offering assistance "to any municipality desiring to test the legality of the tax evasion, but which alone could not afford to come to grips with such a powerful corporation."[12]

The C.P.R. handled land policy through its Land Department, and the sale of land through the Canada North-West Land Company. These two agencies were instrumental in developing towns. Following the example of railways in the United States, the railway sold all town and village plots located on its line to the Canada North-West Land Company. Town sites were entrusted to four trustees: two from the railway and two from the company. The net proceeds were divided equally between the two agencies. The agreement was in effect during the railway's construction and for one year after its completion between Winnipeg and the Pacific coast.[13]

The railway had much to gain from immigration, and everything to lose if large numbers of settlers failed to materialize. A thriving population in the west would not only provide the railway with clientele, but would also provide labourers for railway expansion and increase the value of railway property. The C.P.R. was most conscientious in its promotion of settlement.

Despite crop failures in the 1880s due to droughts and early frosts, the widely distributed C.P.R. literature continued to describe the prairies in glowing terms. Indeed, when a report was circulated that land between Moose Jaw and Calgary was unsuitable for cultivation, the company went so far as to establish ten experimental farms in this region.[14] An immigration department was set up in London, England with Alexander Begg as its agent, while on the European continent H.H. Toe Laer promoted immigration under the supervision of the London office. The C.P.R. also sponsored lectures and a travelling exhibition van which toured England equipped with information and displays of produce. Return men, settlers from the North-West sent home to describe their experiences, were used from 1891 to 1895, but their "accomplishments were not commensurate with the expense involved."[15] The railway's work in both Europe and the United States was hampered by the high cost of transportation.

In North America, the greatest enemy of the railroad's immigration work was competition from the United States. Prior to the completion of the Canadian railway route through northern Ontario, immigration traffic was diverted through the United States, where it fell prey to American agents extolling the virtues of the American west and exaggerating the treacheries of the Canadian North-West. American agents boarded trains carrying settlers from New York to Canada and told stories of milking ice-cream from frozen cows; they did succeed in diverting many immigrants.[16]

The C.P.R. responded with a campaign to capture the attention of Ontarians who might be considering emigration to the United States. A railway exhibition car, "gaudy in appearance," was sent through the province. Return men, notably government officials from the North-West, "preached Manitoba" to eastern Canadians. Excursions were arranged for those seeking homes in the North-West. The first, in August of 1887, was jointly organized by the Manitoba and Northwestern Railway and the Canadian Pacific. At harvest time, railway agents recruited workers in eastern Canada and transported them free of charge to the west. In the first year of these harvest excursions, 3,000 workers arrived in the North-West and were encouraged to settle. Another form of excursion was that reserved for journalists and editors of newspapers. The railway took great care to make these complimentary trips enjoyable, and expected favourable reviews in return.

Although the C.P.R.'s promotional efforts were often in vain, the *Manitoba Free Press* was correct in noting that "the effort of the Canadian Pacific Railway in the matter of settling Manitoba and the North-West has been as great and probably more methodical than the government's."[17]

The Rudiments of an Immigration Policy

The North-West Territorial Assembly and the Manitoba government saw the development of natural resources within their territories as crucial to their future. Both governments took active roles in promoting settlement. They had an uneasy relationship with the Canadian Pacific, and at times supported restrictions of the railway's power. The western governments themselves were severely restricted by the federal government's control over their territories, assets, and funds. It was not until 1892, for example, that the Territorial Assembly was given jurisdiction over the manner in which it spent its federal grants.[18]

In 1888, the Territorial Assembly began to recruit immigrants aggressively. It secured free passes from the C.P.R. for its immigration agents and solicited grants from agricultural societies to cover the costs of sending delegates to eastern Canada to encourage immigration. Charles Mair, N.F. Davin, and Edward Fitzgerald were hired to author immigration literature. Articles and advertisements were sent to British publications and displays of western resources were prepared for agricultural exhibitions.[19] The Assembly also attempted, unsuccessfully, to get funds from the federal government to engage two permanent immigration agents in Great Britain and four temporary agents in Montreal, Quebec, Toronto, and Chicago.[20]

A jurisdictional dispute arose. In 1890 the Assembly complained of "the yearly appeals we have made to the Dominion Government for assistance in the work of populating the many million acres of Dominion land in this country and the cold response with which they have been met."[21] The federal government took the position that Parliament should not vote grants to the provinces or territories because promoting immigration was a federal and not a local matter.[22] This unfortunate dispute created a rift between Ottawa and the North-West on the crucial issue of how best to finance the interests of the North-West and only diverted energies away from the promotion of immigration.

Based on the example of the United States, the federal government's assumption was that once free land was made available and financial interests were rallied, immigration would automatically follow. Such was not the case. The federal government realized only in the 1890s that it had to assume a more active role in peopling the prairies; the financial interests in Canada were not powerful or diverse enough to do the job themselves. They could not force low steamship rates or offer transportation subsidies, and they could not guarantee employment upon arrival. They also did not offer the diverse attractions in terms of employment opportunities that allowed for the open-door policy existing in the United States.

Immigration policy was administered by two government departments: the Department of Agriculture and the Department of the Interior. The Department of Agriculture, through its Immigration Branch, regulated the immigration effort abroad, while the Department of the

Interior controlled immigration within Canada. It was not until 1892 that the entire immigration effort was put under one administrative roof. In that year the Immigration Branch became part of the Department of the Interior.

The earliest criticism of the government's immigration policy was that it was spasmodically and ineptly executed.[23] To 1891, the government had only five immigration agents on the continent: in England, Ireland, Scotland, France, and Germany.[24] The Conservatives begrudged money spent on the cultivation of immigration. From a maximum of $426,860 spent in 1885, immigration expenditures declined steadily to a low of $100,091 in 1890.[25] By that year, the Department of Agriculture had become so atrophied that it was unable to spend the amount voted to it by Parliament.[26] But there were also suggestions that money had been squandered — on useless advertising and incompetent agents.[27] Trade and labour organizations objected to the admission of artisans and mechanics at a time when the labour market was overstocked.[28] Politicians, it seemed, could do no right when it came to immigration. There were complaints because the government was slow to pay agents and shipping companies their bonuses, waiting until they proved that the immigrants had been settled and intended to stay on the land.[29] Other nations paid agents simply for booking the passage of emigrants to their lands. Furthermore, the government did not understand the restrictive emigration laws of some European countries. A rude shock was received when John Dyke, Canadian immigration agent in Hamburg, was arrested and jailed six months for inciting emigration.

Although the Department of Agriculture reported that more than 900,000 immigrants were brought to Canada from 1882 to 1891,[30] it was criticized for sweeping all newcomers entering Canadian ports into the statistics regardless of their final destinations. As one politician noted, Canada was often just a stop along the way to the United States.[31] The inflated head count only raised false expectations for the North-West. And of course the government neglected to report the number of emigrants leaving Canada for the United States.

Unfortunately for those who anxiously awaited the development of the North-West, the government learned the rudiments of immigration work by trial and error. Procedures improved somewhat under the guidance of Thomas Mayne Daly, minister of the newly consolidated Department of the Interior from 1892 to 1896. The aggressive Daly replaced incompetent immigration agents and paid the competent ones faster, arranged with steamship companies to distribute literature in Great Britain and Ireland, raised the commission for booking agents to equal that offered by Australia, and provided an additional bonus of $5 for every agent making a booking to Winnipeg. To end the practice of inflating immigration statistics he devised a system which recorded homestead entries only. Immigration agents were sent to work in France, Belgium, and Norway.

Daly also reformed the system of immigrant reception. A government agent accompanied all immigrants travelling across Canada to prevent American agents from diverting settlers to the United States. He arranged a "very thorough system of taking care of the immigrant and seeing that he is properly dealt with, from the time he arrives in Canada until he is finally located on his homestead in Manitoba or the Territories. . . ."[32] To this end, government immigration buildings were upgraded to provide more space and better facilities and train service was improved for a faster, more comfortable journey westward.[33]

Clifford Sifton as Minister of the Interior

Despite the efforts of Thomas Daly and various governments, business interests, and individuals, the total number of immigrants entering the country actually declined severely in the first half of the 1890s, reaching an all-time low of 16,835 in 1896.

But the election of Wilfrid Laurier's Liberal government and the appointment of Clifford Sifton as Minister of the Interior in 1896 signalled a dramatic turn in Canada's ability to attract immigrants. Although changing world economic conditions and the shift of emigration centres from northwestern to southeastern Europe contributed to the sudden influx of settlers, much credit has to be given to Sifton.

Born on 10 March 1861 near London, Ontario, Sifton grew up in a tough-minded, sober Irish household where business acumen and politics were allied with the Protestant work ethic. His father, a farmer cum oil producer, railway contractor, and Grit politician, moved his family to Manitoba in the late 1870s after the Mackenzie Liberals awarded him a contract to build part of the Pacific Railway. The younger Sifton went east, however, where he received a first-rate classical education at Victoria College, Cobourg (1876–1880). Returning to Manitoba after receiving his B.A., he was called to the bar in 1882 and for a brief period practised law in Brandon where his parents were comfortably settled.

Intense, ambitious, and well-tutored in the art of politics, Sifton was elected Liberal M.L.A. for North Brandon in 1888. Thomas Greenway, the Liberal premier, recognized Sifton's oratorical and organizational talents, appointing him Attorney-General and Minister of Education (1891–1896). The youthful cabinet minister rose swiftly to prominence, overshadowing Greenway and in effect becoming the real leader of the

Manitoba Liberals. When Laurier assumed power in 1896, it was Sifton who negotiated controversial amendments to the province's education act with the new Prime Minister. Sifton's skilful, hard-nosed bargaining impressed Laurier, who lost no time in conscripting Manitoba's leading politician into the federal cabinet.

Sifton brought to Ottawa not only an understanding of the economic needs of the North-West but also the ability to negotiate profitably with the government of Manitoba, which at that time was the only provincial government in the prairies. He had no doubts about the enormous economic potential of the west, but first and foremost it had to be populated. He energetically proceeded to put the government's immigration policy in order.

First he dealt with the railways and the huge tracts of land that had been set aside for them. The railway companies had delayed selecting their land not only, as in the case of the C.P.R., to prolong tax exemptions, but also to determine which lands would be most valuable after settlement patterns had developed. As a result, about 24,000,000 acres lay idle. Sifton terminated this system of granting land and pressured the railway companies into choosing their allotments. Thus, by 1900, large chunks of "railway lands" had been freed for general settlement.

Sifton next moved against land companies, which were also tying up substantial blocks of productive land. These blocks had been sold by railways or granted by the government throughout the 1880s and 1890s. The land companies had also been unsuccessful in their settlement schemes. By forcing land companies to meet settlement requirements within a specified time, Sifton put new vitality into the settlement process. Few land companies survived his term in office, and only one was granted a charter.[34]

While land in the North-West was being cleared for settlement, Sifton set about offering the immigrants a better welcome. C.P.R. freight and passenger rates to western Canada were lowered.[35] A commissioner of immigration at Winnipeg became responsible for seeing that immigrants were received, cared for, transported, and settled on homesteads.[36] The Department of the Interior had worked directly with agents in Europe, but in 1903 the Canadian Immigration Office was established in London under the High Commissioner. And a Superintendent of Immigration was appointed to oversee all aspects of immigration work from Ottawa.[37] Immigration halls were developed in about 100 western centres,[38] and those en route were improved.

Sifton proceeded to refine the nation's immigration policy on three premises. First, the North-West and Canada would not prosper in the long term without farmers and farm labourers.[39] Second, no nationalities would be excluded if they were likely to become successful agriculturists. Third, immigration work would be carried on "in the same manner as the sale of any commodity — on practical business principles through advertising."[40]

Sifton's immigration policy was distinctly different from its precursors. Not only did his department expend enormous financial and human resources to attract newcomers from the traditional sources — the British Isles, the United States, and northwestern Europe — but it also made concentrated efforts in eastern Europe. Throughout his term as minister, Sifton staunchly defended this course of action. He even went so far as to characterize the preferred immigrant as a "stalwart peasant in a sheep-skin coat born on the soil, whose fore-fathers have been farmers for ten generations, with a stout wife and a half-dozen children."[41]

By 1896, East Europeans had already begun emigrating to Canada, although in limited numbers. As early as 1872, for example, the Canadian government began negotiations with Mennonites, who, although technically of German origin, were considered to be Slavs because they came from southern Russia. A block of land, exemptions from military service and oaths, freedom of education, and low rates from Hamburg to Winnipeg had attracted more than 6,000 of them by 1879.[42] Hungarians from the coal mines of Pennsylvania had been encouraged to migrate to Canada by one of their leaders, Count Esterhazy. By 1885 they had established themselves as farmers in the Hun Valley of Saskatchewan. They were so successful that they prompted the Department of Agriculture, the Allan Shipping Line, and the C.P.R. to send Theodore Zboray back to his homeland to recruit more Hungarians for the Canadian west. It was not long before Ukrainians learned from their Hungarian acquaintances in the Austro-Hungarian Empire of the advantages offered in Canada. By 1891, the first Ukrainian settlers had arrived.

More significant to the advance of Ukrainian immigration, however, was the arrival in 1895 of Dr. Joseph Oleskiw,* a Ukrainian professor of agriculture. He ventured to Canada to acquire first-hand, detailed, and accurate information on settlement opportunities, outlining the requirements of his Ukrainian countrymen who were seeking "a country with ample food, free land . . . willing to accept thousands of farmers who, although possessed of modest means, are diligent and thrifty. . . ."[43] Oleskiw was welcomed in London by the Canadian High Commissioner and Thomas Daly met with him twice: for two hours on 26 August in Edmonton and later in Ottawa on 2 October. Oleskiw was asked to prepare a memorandum of general proposals regarding Ukrainian immigration, which Daly promised to submit to

---

* For a discussion of Oleskiw, see Chapter 4.

cabinet. Oleskiw did so but nothing of substance occurred until Sifton took office. Sifton gave Oleskiw's proposals serious attention and appointed him Canada's unofficial immigration representative of Galicia, a province in the Austro-Hungarian Empire heavily populated by Ukrainian peasants.

The results were impressive; when Oleskiw said thousands, he meant it. In 1896 Canada received only 1,275 Ukrainian immigrants; this figure rose to nearly 5,000 in 1897 and continued to escalate in the subsequent years until by 1900 more than 27,000 Ukrainians had made the Dominion their home. By 1914, when the Great War cut off immigration abruptly, approximately 170,000 Ukrainians had entered Canada.[44]

The Numbers Game: Recruitment in Europe

Clifford Sifton's efforts to tap the vast pool of agrarians in continental Europe were persistent. In January of 1899 he appointed W.T.R. Preston Inspector of Emigration in Europe. His instructions to Preston were blunt: "Immigration we must have. Go overseas and look over the ground. None of the old officials know anything about it. If you can solve the problem or make any reasonable suggestion likely to be successful, it will be adopted. You will have all the money that may be necessary."[45]

Preston and his small staff began by compiling a list of all booking agencies on the continent whose addresses they could track down. Then Preston set off on an "inspection and investigation" tour which took him to all parts of Europe.[46] He found that Canada's promotional work on the continent was in a state of chaos. The government had arranged to pay booking agents a bonus of £1 per head on agricultural workers and domestic servants who were booked for Canada and who actually settled there. The results were quite unsatisfactory. Preston discovered that Canadian immigration literature sent to these agents commissioned by the Canadian government was simply piled up in storehouses or cellars.[47]

The reason for this state of affairs was evident to all but the Canadian government. Most European countries had restrictive emigration laws. While the authorities in Germany, Austria-Hungary, and the Scandinavian countries, for example, did not prohibit emigration outright, they did thwart those who would induce citizens to leave their country.[48] Those directly involved in immigration propaganda were liable to prosecution and imprisonment. To complicate matters, Preston discovered that emigration laws and police regulations throughout Europe were, in many cases, contradictory. Even if agents were operating within the law of the country, local regulations left the agents open to the "most summary action on the part of the police."[49] Indeed, in most European nations the police had arbitrary powers; they could seriously interfere with legitimate business.[50] Consequently, some agents Preston called upon declined absolutely to discuss immigration matters and advised Preston to return to London.[51]

It was sober advice; Canadian government officials engaged in immigration promotion were generally not welcomed by the authorities. Sir Donald Smith (Lord Strathcona), Canadian High Commissioner, found himself in difficulty when early in 1899 he travelled to Hamburg, rented a room at the Hamburger Hof, and proceeded to invite booking agents to confer with him. Fortunately, he stayed in Hamburg for only one day, because on his return to London Lord Strathcona discovered that he had created a small diplomatic crisis. J. Chamberlain, Secretary of State for the Colonies, informed him that "the Prime Minister, Lord Salisbury, had received an official visit from the German ambassador, Count Hatzfelt, who pointed out to him that the High Commissioner . . . had broken the German law and also violated the police regulations of Hamburg in his attempts to incite booking-agents to perform emigration work."[52] The German ambassador bluntly told Lord Salisbury to advise Lord Strathcona to keep out of Germany in future or he would be arrested.[53]

Despite the odds, Preston did meet with certain "influential individuals"[54] who were willing to work on Canada's behalf if suitable arrangements could be made to protect them. Through "judicious contacts" Preston arranged for a number of booking agents and their representatives from Holland, Sweden, Norway, and Germany to confer with him in Bremen and Hamburg in May of 1899. At these meetings a consensus was reached: a syndicate could be established to carry on emigration propaganda throughout Europe if the Canadian government redirected its bonus system to the syndicate and gave it exclusive rights to the project. There was a third condition: the Canadian government had to protect the anonymity of the syndicate members.[55] The syndicate, in return, was willing to be judged by "actual results at the ports of debarkation in the Dominion."[56]

Preston cabled this information to Ottawa in code, representing the syndicate as "a combination of people who would make a success of immigration work because they had representatives in practically every country in Europe and they would make such a combination as could make a very successful propaganda."[57] Sifton cabled his approval in principle and suggested that a provisional agreement be drafted.[58] He also sent his Deputy Minister of the Interior, James Smart, to London, where he was to confer with Lord Strathcona, aid Preston in the negotiations, and make final recommendations to Sifton.[59] Through September and October of 1899 Preston and Smart held a number of conferences with representatives of the syndicate, which was officially designated the North Atlantic Trading Company (NATC). On October 20 an agreement was concluded. Sifton had two reasons for sanctioning this clandestine contract: the promotional efforts of Canadian officials had been obstructed, and the system of paying bonuses to individual booking agents had failed.

Two key groups made up the NATC: booking agents and officials of steamship companies. Both groups shared a common goal — to profit from emigrants. Steamship lines made huge profits not only from human cargo but also from the "emigration hotels" which they built in every major port city on the European continent.[60] The booking agents were hired by the steamship lines to recruit the emigrants. The NATC was a convenient central agency for both signing parties; Canada secured its immigrants, and the "trading company" got its business.

Booking agents were in a position to carry on propaganda activity that was generally illegal. They were licensed both by the steamship lines and by the government for the purpose of selling tickets on behalf of steamship lines. As long as they simply sold tickets, they did not violate emigration laws. In selling tickets they had some latitude vis à vis propaganda. As licensed agents they could, for example, send immigration literature from one country to another without transgressing the statutes of the country in which they were residing.[61] Those booking agents associated with the NATC were supplied with Canadian immigration literature and paid to pass it on to potential emigrants across national boundaries.

Distributing information through official booking agents, however, was but one method employed by the NATC. The NATC also employed unlicensed agents (most of whom worked as secret emigration agents for steamship lines) to conduct personal visits to "restrictive" nations. They visited communities not as representatives of a government or company but as private individuals. They stayed in a village or town for a short period (usually not more than a month), circulating among the populace to identify potential emigrants. In some cases they distributed literature clandestinely. When it was feasible they enlisted the aid of local figures — mayors, teachers, clergymen, and minor officials (such as passport officers) — who, for financial considerations, could provide lists of possible emigrants.[62] A network of covert emigration agents and local contacts was well established in Europe.[63]

The NATC also made considerable efforts to contact immigrants already bound for Canada from whom they could obtain the names and addresses of relatives, friends, or other connections in the countries from which they had emigrated. Indeed, the company employed a Mr. Salinger who was a Canadian government employee with the Department of the Interior in Liverpool. Because of his knowledge of seven languages, his job was to interview immigrants for the department. He also had access to the "emigrant hotels" of the different steamship lines. He obtained thousands of useful names and addresses for the company. The NATC paid him a stipend through W.T.R. Preston.[64]

The activities of the NATC involved substantial expenditures and a certain number of risks which could only be undertaken for a "suitable" reward. The company was not actually paid for direct bookings but for the propaganda work it performed. This accounts for the vagueness of the contract. No precise mathematical formula was instituted for bonuses other than a head count of the immigrants disembarking at Canadian ports. The company did not have to prove that it had in fact provided the inducement for the immigrants who came to Canada. Conceivably, a large number of the immigrants for whom the NATC received bonuses came to Canada without the assistance of the company.

The actual procedure for ascertaining the amount owed to the company was simple. All "continental immigrants" landing in Canadian seaports were met by officers of the Department of the Interior. After a medical examination, all immigrants were questioned on a variety of subjects, including their occupation and what their intentions were in coming to Canada. If they indicated that they were agriculturalists (or domestic servants), they were then credited to the NATC, provided all the other stipulations of the contract had been fulfilled. Afterwards the reports of American immigration officers were checked to see which immigrants had applied to cross the border into the United States; those immigrants were then deducted from the credit of the company. W.P. Scott, Superintendent of Immigration, was in charge of counting immigrants and deciding which fulfilled the requirements of the contract. When Scott was satisfied that the number of immigrants who fulfilled the agreement was correctly noted, he sent a cheque (usually monthly) to W.T.R. Preston, who countersigned it over to the NATC.[65]

Despite this imprecise method of accounting, the Department of the Interior considered the contract to be effective within the parameters of "general propaganda work." Preston, for example, firmly believed that between 1900 and 1906, "we have got 100,000 to 125,000 people, who, but for this company would not have known about Canada."[66] The total number of immigrants who arrived from the countries covered by the NATC contract (which ran from 1899 to 1906) was 128,108. The total sum in bonuses paid to the company was $241,099.51, which amounted to payment for only about 25 per cent of the total number of immigrants who arrived in Canada.[67] Obviously then, the terms of the contract were strictly enforced by the Department of the Interior. The Department was, in fact, satisfied with the results; on average it spent $1.72 per head on immigration from the continent of Europe compared to $4.64 per head on immigration from the United Kingdom.[68]

The extent of the government's contract with the NATC was not revealed to the Canadian Parliament until July of 1905 when the information was leaked from the Auditor General's account.[69] The government was bitterly attacked by the Conservatives. Under intense scrutiny from the opposition and the pressure of adverse public opinion, Frank Oliver, who in 1905 replaced Sifton as the Minister of the Interior, cancelled the contract on 30 November 1906. Any further probes into the company, especially into the identity of its members, might have resulted in negative repercussions for its members and Canadian officials in Europe.

Yet the NATC was not a fraud. Evidence suggests that it carried out its obligations diligently; certainly its promotional work on behalf of the Canadian government was extensive. Sifton and his officials believed that they received full value for the cost — value which continued to be translated into immigrants long after political pressure forced the government to curtail its agreement with the company.

Sifton's follow-up of Oleskiw's initiatives and his bold and ingenious (if not strictly legal) dealings with the NATC facilitated the arrival of large numbers of Ukrainians as well as many other groups. It also added to the tension between socio-cultural and economic motivations and concerns. Although the arrival of these Slavs could easily be defended and their contributions judged on economic grounds, the tensions, problems, and frustrations throughout future decades would amplify and aggravate the social differences between the existing population and the foreign newcomers.

The vision of the Canadian west as the last British outpost was to be shattered. It would be impossible to make Britishers out of Ukrainians. Instead, the intertwining of the old and new communities would call up a definition that required mutual concessions. In the Canadian west, institutions retained their British traditions, but the character of the population changed. Sifton's policies were the fatal blow to the Imperialist notion of a British-Canadian west. They also cleared the way for the growth of Canada's unique multicultural character.

CHAPTER 3

THE SEEDS OF EMIGRATION

While the Canadian North-West lay empty, the Austrian crownlands of Galicia and Bukovyna staggered under the weight of humanity. Every patch of soil was replete with redundant peasants preoccupied with the realities of life — overpopulation, shortage of land, unemployment, political and social oppression, and starvation. By the latter half of the nineteenth century, their precarious existence had triggered the forces of emigration. For hundreds of thousands, emigration presented the only hope of survival. In the context of basic human needs it was "an absolutely natural, indispensable and inevitable phenomenon."[1]

Peasants of Galicia and Bukovyna came to Canada to escape their native environment, yet in a mental sense that environment came with them. It was evident in their attitudes and in the institutions they transplanted, at least in part. Old world baggage served a myriad of purposes, from promoting characteristics palatable to the host society to acting as a barrier against assimilation. Also contained within it were the seeds of internal political and religious factionalism. The roots of these emigrants cannot be ignored, then, because to appreciate the Ukrainian *Weltanschauung* that existed in Galicia and Bukovyna is to understand the experience of the Ukrainians in Canada.

Peasant Life in Galicia and Bukovyna

Galicia and Bukovyna were a microcosm of the patchwork of nationalities that comprised the Austro-Hungarian Empire. Among the multitude of ethnic groups contained within the two provinces, the Ukrainians were the most numerous. Of the 4,100,000 Ukrainians in the Empire on the eve of the First World War, more than 3,350,000 lived in eastern Galicia and 300,000 in northern Bukovyna. In Galicia, they made up 43 per cent of the population, followed by the Poles and Jews at 40 per cent and 10 per cent, respectively. In Bukovyna, more than 40 per cent of the population was Ukrainian, with the bulk of the remainder consisting of Romanians, Germans, and Jews.[2]

Despite their numerical strength, the Ukrainians were at the bottom of society in both provinces. Romanian boyars (noblemen who owned grand estates) formed the upper class in Bukovyna, garnering economic and political power, while in Galicia it was the Polish nobility which controlled the affairs of state.* The most striking characteristic of the Ukrainians in the two crownlands was their predominantly rural, rustic nature; more than 90 per cent of all Ukrainians in the Empire were engaged in agriculture.

Galicia, although the largest province, occupying more than one-quarter of Imperial Austria's total area, was grossly overpopulated. In 1869, it contained 5,444,689 inhabitants; by 1890, the figure had risen to 6,607,816.[3] Ivan Franko, a noted Ukrainian historian and publicist, has calculated that in 1869 there were 69 people per square kilometre; in 1880 there were 76, and in 1890, 84.[4] The Galician population increased annually by about 60,000; the average birth rate was 45.2 per thousand, 7.2 higher than in the rest of Austria-Hungary.[5] Correspondingly, there were 8.6 marriages per thousand, while in other Austrian provinces the figure stood at 5 to 6 per thousand.[6]

Marriage, by both the Galician and Bukovynian peasant, was deemed very important. A wife meant another pair of hands and a new piece of farming equipment or possibly a patch of land as dowry. She would also bring children; the birth of as many as ten was not unusual. Indeed, the inability to bear children was considered a disgrace, and lawful grounds for separation.[7]

As these peasants divided their diminutive landholdings among offspring, the number of even smaller farms increased. This division of land gained rapidity toward the end of the nineteenth century. In 1859 there were 799,783 taxed landholdings in Galicia; in 1882, this figure stood at 1,420,000.[8] Small landowners, with property averaging three to four hectares, numbered 500,000 in 1848. This rose to almost 800,000 in 1875.[9] In 1900, 49 per cent of the landholdings in Galicia and 56.6 per cent in Bukovyna were less than two hectares.

At the same time, estates held mainly by the Polish nobility grew

---

*See Appendix I for discussion of political status

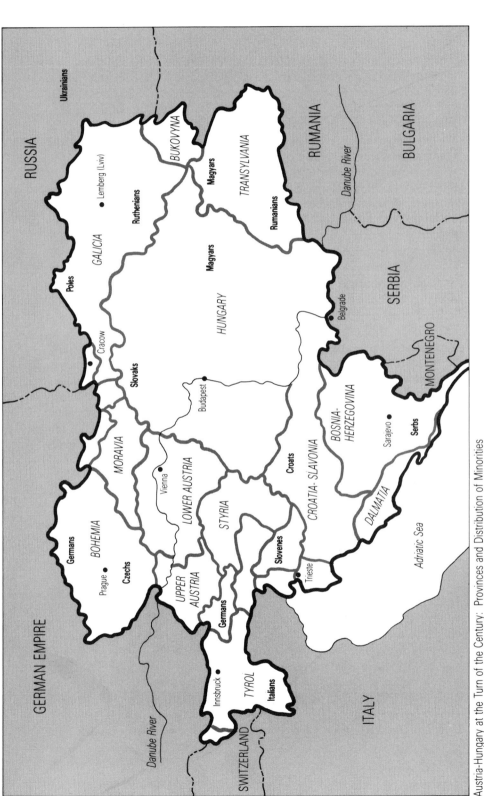

Austria-Hungary at the Turn of the Century: Provinces and Distribution of Minorities

larger in size and smaller in number. In 1848 there were 5,000 large estates; in 1859 this figure shrank to 4,500, and in 1876 to barely 2,000. The average large estate in 1848 was not more than 500 hectares; by 1887 it was about 2,400 hectares.[10] In 1900, 61 per cent of the land in Bukovyna and 55.3 per cent of the land in Galicia was held by 5.3 and 5.4 per cent, respectively, of the total number of landowners — the holdings in each case being over 10 hectares.[11]

The peasant found himself in a precarious position. Using primitive tools — wooden ploughs, flails, and sieves —, unable to secure artificial fertilizer because of the expense, and ignorant of crop rotation, his productivity per hectare was dismally low. By comparison, the large estate owners could afford factory-built steel ploughs and threshing machines. Moreover, many owned distilleries, cheese factories, and dairies. As Galicia and Bukovyna moved toward a capitalist economy in agriculture, the peasant discovered that he could not support his family, let alone compete with the estate owner.

Land taxes and limited access to pastures and forests also contributed to the depressed condition of the peasantry. With the abolition of serfdom in 1848, peasants no longer had free use of manorial grazing land or wood for heating and baking. A peasant from the village of Lytvyn, for example, reported that an oak tree cost 25 gulden.[12] A gulden, worth 46 cents U.S. or 2.5 French centimes in the early 1870s, could support an agricultural worker for two days.[13] Although peasants argued their claims to pastures and forests before the courts, by 1881, out of 32,000 cases, the peasants had won only 2,000.[14] The court costs involved — by 1881, an estimated 15-million gulden[15] — were a sufficient impetus to cause bankruptcy.

The peasants were victims of a second economic change. After the abolition of corvée in 1848, which meant that peasants were no longer required to provide some free labour to their lord, the central government in Vienna assumed the responsibility of paying the lords compensation. In the 1850s, however, the burden was shifted from the state treasury to the Galician and Bukovynian peasantry. As late as the 1880s, these indemnization payments amounted to 50 per cent of regular taxes. In comparison, Bohemian, Moravian, and Silesian payments amounted to only three to seven per cent of regular state taxes.[16] Additional payments to nobles included a compensation in the amount of 66-million gulden for their abandoning of the monopoly on the production and sale of alcohol in the late 1880s.[17]

In addition to court costs and taxes, there were young children to be christened and older children to be wed, relatives to be buried and feast days to be celebrated. Feeding and clothing families in the long winters after bad harvests also depleted resources. To cover costs, peasants borrowed money. In some regions of Galicia in the 1870s, nearly 90 per cent of the population was in debt.

Indebtedness frequently led to total financial ruin. With interest rates on loans ranging from 52 to 104 per cent, many peasants defaulted and were forced by the courts to auction their land. Others voluntarily sold their plot to pay off debts. Between 1867 and 1883, approximately 35,000 peasant farms in Galicia were auctioned. By 1875, the landless peasant proletariat exceeded 500,000.[18] In Bukovyna, nearly 90,000 peasants sold part or all of their land between 1868 and 1892.[19]

The money-lender was usually the tavern-keeper, and most of the tavern-keepers in Galicia were Jewish. According to the census of 1900, Jews made up 85 per cent of those who produced or distributed alcoholic beverages. This explains much of the anti-Semitism of the East European peasantry; a peasant who lost his land through default on a loan usually vented his feelings on the village money-lender.

Political and social problems blighted the peasant's life, making death from malnutrition and disease all too common. Starvation was particularly widespread in Galicia during 1847, 1849, 1855, 1865, 1876, and 1889.[20] Although central Poland, for example, had the same population, the number of deaths caused by malnutrition-related diseases was higher by 50,000 in Galicia. Epidemics also took their toll. In 1873, more than 90,000 Galicians died of cholera.[21]

The state of economic depression was common not only among Galician peasants but within the entire crownland. One commentator noted that within the Austro-Hungarian Empire "the taxes coming principally from the rich industrial and agricultural districts of Bohemia, Moravia, Silesia, Lower Austria and Styria, are spent largely on the hopelessly bankrupt province of Galicia."[22] The Polish overlords were blamed:

> A dozen or more years after the administration of the province had completely passed into Polish hands it was still one of the poorest crown lands of the monarchy. . . . There is no doubt that during the first 25 years of Polish rule little was done to raise the country from poverty and that Galicia's great landowners and bourgeosie [the large majority of whom were Polish] showed insufficient economic and social initiative.[23]

Generally, the transfer of Galicia from Polish to Austrian rule in 1772 had not significantly altered the position of the vast majority of Ukrainian peasants vis à vis the Polish landlords. The Poles still held their political and economic rule, although now in the name of the Austrian government. Meanwhile, "the government in Vienna showed little interest in developing a distant and strategically exposed province."[24] Neglected Galicia shared a border with Austria's rival, the Russian Empire.

Galicia's lack of industrial development was critical: in 1900 there were only 100,000 industrial workers in a population of 7.3 million.[25] The artisan's workshop, not the factory, dominated local industry. Cottage industries explain why in 1869, for example, there were only 1.7 workers for every industrial employer in Galicia.[26] Given this state of affairs, the landless or debt-ridden peasant had few choices: he could work for the large estate owner; he could attempt to obtain at least seasonal employment; he could join the ranks of the unemployed and look forward to death by starvation. Or, he could emigrate.

On the estates of large landowners, the working hands earned, on the average, 15 to 25 kreuzers daily (100 kreuzers made up one gulden). Because of the large surplus of labour in Galicia, men earned 11 to 30 kreuzers for a 14 to 18-hour day; women and girls earned 12 to 15 kreuzers. In Bukovyna wages were even lower: agricultural workers earned 10 to 14 kreuzers daily.[27] This pittance was usually accompanied by scolding and whipping. Even on these terms, it was difficult to obtain continuous employment. Peasants considered themselves lucky when they could find employment for two days a week.

Other peasants searched for employment in the oil fields of Galicia. Extracting and refining oil and ozocerite (earth wax) employed some 15,000 workers in the 1870s.[28] Most of the unskilled labour was recruited locally and was seasonal. Companies were allowed to buy small lots of land, and many rivals would locate their rigs on the same deposit. The extractor of the natural resource became its owner. Oil was collected in a primitive manner — workers carrying buckets were lowered into shafts on ropes — and the work was dangerous. Broken ropes, explosions caused by gases, cave-ins due to poorly supported shafts, and asphyxiation from lack of proper ventilation were common. The oilmen recieved 35 to 50 kreuzers daily.[29]

Galician peasants were familiar with both seasonal labour and seasonal emigration. In 1910, more than 82,000 Ukrainians from Galicia worked in Prussia, either in agriculture or industry. The emigrant who found employment in Prussia could save 100 to 200 gulden after 8 to 10 months.[30] Others, more adventurous, journeyed to the United States to work in the coal mines of Pennsylvania. There a worker might earn as much as 600 gulden a year[31] and be relatively wealthy upon his return.

The economic conditions in Galicia and Bukovyna completely justified the upheaval the peasants would suffer by emigrating. Yet the intimate knowledge of what constituted poverty would be, ironically, invaluable to the Galician and Bukovynian in Canada. Homesteading in the wilderness of Canada would not be very different from their attempt to eke out an existence in Galicia and Bukovyna.

There would be one essential difference, however. In Galicia, overpopulation and the lack of industrial development overshadowed any hope the peasants may have had for the future. The environment of the peasant seemed hopelessly arbitrary and limited. As one scholar has noted, the pattern of peasant behaviour suggests that the world seen by the peasants was one in which all desired things "exist in finite quantity and are always in short supply."[32] Canada, however, was a country of abundance; it inspired optimism in the peasants who had all but accepted their circumscribed existence. In Canada, the intensity of their hope would make the new ordeals bearable.

The Rise of National and Political Consciousness

Although the economic state of Galician and Bukovynian peasants was appalling, there were movements in the nineteenth century to enlighten and educate, especially in a political and national sense. By 1914, great progress had been made. One historian has written: "in the short span of twenty years preceding the Great War a tremendous change took place in Eastern Galicia. In the place of a depressed peasant mass arose a politically-conscious peasant nation."[33]

With the dawn of the constitutional era in the Austro-Hungarian Empire in the 1860s, many nationalities took advantage of the extended civil liberties granted to them. These included freedom of assembly, association, speech, and press. In Galicia, these freedoms were revolutionary, especially when compared to the total repression some 17-million Ukrainians were experiencing in Russia.

The Ukase of Ems (a Tsarist order) in 1876 prohibited all forms of Ukrainian political activity in the Russian Empire. Fearful that the "toleration of literature in the popular Ukrainian idiom would give permanent footing to the idea of the possibility, in the distant future, of the separation of Ukraine from Russia,"[34] the Tsar banned the printing and importation of Ukrainian publications, together with Ukrainian theatre and music, and disbanded all groups that acknowledged and promoted the Ukrainian nationality. With the development of a Ukrainian national consciousness nipped in the bud in Russia, Galicia became fertile ground for the activities of intellectuals after 1876. Although Bukovyna was cut off from its neighbour politically and religiously, it had the same freedoms and echoed developments in Galicia.[35]

Ukrainians did not become a nationally conscious people overnight.*

---

*For a summary of Ukrainian nationality and religions, see Appendix I.

Those in Galicia referred to themselves as Ruthenians rather than as Ukrainians. Before 1890, the designation "Ukrainian" was used only to identify the Ukrainian nation in the Russian Empire. Ukrainians in Russia, as in Bukovyna, were of the Eastern Orthodox religion. The Ruthenians in Galicia, who were Greek Catholics, rejected the term "Ukrainian" in order to separate themselves from the Orthodox Bukovynians and Russian Ukrainians. Many Galician Ruthenians, in fact, did not consider themselves Ukrainian at all. With little sense of their historical origins, they had varying opinions of their classification. Some believed that Ruthenians constituted an independent nationality; others were accustomed to thinking of themselves as part of the Russian nation or part of the Polish nation. In the latter third of the nineteenth century, the Greek Catholic Galicians — not surprisingly — suffered an identity crisis. To quote one historian, "the use of the term *Ukrainian* to refer to nineteenth century Galician Ruthenians is a commonly accepted anachronism in historical scholarship, but it unfortunately permits hindsight to settle a question that at that time was by no means settled."[36]

Two intellectual groups surfaced among Ruthenians in Galicia in the 1860s: the Ukrainophiles and the Russophiles. The Ukrainophiles, or national populists, believed that the Ruthenians were part of the Ukrainian nation. Their populist bent was heart-felt: "We shall always stand on the side of our poor rag-covered people."[37] Before 1876, the Ukrainophile movement had its headquarters in the Russian Empire. The key figure was Mykhailo Drahomanov, an historian at the University of Kiev who continued to supervise the movement even after his exile to Geneva, Switzerland.

Russophiles, on the other hand, idolized Russia and claimed that the Ruthenians in Galicia were part of the Russian Empire. "By identifying with the Russian nation, the Ruthenians in Galicia could bypass their native plebian culture, their peasant vernacular, their lack of a state tradition, and claim as their own a high culture, a developed literary language and a powerful State."[38] This orientation offered a cure for the inferiority complex shared by the Ruthenian clergy and intelligentsia. It also attempted to do away with the bitter disappointment over the Ruthenians' record as a *kaisertreu* people who had submitted almost too willingly to the Austrian state. Russophiles were also confident that they could challenge the "aristocratism" and power of the Poles in Galicia. The Galician Russophiles received financial support from Russia.

Both the Ukrainophile and Russophile movements were distinctly Ruthenian, and distinctly the formulations of the intelligentsia and clergy. The Ruthenian elite in Galicia, however, was quite small, as many of its members had been Polonized in the seventeenth century.

The Ruthenian intelligentsia was also constricted by the underdeveloped state of education. With Polish becoming the official language in Galicia in 1869, the two universities in the province, Lviv and Cracow, which had been German during the absolutist era, were Polonized.[39] The Ruthenians did have their Chairs of Study at the University of Lviv, but for many years, there was only one gymnasium for secondary-level study available to Ruthenians. After the signing of the *Ausgleich*[40] in 1867, elementary instruction was given in the native language; education past the elementary level, however, was an expensive undertaking. Few Ruthenian students proceeded to the post-secondary level. At Lviv Polytechnic between 1861 and 1901, for example, 83 per cent of the students were Polish, 11 per cent were Jewish, and 6 per cent were Ruthenian.[41] The illiteracy rate among the Ruthenians in Galicia was high. One scholar has written:

> Excluding children under six years of age, illiterates made up 77 per cent of Galicia's population in 1880, 67 per cent in 1890, and 57 per cent in 1900. . . . The illiteracy rate for Ukrainian peasants, however, was higher, for a great number of Galicia's literate inhabitants lived in cities, not in the countryside; Western Galicia was more literate than Ukrainian-inhabited eastern Galicia; and in the countryside, non-peasants (nobles, stewards, tavern keepers, priests, teachers) made up a significant percentage of the literate group.[42]

The universities had four facilities: theology, law, medicine, and philosophy. As the chart[43] below illustrates, Ukrainians overwhelmingly favoured the theological faculty, and with good reason. The clergy had an economic advantage in Galician society. They received a salary from the state, fees for sacramental rites, and sizeable farms. In Bukovyna, the Greek Orthodox Church held 286,000 hectares, or one-quarter of the area of the province. In Galicia, the average landholding per parish was 50.6 hectares.[44] The Uniate Church also held the rights to considerable pasture and forest lands in Galicia. The Austrian government granted the Uniate Church and clergy equal status with their Roman Catholic counterparts, although the Uniate Church was regarded as an inferior church, the church of the peasants.

Given the general lack of education among the majority of Ruthenians, the Ukrainophiles were faced with a problem. Their movement could not be successful if it remained a movement of the intelligentsia. Mass support from the peasantry was required, as there was no other large class from which to draw. The artisans were a small group and there was no responsive working class. Yet how could the destitute peasantry be harnessed? The key became the education of the peasant.

Table 3-1
**University Students by Faculty
and Nationality, 1861-1901**

Nationality	Theology	Law	Medicine	Philosophy
Polish	9	55	17	19
Jewish	—	69	22	10
Ukrainian	55	31	5	10

In 1868, the national populists founded an adult education club — the Prosvita (Enlightenment) Society — as a first step in the development of mass support. To 1874, only two member clubs existed; however, by 1886 there were 461, and by 1908, 2,048.[45] The clubs, with an average membership of 50, gathered for public readings; literate peasants would read aloud from popular newspapers and booklets on saints, agricultural techniques, and, most often, politics. Prosvita published and distributed booklets through agents, which included associations, merchants, booksellers, and priests.

Russophiles, to be equally effective, also needed peasant support. In 1874, the Mykhailo Kachkovsky Society was established in Kolomyia as a rival to Prosvita. In 1869, the Bukovynian equivalent, Ruska Besida (Ruthenian Club), was founded. It had a Russophile orientation until the mid-1880s; thereafter, it was closely allied with Prosvita.[46]

The network of reading societies in Galicia and Bukovyna brought extraordinary results: "joining an organization to listen to or read newspapers and booklets gave the Ukrainian peasant membership in a community wider than the village commune, a community that included other peasants in other villages as well as editors and writers in the capital."[47] Through the reading societies, the peasants developed into a receptive, highly politicized group.

At first, the national populists relied on priests in villages to promote the establishment of local Prosvita societies. The clergy reacted favourably; they were anxious to see the improvement of the peasantry, and the societies gave them a forum to preach, among other things, sobriety. In fact, between 1868 and 1874, the clergy made up 65 per cent of all Prosvita's members in the countryside.[48] The priest was "spiritual father and counsellor" to the peasants; he was, too, the predecessor of the secular intellectual, "the natural bridge from the intelligentsia to the peasantry."[49]

However, it did not take long before there were serious disputes with the clergy over ideology and economic matters. The enlightened peasants agitated through local reading clubs for reductions in sacramental rites fees, or demanded that the priest share his pasture. The priests, however, took enlightenment only so far; they were unwilling to lower sacramental fees or to share their pastures and forests. Incidents such as the one in the village of Volia Iakubova contributed significantly to anti-clerical sentiment:

> For years, Fr. Harbinsky has rented his pasture to the speculator Chaim for 90–110 gulden, who in turn subleased it to the peasants for an additional 100 gulden. When villagers asked the priest to rent the pasture directly to them he agreed and asked 200 gulden, the same rate as Chaim.[50]

By the mid-1880s, the reading clubs were engaging in blasphemous agitation against the church.

Conflicts also arose between the rich and poor peasants over local government officials and electors to Parliament and the Diet. Each province in the Austro-Hungarian monarchy had a Diet which legislated provincial affairs and set provincial taxes, but had no power to alter state laws. The federal legislatures were parliaments in Vienna and Budapest. The peasants voted for electors — the village chief, scribe, and councilmen — who, in addition to running the village governments, participated directly in provincial and federal elections. These village electors were invariably the richer peasants, who used their advantages. The local government, which they controlled, often "abused its considerable powers when assessing taxes, making loans, aiding the poor from the communal treasury, assigning peasants to repair roads, functioning as the village police, issuing certificates of poverty (useful in court cases) and granting exemptions from military service."[51] These small groups of village officials were also not above swaying their votes when bribed or threatened by the nobility.

Local reading clubs monitored the revenues and expenditures of the village government, as well as whether the local electors were voting "correctly" in elections to Parliament and the Diet. Complaints were submitted by reading club members to popular newspapers:

> Our chief also for some reason doesn't like to hear about a reading club. But how could a chief like ours like it if people read newspapers in a reading club, because from newspapers people would find out how our chief voted in the elections. And our chief, who was an elector in the recent elections to the Diet . . . paid no attention to the national cause, but only paid attention to who was giving out kielbasa

and other treats. So he voted for Pan Sznel and not for the Ruthenian candidate.[52]

Reading clubs advanced candidates for local offices to replace incumbents considered unworthy and often supported deputies, which the village government opposed, for Parliament or the Diet. In 1897, the direct franchise was extended to all adult males, but electors continued to be chosen through indirect franchise and had the privilege of voting twice. It was not until 1907 that a universal male suffrage replaced the indirect franchise.

Meanwhile, in the 1870s, the priests oversaw the establishment of local "temperance societies, church brotherhoods, cooperative stores, communal granaries, loan funds, schools, choirs, amateur theatrical troupes, gymnastic clubs, and volunteer fire brigades."[53] By 1883, village cooperative stores had joined a larger organization, Narodna Torhivlia (National Commerce), founded in Lviv. Krayovyi Soiciz Kredytni (Crownland Credit Union), a credit cooperative, was founded in Galicia in 1898, and agricultural cooperatives became branches of Silskyi Hospodar (Village Farmer) in 1899. A dairy cooperative was established near the town of Stryi in 1907.[54] As well, a special land bank was formed in 1908 to aid peasants with land purchases; the result was that holdings of large landowners decreased from 40.3 per cent of eastern Galician land in 1889 to 37.8 per cent in 1912.[55]

All the socio-economic activities, however, were supplementary to the purpose of Prosvita societies. Their primary goal was political. Through their periodicals, the national populists imbued Prosvita members with a sense of Ukrainian nationalism. Peasants were taking an interest in politics and elections, supporting Ukrainian candidates. However, the Ukrainophiles' necessary alliance with the clergy allowed the clergy to assume influential positions in the movement. Consequently, national populism, although it defied the priests for a time, finally retreated from a democratic ideology to an acceptance of a more clerical world view.

The national populists' association with the clergy alienated younger intellectuals within the Ukrainian student clubs at the University of Lviv. Advised and prodded by Mykhailo Drahomanov, these students took a new intellectual course. Drahomanov maintained that the plight of the peasants had to be remedied through socialism directed by the Ukrainophile intelligentsia. But first a number of conditions had to be met. These included educating the peasants so that they could share in European intellectual life and ultimately achieve socio-economic emancipation.

The first manifestation of the new intellectual current was the adoption in 1876 of the Ukrainian vernacular in the formerly Russophile student newspaper *Druh*. Other manifestations included an interest in ethnography and the ideological union of the Russophile students' club with the Ukrainophile club.[56] The new ideology became Drahomanovite-Ruthenian socialism.

The socialism of the new intellectuals did not go unnoticed. They became "in the sterile Galician intellectual life, something new, shocking, and promising."[57] Russophilism and national populism had been rejected as unsatisfactory. Like their forerunners, however, socialists were faced with the problem of disseminating their views to gain mass support. The groundwork had been laid by the reading societies in the 1870s, and by the surfacing of social conflicts. Peasants, in their struggle against village governments, clergy, and money-lenders, turned to the socialists. Indeed, the "transformation from a national reading club to a socialist reading club, a common transformation in the 1890s, would involve little more than switching subscriptions from nationally-oriented periodicals to socialist periodicals."[58] Socialists also organized mass assemblies and coached peasants to speak. One commentator noted the effect of seeing the audience and hearing the speakers influential in local societies:

> Anyone who has ever been present at an assembly of Ruthenian Radicals and has seen peasants in their sheepskin jackets, with their hair plastered down with grease, making notes on scraps of paper supported on their knees in order to participate in the discussion; anyone who has heard Huryk, Novakiwsky, or Ostapchuk speak . . . that person perforce has been filled with wonder and respect for this nation's intelligence and its capacity to develop.[59]

In 1890 on October 4 and 5, about 30 socialists met in Lviv at the founding congress of the Ruthenian-Ukrainian Radical Party, the official organization of Drahomanovite-Ruthenian socialists. Their program included demands for "state financial reforms, universal suffrage for both men and women, the abolition of the standing army, free elementary and secondary education, and the widest possible autonomy for Galicia."[60] A plan to nationalize the land in Galicia for cooperative agricultural production was developed by Ivan Franko, the noted publicist, and became the basis of the party's economic program. According to Franko:

> Peasants had a *right* to plots of land large enough to support themselves and their families. Since, however, there was not sufficient land for every peasant to own an independent homestead that could main-

tain his family, it was necessary to establish collective farms and, in general, to encourage collectivity in agricultural production as the only antidote to proletarianization.[61]

Systematic agitation using improved propaganda techniques was conducted in the villages. Socialism took on the "proportions of an institutionalized, radical social movement"[62] among the Ruthenians in Galicia.

In 1895, the year Drahomanov died, the nationalist wing broke away from the Ruthenian-Ukrainian Radical Party, merged with national populists, and formed the Ukrainian National Democratic Party. This party's platform was based on democratic nationalism and social reform. The National Democrats became the dominant political party, while the Radical Party served as a permanent opposition. The Radicals continued as the party of "agrarian socialism and militant anticlericalism."[63] Both parties championed independence for the Ukrainian people and worked together, most of the time, in the Parliament and Diet.

The Marxist wing also broke away from the Ruthenian-Ukrainian Radical Party, forming the Social Democratic Party in 1895. Although it had little influence, it aided in the organization of the trade union movement in Galicia. A fourth party, the Christian Social Party, also existed, but it exerted minimal influence.

The development of the political consciousness of the Ruthenian peasants in the last third of the nineteenth century proceeded at a rapid pace. Practical changes in the quality of life, however, lagged behind. In the 1890s, reformers were only beginning to build a legitimate, institutionalized base. The programs and reforms set in motion would continue to evolve well into World War I.

These accomplishments would be important in the Canadian context. Those peasants who emigrated to Canada transplanted ideas and institutions which were still germinating. In the new land, they continued to grow and develop, at times being altered or hampered, at times encouraged by Canadian circumstances.

Immigrants from Galicia and Bukovyna were viewed in Canada as illiterate peasants ignorant of free institutions and the democratic way of life. Consequently, they were perceived as potentially dangerous. Would they not, in their ignorance, turn freedom into licence, or disregard democratic institutions? Were they not inferior, debased by centuries of oppression? Could they function as members of a "civilized" society?

Even a cursory examination of socio-political life in Galicia and ~a during the latter half of the nineteenth century undermines this stereotype and its connotations. It was true that the large majority of them were unable to read and write, and that they had come from an economically underdeveloped region, but ignorance, when defined in social, economic, and political terms, was not characteristic of the Galicians or Bukovynians. The peasants were quite familiar with the electoral system and with free and voluntary institutions.

There were parallels between Austria-Hungary and Canada. In each, the most recent constitution had been drawn up in 1867. Both had provinces, with provincial governments joined in a federation headed by a central regime. Representatives to the government were elected (even if indirectly, as was the case in Austria-Hungary until 1907), and in both, to a greater or lesser extent, there were unsavoury electoral practices. Corruption and bribery, most evident in the Austro-Hungarian Empire, was not unknown in Canada.

Citizens of each country also suffered from an identity crisis — the Ukrainian peasants pondered whether they were Austrian, Ukrainian, Ruthenian, or even Polish. The issue was still being debated intensely during the years of emigration. But what of the Canadians? They had a dualistic component — Anglophone and Francophone. And were not the Imperialists, in their quest to make Canada the "belly-button" of the British Empire, searching for their identity as well? Were they truly Canadian, or British, or hybrid Americans? It was impossible to present a unanimous definition of the Canadian identity, and the arrival of the Ukrainians and other immigrant groups only complicated the matter.

There were, of course, conspicuous differences between Ukrainians and established Canadians. First, there were the most obvious external aspects: language, culture, religion, and dress. These visible manifestations were intolerable for many Canadians, who urged assimilation at all costs. Yet the Ukrainians had resisted intense Polonization efforts in their homeland, and would resist Anglicization in Canada. There were some who conformed to the dominant culture in both cases, but for the majority the Ukrainian identity, however ill-defined, was to be preserved. Second, although the Galicians and Bukovynians were acquainted with a system of relatively free representational government, they were attuned to a social and political tradition closely tied to their needs and circumstances. When compared to the conservative and liberal traditions in Canada, their frame of reference appeared alien — even extremist. This difference in political thought would be another point of friction, especially when hardships and injustices similar to those in Galicia and Bukovyna were encountered.

In the end, a reciprocal relationship emerged. Canada did alter the Ukrainian peasants, but they also altered Canada.

CHAPTER 4

CROSSING THE RUBICON

The swift development of the industrial age stimulated the mass migration of peoples. Labour-hungry countries offered attractive economic opportunities to citizens of those countries where industrial growth lagged behind. Attendant upon industrialization was the transformation of agriculture from farming for personal consumption and sustenance to market production. In Galicia and Bukovyna, the unemployed peasant's sense of futility was amplified by stories of wealth and opportunity elsewhere. Whether one emigrated permanently or temporarily to better one's position at home, the solution to the economic ills had to be sought outside Galicia and Bukovyna.

However, all-encompassing generalizations, especially economic ones, do not tell the whole story. Freedom promised in the new lands was, for some, sufficient reason for emigration. For others, emigration was simply a matter of reuniting with families. The reaction of local governments against the mass outflow also had its effects; ironically, the disapproval caused many peasants to re-examine their status in Austria-Hungary. Still others emigrated purely to satisfy their adventurous spirit and yearning to become "worldly." Indeed, each emigrant had his own reason for leaving. One peasant, for example, witnessed his horse break a leg in a pond during a winter storm, and was unable to recover damages from the landowner who was responsible for the roads on the land. A lawyer's promise that the case was simple and victory would be easy pacified the peasant temporarily. When the case was lost, the peasant sought revenge, but his hostile energies became diverted by acquaintances who championed emigration. Without telling his wife, the peasant left for Canada.[1]

The methods of acquiring knowledge about the lands of opportunity also varied with each case, as did the means of financing passage. Many factors affected the choice of country. Friends, relatives, educational societies, periodicals, and agents were influential. The opportunities promised by various countries and the potential for a better future, especially for the children, were often essential considerations. Once the decision to emigrate was made, financing the passage and departing safely were the final concerns, although in some cases they were the biggest hurdles. Money-lenders, land speculators, friends, relatives, agents, and authorities all either helped or hindered.

The decision to emigrate, the parting with loved ones, and the journey through unknown territory to an unknown land were painfully disorienting. The totality of the immigrant experience, starting in the old world where much that was cherished was left behind and not ending until long after their arrival, was incomprehensible to most of the Canadian population.

Ukrainians in Brazil and the United States

Emigration was a fact of life in Galicia and Bukovyna long before Canada was discovered to be an attractive land for settlement. Brazil was the first overseas destination that pacified emigration fever. In Brazil during the first half of the nineteenth century, the rapidly expanding coffee-growing industry experienced a depletion in the free labour supply. Plantation owners used all the incentives possible to encourage an influx of labour. Agents were sent to Austria and Germany, promising a prosperous future for those who went to Brazil. The German immigrants who were the first to go, however, were treated like slaves on the plantations. Consequently, in 1859 the Prussian government vetoed the emigration of its own citizens to Brazil.[2]

Thereafter, Brazilian agents concentrated their efforts elsewhere in Europe. The abolition of slavery in Brazil in 1888 increased the need for labour, and encouragements were made more attractive. To the peasants in Austria-Hungary, free transportation, land, buildings, cattle, and agricultural implements were promised.[3] The peasants were also overwhelmed by the "news" that Prince Rudolph (the crown prince of Austria) did not die (he committed suicide in 1889) but was residing in Brazil from whence he was beckoning Galician and Bukovynian peasants to come to join his Empire. The success of the deceit was immediately evident in the large number of letters sent to Princess Stephanie in Austria from various Galician districts, informing her of the good news.[4]

The unfortunate result of the enticements was that many peasants did emigrate to Brazil. Most were taken to coffee plantations in San Paolo to provide what was, essentially, free labour. The cost of passage, even though largely subsidized by the Brazilian State Treasury after 1887, and the cost of room and board set by the plantation owners were deducted from salaries. Workers retained little or no money. Among the 109,502 Russians and 85,970 Austrians who entered Brazil between 1884 and 1939, there were many Ukrainians. Some immigrants were able to proceed to southern Brazil, where they took up homesteads. Many simply perished, being ill-adapted to plantation work.[5]

In the United States, immigrants were required to work in coal mines and act as strikebreakers. In 1877, a Pennsylvania coal company representative appeared in Austria to persuade people to emigrate.[6] Under contract for labour, the peasants had the cost of passage deducted from wages. There were no restrictions to entry, but movements soon developed to oppose the importation of "undesirable" southern and eastern Europeans. The depression in the early 1880s added to the back-lash and immigration laws were reconsidered. Objections to free entry were voiced by trade unions forced to compete with the cheap and abundant labour supply. Even business no longer defended free immigration but became concerned with the deterioration in the urban environment caused by the large concentrations of immigrants in cities. Business also feared the infiltration of the labour movement by radical immigrant elements.

Immigrants to the United States before 1880 had come mainly from western Europe: Great Britain, Germany, Switzerland, France, and the Scandinavian countries. These were nationalities that had colonized the United States, aided in its growth and development, and were readily welcomed. But by the 1880s this desirable immigration decreased and was replaced by waves of "lower races." Nativism soon became aroused. The American Protective Association (APA), born in Iowa in 1887, opposed all Catholics and, especially, Catholic foreigners.[7] The APA gained support from American workers and bitterly opposed Slavic and Italian immigration.[8] The Immigration Restriction League, created in Boston in 1896, released fervent anti-immigration literature.[9] The ever-vigilant Ku Klux Klan also took up the anti-foreigner cause. The combined opposition of these groups forced restrictions on immigration.

The first immigration law in 1882, restricting Chinese entry to California, was followed by another in 1885 which forbade contract labour. Limitations on immigration were subsequently strengthened and in 1897 culminated in legislation which imposed a literacy test on immigrants — directed mostly at Slavic and Italian newcomers. Designed to "protect" the people of the United States from the social and economic problems accompanying immigration, the test set comprehensive and detailed qualification requirements. In effect, it prevented the entry of immigrants who could become public charges (because of illness, weakness, or poverty). The test was also used as an excuse to close the doors in the name of public morality, public peace, and the continuity of American political life.

Another restrictive measure was the head tax, payable with the cost of the steamship pass, which was raised from 50 cents in 1882 to $4 in 1907.[10] Immigrants were also required to have sufficient funds to support them during the initial job-hunting period. This sum was normally $10. But in New York City, William N. Williams, the Commissioner of Immigration appointed in 1909, raised the figure to $25, requiring the address of a resident relative or friend from immigrants and additional money to cover the cost of railway fare to the location given.[11] Those unable to meet the requirements were deported within 48 hours of arrival. Fines ranging from $1000 to $5000 and jail terms of up to five years were imposed on people who brought in immigrants contrary to immigration laws.[12]

That the American government undertook to control immigration is understandable. With homesteads in the American west being filled and the labour market being flooded, the authorities were forced to reconsider the "come one, come all" policy. The United States, whose population increased from 3.9 million in 1790 to 91 million in 1910, had trouble with the concentration of immigrants in the northeast. In 1905, 90 per cent of the arrivals remained in the northeastern states, 1 per cent settled in the southwest, 4 per cent in the western states, and the remaining 2 per cent went to Alaska, Hawaii, and Puerto Rico. The census of 1900 showed that 36.9 per cent of New York City's population was comprised of immigrants. By the end of the nineteenth century, the United States had had its fill of immigrants and was seeking, if not to repel, at least to control the tide of people.

By the turn of the century, Ukrainians had already established their community in the United States. The Ukrainian immigrants who had begun to arrive in 1870 were drawn to the coal mines in Pennsylvania. Exact figures are not available on the first wave of immigration, which spanned the last three decades of the 1800s. Estimates range from 200,000 to 300,000.[13] Such calculations are complicated by the fact that Galicians and Bukovynians were often vague when it came to stating their nationality. Immigration officials often listed them arbitrarily and variously as Poles, Ruthenians, Austrians, Hungarians, Russians, Galicians, or Bukovynians.

An important accomplishment for the Ukrainian immigrants of

Pennsylvania was obtaining a priest — the focus of a Ukrainian community, in this case Catholic — from Europe. In 1884, the Metropolitan of Galicia, Sylvester Smbratovich, Archbishop of Lviv, sent Father John Voliansky.[14] In 1886, Father Voliansky began publishing a weekly Ukrainian paper, *America*, as a vehicle for immigrants living outside their homeland.[15] *Svoboda* (Freedom), a weekly newspaper, was founded in Jersey City, New Jersey, 11 September 1893, by Father Hryhorii Hrushka. It continued the work of *America*, which folded in 1890.[16] The development of the community was witnessed by the establishment of the Ukrainian National Association, 22 February 1894, by which time there were already 30 Ukrainian priests in the United States. The need for the circulation of news increased. *Svoboda* became a bi-weekly newspaper on 1 March 1894, a tri-weekly on 8 August 1914, and a daily on 3 January 1921.[17] The second wave of Ukrainian immigration between 1899 and 1910 brought 147,375 people (not including those registered as Austrians, Russians, or Poles).[18]

The Ukrainians, concentrated in the northeastern states, worked in coal mines, in industries, and on railroads. A few established small businesses. They were thrifty, not only out of need, but out of habit. Saving money to improve the condition of any family members at home was also a major consideration.

By the time Ukrainians began to look toward Canada, the Ukrainian community in the United States was developed enough to benefit immigrants north of the border. *Svoboda* was their most important contribution. It became the mouthpiece for Ukrainians in North America. Like the periodicals in Galicia, which were effective in revealing problems common to all, the American periodical played an important role in the sharing and solution of difficulties. *Svoboda*, prior to the establishment of Ukrainian-Canadian periodicals, also became a good source of knowledge about the early emigration to Canada. The American religious community, although not directly beneficial to Ukrainian-Canadians — only Father Nestor Dmytriw travelled through Canada in the earliest period — lessened their religious isolation. The very presence of Ukrainians in the United States, in fact, encouraged Ukrainian emigration to Canada.

In some cases, Canada became a second destination for Ukrainians who had emigrated to the United States. The negative response of some vocal Americans to foreigners, and the restrictions placed on their admittance, caused some Ukrainian-Americans to examine alternatives. Canada became an obvious choice for Ukrainians.

The Prospect of Canada

Information about immigration was usually designed to incite relocation rather than to explain what it entailed. Publications and hearsay appealed to the frustrated needs of the peasant, interpreting conditions in the most favourable light. Agents were the masters of this deceit. Verbal promises were easy to make and difficult to disprove. Middlemen wandered through villages impersonating priests and officials to gain credibility with the peasants. Rumours spread quickly through the villages. Influential and widespread families transmitted the news over large districts. Workers returning from Germany or Hungary also brought back a mixture of truths and tales which they had learned from the families and friends of emigrants.

Once Ukrainian emigration began, the peasants received information first-hand. Letters postmarked Brazil or the United States of America were viewed as bearers of truth. As can be expected, some letters were fabricated, telling tales of wealth and success, while others told sorrowful stories of misfortune, hardship, and poverty. The confused peasants sought out reliable sources.

The lessons learned by the time emigration was directed to Canada resulted in a most practical approach to gathering information. Prospective emigrants, and reading societies concerned with the best interests of the peasants, sent scouts to determine the feasibility of settlement. Ivan Pillipiw and Wasyl Eleniak, from the small village of Nebiliw, arrived in Canada 7 September 1891 "to investigate reports which they had heard about the vast uninhabited stretches of fertile land in Western Canada."[19]

Eleniak had learned about Canada from German families while working on river boats.[20] In Canada, he and Pillipiw travelled to Yorkton and Calgary, but were not impressed with the land and returned to Winnipeg. A visit to the German settlement at Gretna, about which Pillipiw had heard, changed their minds. Eleniak remained in Canada, hiring himself out locally, while Pillipiw returned to Galicia to gather their families for emigration. While in Hamburg, Pillipiw made an agreement with a steamship agent. Pillipiw would get the standard bonus of $5 per head for members of emigrant families and $2 for each other individual whom he inspired to emigrate to Canada.[21] But as a sub-agent, he was arrested on a charge of sedition for inciting people to emigrate. The subsequent trial and one-month jail term strongly publicized Canada and its possibilities. In June of 1892, 12 families from Pillipiw's village emigrated to Gretna, Manitoba. Eleniak's family arrived a few years later and settled in Chipman, Alberta.

The scouting expedition of Eleniak and Pillipiw had borne fruit. Celebrated as the first Ukrainians in Canada, the real significance of their arrival and the subsequent arrival of their families and friends is that it was the best possible advertisement for Canada as a destination. The approval of Canada was a much stronger incentive to emigrate there than any agents or literature could muster. The reaction was, at first, slow, but Ukrainians trusted the voice of experience, especially when the voice was one of their own. The logic was simple: "that they are not returning means that life there is good."[22]

When Joseph Oleskiw embarked on his scouting expedition to Canada, he, unlike Pillipiw and Eleniak, was on official business. The Prosvita Society, based in Lviv, had become concerned about emigration to Brazil. It attempted to counter the false claims of agents and to discourage immigration there, informing the peasants of the realities of emigration and the conditions in various lands. Oleskiw was the obvious choice to collect first-hand information and to author brochures.

Joseph Oleskiw was born 28 September 1860 to a priest's family in the village of Nova Skvariava, in Galicia. He completed secondary school in Lviv and proceeded to the University of Lviv, where he received a doctorate, specializing in natural sciences, chemistry, and geology.[23] His studies were continued in Erfurt, Germany, in botany and agriculture.[24] Oleskiw then returned to Galicia and lectured at the Agricultural College in Dubliany, near Lviv. After successfully completing examinations, he was appointed Imperial and Royal Professor at the teachers' seminary in Lviv. Oleskiw was a director of the Prosvita Society and a friend of Ivan Franko.

On his trip to Canada, Oleskiw carried a letter of introduction to the Minister of the Interior from Sir Charles Tupper, the High Commissioner in London. Upon his arrival in Montreal on 12 August 1895, he met with the Austrian Consul General, Edward Schultze, and received a second letter of introduction. His travels through Canada took him to Edmonton, where he met the Honourable T. Mayne Daly, Minister of the Interior, and proposed a plan for the settlement of Galician peasant farmers in Canada. His proposal was favourably received. Oleskiw met with Daly once again on 2 October, in Ottawa. His proposal was awaiting a decision by the Cabinet at that time, and it was subsequently accepted.

Oleskiw was instrumental in placing an immigration agent at Winnipeg to serve the needs of Ukrainian arrivals. Kyrylo Genik, a postal official in Lviv, was chosen for the position. Prior to his departure, Genik secured literature about Canada and distributed it at village meetings. Arriving in Canada with a score of families, he took up his new post in the fall of 1896. Canada was gaining not only publicity, but legitimacy as a preferred destination.

Oleskiw's travels also took him to the United States. Upon his return to Galicia in 1895, he published two pamphlets — *O Emigratsii* (On Emigration) and *Pro Vilni Zemli* (About Free Lands) — describing, in detail, conditions in North America. About the United States, Oleskiw was pleased to report good news:

> At the end of this year [1895] a renewal of interests began — factories went into motion. There is work in the factories, in the coal mines in the United States, especially in Pennsylvania, where there are 200,000 Lemkos and Hungarian-Ruthenians, and up to 30 of our priests. The daily pay is a minimum of $1.00 and our modest man can save nearly half of that.[25]

Oleskiw's report of his trip to the United States no doubt added to the already high numbers of Ukrainian immigrants there. His differentiation between Canada and the United States was based on the occupational choices in the two countries. Canada provided land for agriculturalists, and farming could be supplemented by seasonal jobs, whereas the United States offered primarily jobs, supplemented by the existence of a Ukrainian community.

Immigrants continued to depend on the latest news about Canada and other countries. Stories written in *Svoboda*, which was received in many Galician and Bukovynian villages, were helpful guides to the situation in Canada as well as the United States. Oleskiw's booklet about Canada, included in packages of information provided by agents, was particularly convincing because it was in Ukrainian. As a result, agents who distributed it gained respectability. Letters from relatives and friends were also effective, especially when money was enclosed. In later years, accounts of travels through Canada reinforced the country's suitability. One author described Canada in terms of familiar sights:

> In the western Canadian provinces there are fields of a few hundred kilometres in length and in width, where a Galician immigrant settled next to a Bukovynian and lives the same life of the "old country" and abides by the views which he brought with him. Among these homesteads a traveller can drive for days, and will see nothing more than houses, built in Galician style, and here and there, wood churches, similar to the old country ones.[26]

Such descriptions decreased the prospective immigrant's fear of dislocation in a foreign land.

However, not all reports of life in Canada were complimentary. One pioneer wrote of an incident that would have daunted a less hardy soul:

It was difficult to imagine what Canada was really like — some praised it, others criticized it. I remember one peasant, I Vowk from the village of Zavalya, who returned from Canada and, in Sniatyn in the market, in the midst of large crowds of people, kissed the ground and warned people not to go to the "Canadian hell."[27]

In the end, the decision of where to emigrate was, in part, a gamble based on hope. The elementary need to emigrate was strong, but the destination depended on as many abstract and idealistic factors as it did on practical economic, political, and social considerations.

Obstacles to Departure

About one million Ukrainians emigrated from Galicia and Bukovyna from the mid-1880s to World War I.[28] Although the mass exit alleviated some of the overpopulation and unemployment problems, it threatened to disrupt the fabric of the society seriously. The peasant masses were seen to be the most stable element of the society — the base that upheld the whole hierarchical system. Any turmoil in the peasant way of life was feared as a direct infringement on the power and authority of the richer elements in the society. And mass emigration certainly shook the structure.

Emigration was feared most by estate owners. The abundant labour supply, over which they wielded complete control, was no longer guaranteed. For example:

One evening on a gentleman's estate the masses gathered. They were numerous, but happy and satisfied — an obedient crowd, faithfully devoted to the landowner. The next morning, the superintendent arrives and awakes the tender gentleman from the sweetest morning sleep. "Please, tender gentleman, wake up!" the superintendent speaks obediently. "The two of us must go and feed and water the cattle and horses, because we are the only two males left on the estate. Last night all the help left and disappeared."[29]

Such incidents (or stories) horrified the landowners. The Austro-Hungarian constitution allowed freedom of departure, and no one had taken any action to protect the landlords.

But pressure from the landowners soon forced authorities, especially at local levels, to stop emigration at all costs. In April of 1877, a secret circular was issued by the Galician vice-regency. It ordered village elders and police to stop the emigration of poor peasants and to return them to the manorial estates. In another circular, issued in June of that year, poor peasants were defined as those who did not have, in their possession, 160 gulden. This restriction was extended to include all females under 35 years of age. These circulars were quickly replaced by stricter ones. In the end, an order was issued to patrols on the Austro-Prussian border, which emigrants crossed en route to sea ports, and to Cracow police to allow no peasants to cross the border.[30]

In the meantime, all other possible obstacles were placed in the path of prospective emigrants. Mail carrying money or emigration literature rarely reached its destination. The recipient was normally shown the envelope, stamped "delivery forbidden," and then the letter was returned to the sender or confiscated.[31] Even registered letters sent from within Galicia were not assured delivery.[32] District councillors and village elders refused to authorize the documentation and passports required for travel. Authorities spread stories about the severe climatic conditions, dangerous voyages, and any other torments that could be attached to emigration. Local police kept anyone who showed any interest whatsoever in emigration under surveillance, and there was frequent harassment. Emigration literature, passports, and money were searched out and confiscated. Railroad stations were watched, and emigrants were turned back. Wives who received passes from husbands overseas were turned back and had their passes confiscated, in the hope that the husbands would return. Even priests, accused of inciting peasants to emigrate and fearing for their favoured positions, preached against emigration to disprove the accusations.

Amendments to the Austrian Criminal Code limited the work of agents: "Whoever without permission of the authorities is engaged in emigration matters . . . will be punished by 8 days to 6 months in jail," read one paragraph.[33] Another stated: "whoever incites others to emigrate by presenting untrue facts or by other means . . . will be punished by 6 months to two years in jail."[34] Extreme breaches of the law carried maximum penalties of three years' hard labour and 3,000 gulden fines.[35] However, agents licensed by the authorities were allowed to work in Austria-Hungary as long as they did not overstep the boundaries of agitation. Laws that indirectly regulated emigration were passed by both the Austrian and Hungarian parliaments. Hungarian authorities bowed to public pressure which opposed the arbitrary power to control emigration assumed by local authorities and vetoed all "committee regulations" in 1888. Complete freedom of emigration was restored by additional orders in 1892. In 1903 and 1909, Hungary passed laws dealing specifically with emigration. These laws were based on the premise that while emigration was an unfortunate development, it could not be stopped and the emigrants should be protected. The laws, basically, forbade emigration by those who did not meet immigration restrictions in the countries they intended to settle in. Austria, meanwhile, did not manage to put together an emigration law before 1914.[36]

Shipping company agents managed to get around most obstacles. When forbidden to incite emigration themselves, they took advantage of enterprising individuals. Contacts in villages were promised free passages or a sum of money for every emigrant brought or sent to the agency. Agents were able to use the disappointed emigrants who returned from Brazil, a country which refused many of those who came. Eager to find an alternative destination, these experienced travellers quickly brought their business, and the business of family and friends, to the agents who offered them free passage. Agents found that business was much improved through the use of these returned emigrants, who were more persuasive among the peasantry. Needless to say, these emigrant sub-agents were subject to the legal consequences of such activity, and if apprehended would suffer the same penalties as full-fledged agents.

To overcome the obstacles set by local authorities and police, peasants tried to pack and depart in secrecy. To help the emigrants across the borders, a veritable army of middlemen, sub-agents, and others was created. These people, paid by both the agents and the emigrants, did nothing else but lead emigrants out of Galicia, attempting to go undetected. Once outside Galicia, these leaders sent the emigrants by train over routes which bypassed major cities and, although longer and more expensive than regular routes, were lightly patrolled, if at all. Another popular method of eluding emigration restrictions involved obtaining passes from Hungary for work in Austria, or vice versa. These were far more readily accessible than emigration passes. Once out of one's district, departure was much easier from a point where the emigrant's true intentions were not suspected.

Local money-lenders and land speculators, although looking out for their own interests, were also cooperative. As most emigrants sold or took out loans on their land and belongings to pay passage, speculators with cash bought out land and chattels. As many emigrants left in large groups from concentrated areas, the selling price reflected the need to sell quickly and was very depressed. It was possible for speculators with plenty of cash to become estate owners almost overnight.

Shipping houses, as the exodus became more and more profitable, took steps to ensure business. To prevent competition between themselves, two rival companies — the Packetfahrgeselschaft and Union (Hamburg) and the Cunard (England) — joined forces in the so-called Clearing-hous and managed to obtain a concession from the Austrian government. The company set up headquarters in Osviencim. With pooled resources, it conducted operations in Galicia and Bukovyna. To render the restrictions imposed on emigration ineffective, the Clearing-hous bribed officials. With apparent immunity, the company was able to buy the free movement of peasants.

The Clearing-hous also organized bands which attacked agents of other companies and diverted their emigrants. Bloody battles often resulted. Diverted emigrants were usually boarded onto trains for Hamburg. Railway authorities, border patrols, and conductors were all agreeable because, if cooperative, they were assured a share. During the journey, many emigrants were robbed or swindled out of their accumulated savings.

Other steamship companies were naturally outraged by the situation. The Belgian Red Star Line (Antwerp), the Dutch Holland-America Line (Rotterdam), and especially the German Norddeutscher Lloyd (Bremen) companies sought revenge by informing Galician and Bukovynian authorities of Clearing-hous dealings. But authorities in these districts, which received up to 12 per cent of the net profits of the Osviencim agency, deemed the accusations unsubstantiated. In the end, it was the pressure of public opinion that forced an investigation. The celebrated Vadovytsi Inquiry lasted from 14 November 1889 to 8 March 1890, and heard 65 defendants and more than 400 witnesses.[37] Subsequent laws, however, solved little.

Passage to the New World

That most Ukrainians were poor on arrival in Canada is true. But this did not mean that they were penniless on departure from the old country. Peasants took advantage of a number of methods to acquire money for emigration. The most obvious of these was personal savings. Poorer peasants turned to money-lenders, speculators, families, and friends, all of whom considered the emigrant an investment — in many cases, a sound investment. Money loaned or given was recoverable in most cases. The large family unit played an important role. With pooled resources, a few family members were financed to emigrate and, in a few years, sufficient money was sent back or saved at home to allow the whole family to depart.

The emigrant was issued a passport by government or shipping company officials only when he could prove that he had sufficient money for passage; those who managed to reach the Osviencim agency without sufficient funds were turned back. The emigrant required approximately 200 gulden for the journey.[38] The cost of a steamship pass varied according to season (summer was most expensive, winter was cheapest) and according to type of steamship. Time of travel, which could be as high as 20 to 28 days or as low as 9 to 12 days depending on the steamship line, did not affect price. The longer trips cost the companies more, but they made up for their losses through poorer service and food.

Even when an emigrant was able to raise more than sufficient funds for passage, there was no guarantee that he would arrive in Canada with the surplus cash. Agents frequently robbed emigrants of all their money. Emigrants were often so afraid that the authorities would cause a delay or turn them back that they resorted to bribery willingly, and at times needlessly.

This susceptibility created opportunities for unscrupulous characters who promised a free and safe journey and were never seen again. Doctors could also be shameless; a certificate of health was required in order to obtain passage, and if a child fell sick a bribe to the medical official was sometimes the only way to continue the journey. Doctors were known to take wedding rings if the family had nothing else to offer. Train conductors, border patrols, workers at lodgings where emigrants stayed before departure, all were potential adversaries. Those emigrants who refused to part with their cash did so with the fear that they might be stopped and turned back at any point.

A departing emigrant required a health certificate, a passport, and a certificate of sanity, which were issued by local authorities. En route, the emigrant paid a deposit on the steamship pass at one of the agencies, which were located in most major cities, and obtained a pass to Osviencim. At Osviencim, certificates were checked and the emigrants were given their departure dates. In many cases, the agency put the emigrants through medical and sanity examinations. The emigrants were then boarded onto trains which took them to the seaports. There, at the headquarters of the steamship company handling their business, the remainder of the cost of passage was required and personal data was collected. The emigrants again underwent medical examinations. Those in ill health or deemed to be insane, and those with insufficient funds, were turned back from Osviencim or the seaport. Most of the Ukrainian emigrants who did manage to leave departed from Hamburg or Bremen. The emigration hotels in Germany, like the one in Fiume, Hungary, were under government control. For 2 to 2.40 marks a day in Germany, or for 2 to 3 crowns in Hungary, emigrants were housed, fed, and generally protected from exploitation.

Emigrating, especially for peasants who had lived in small, tightly knit villages, and who had rarely travelled, was a highly emotional experience. They were leaving behind family and friends they would never see again. They were abandoning traditions and lifestyles which went back centuries. The more sentimental ones packed a handful of Galician or Bukovynian soil. The pain and nostalgia would not be overcome quickly or easily.

Once on board the steamships, emigrants were herded into large halls filled with rows of bunk beds. Women and children were usually separated from the men, or the passengers were divided in rooms for families, single women, and single men. Some ships provided life buoys as pillows on linen bunk beds, while others had seaweed mattresses with pillows and light blankets. The smell of disinfectant in the unventilated quarters was particularly strong. Meals consisted of tea or coffee and bread or crackers for breakfast, bread or crackers, soup, meat, potatoes (or cabbage or rice), and often pickled herring for lunch, and a snack of vegetables for dinner. Some ships allowed emigrants to eat as much as they wanted; others handed out carefully divided portions. As the supply of fresh water on the ship was limited, drinking water was scarce and fresh water for washing was not available.

During the first few days of the trip, the emigrants were naturally excited about their new adventure on the seas. They passed the time singing, playing cards or dominoes, telling stories, or just resting. But when the ship reached the high, stormy seas, its movements, the poor food, and the smell of disinfectant combined to cause the dreaded seasickness. Halls were transformed into smelly, dirty infirmaries where one heard only the moans and groans of the sufferers. It was difficult even for the healthy to escape illness in such surroundings. The ship's staff milled around, cleaning and disinfecting the halls, but the sickness would let up only on calm seas. The emigrants were unable to eat for long stretches of time. They suffered from the prolonged weakness associated with seasickness.

For most of these formerly landlocked peasants, the ocean voyage proved a horrifying experience both physically and mentally. Yet it reinforced the need to look to the future and reaffirm their belief that once across the Rubicon, life in the promised land would be worth their ordeal.

PART II

IN THE
NEW LAND,
1891–1905

CHAPTER 5

THE SETTLEMENT FRONTIER

To the Ukrainians who crossed the ocean, Canada was the promised land. Yet their hopes were soon dimmed. Sickness took its toll and delayed prospective settlers at quarantine stations. They finally reached their land, but few had anticipated being left alone to conquer the elements on a square mile of utter wilderness.

First and foremost, shelters were erected and land was cleared; survival at the subsistence level was the immediate goal. The lack of tools and livestock made a heavy dependence on manual labour essential. Isolation made the acquisition of supplies or help a major undertaking. Often, sub-marginal land and severe climatic conditions only compounded the burdens. Adaptation to a foreign society also presented problems; the language, dress, implements, buildings, and agricultural organization were all strange to the newcomers.

How did the Ukrainian immigrants survive? Why were they not overwhelmed? The pioneering lifestyle required of them in Canada was similar to the one that they had fled: survival being eked out of the land, death coming to those who failed. Their reverence for the land and mystical superstitions about natural phenomena eased the severity of disappointments. In reality, most of them had no other choice but to endure. Having sold their belongings to cover cost of passage, they could not return. Moreover, in Canada the possibility did exist for a brighter future, if not for the immigrants themselves, then for their children or grandchildren. This ray of hope, which had inspired them to emigrate, underpinned their faith and perseverance. In addition, their attitudes, which so frustrated Canadian immigration officials — obstinacy, restlessness, stubbornness — no doubt helped them endure. A sense of pride developed as the pioneers worked themselves out of the subsistence standard of living, a pride that was passed on through the generations. And their taming of the Canadian west has been defined as the Ukrainians' greatest contribution to Canada.

But there is a more immediate significance of their success. The newcomers were, for the most part, illiterate peasants. The educating process begun in Galicia and Bukovyna by reading societies was severed in mid-stream for those who emigrated. But once the immigrants had gained an economic foothold in the new land, the process of social development was revived. Aided by the compactness of their colonies and the continuous stream of immigration, the growth of Ukrainian cultural institutions defied, in part, Canadian assimilatory influences. The economic base established by the pioneers was the necessary prerequisite to the Ukrainians' social development in Canada.

Arrival in Canada

For the immigrants, arrival on Canada's eastern shore was a most joyous moment. After so many days on the ocean, the sight of land itself filled them with excitement:

> Picture to yourself the father, after disembarking with his family in Halifax or Montreal, leading his little flock to the outskirts of the town. There, in an open field he and his family fall on their knees, kiss the soil of this land; with uplifted hands they thank the Almighty for the safe ocean passage and for their deliverance from the oppression of the landlord and their safe arrival in the land of hope. If one were curious enough, one could have witnessed many such simple moving prayers of thanksgiving of the early pioneers.[1]

After the bustle of disembarking, the immigrants passed through medical examinations and were put on trains bound for the North-West.

Newcomers travelled on special, unscheduled trains which were "side tracked for all the regular passenger and freight trains."[2] The trip from Halifax to Montreal was an especially slow one, as there was much regular traffic on this route. The Canadian Colonist cars seated some 60 people and were equipped with washrooms and heaters. "One could lay down comfortably at night, either on benches on the bottom or on the large shelves on top," wrote one traveller, "There were also stoves for cooking and hot water in tanks."[3] The immigrants were pleasantly surprised at the comfort of the cars. One passenger described boarding the train:

I stepped onto the train, looked around and started to leave. I must have mistakenly gone to the first class coach. But looking around I saw that my co-travellers from the ship had settled themselves in comfortably and were inviting me to join them. I did not expect to see such comfortable Canadian trains. German railway cars were clean and comfortable, but simple and unpretentious. But here in Canada on both sides by the windows are soft green cloth seats for two persons with an empty aisle in the middle.[4]

The luxury of the Colonist cars was most evident to immigrants because the trains with which they were familiar were quite different. The same passenger recalled the train from Lviv to Russian Rava: "It was so tight, that people sat on each others' knees. More people pressed together on the wooden benches than was allowed."[5] Some immigrants even felt that they were not travelling to homesteads but were on "holiday trips."[6] An additional satisfaction was that the bells on the trains reminded the Ukrainian immigrants of church bells in their home villages.[7]

The immigrants exhibited an intense curiosity about the new land: "everyone peered attentively out of the windows to catch glimpses of something interesting, because everything interested us."[8] The first signs of apprehension began to appear at Ottawa:

We were very pleasantly impressed by the massive stone buildings of the Canadian Parliament, built on a hill overlooking the river. Across the river to the west, the landscape was wild through and through. The low, bare, rocky lands and sickly trees made an unpleasant impression on us.[9]

The train was entering the vast wilderness of northern Ontario. The cliffs, rocks, dense forests, burnt areas, and scattered villages were not what the immigrants had expected:

As we sped across Ontario with its rocks, hills, and tunnels, we were afraid we were coming to the end of the world. The heart of many a man sank to his heels and the women and children raised such lamentation as defies description.[10]

Travel through such immense, unpopulated territory for three days and nights filled them with horror:

Our immigrants became fearful that the agents had deceived them, when they promised 160 acres of good flat productive land for each family. Meanwhile, they are travelling for the third day and have not seen one place where they could settle and farm.[11]

The difference between an overpopulated Galicia and Bukovyna and an almost uninhabited Canada was a dramatic one. The Ukrainians had come to Canada on blind faith; very few had knowledge about Canadian topography. They were passing through unknown territory to an inconceivable destination. They had developed, no doubt, a mythological image of their new home. The trip through northern Ontario not only shattered that image, but implanted despair. It also reinforced the impending isolation of the colonists.

Nevertheless, most of the children and adolescents were able to keep themselves amused, much to the chagrin of the federal immigration agents accompanying the passengers. The curiosity among the passengers was difficult to control:

> These people have the fashion that no matter how much you tell them and warn them, they always insist upon being on the platforms of the cars and at all places where the train makes the least stop, they are bound to be out in all directions making it very difficult for the agent to guard them. They are very obstinate and a person travelling with them must have any amount of patience, they insist upon hanging out through windows, standing on the platforms, getting off the train and running all over the country.[12]

So the trips were not without incidents — youngsters fell off the trains or were left behind at stations, which created great panic and commotion among the remaining passengers. Trains frequently had to return to pick up stranded passengers. Others were left behind to be picked up by the following train. With experience, however, immigration officials learned to keep "the children well away from the platforms of the cars, a pastime greatly to their liking."[13]

The running tap water also fascinated the children: "they use or rather waste immense quantities [of fresh water], the youngsters constantly at the taps turning them and leaving them to run."[14] The immigrants' lack of familiarity with the use of washrooms periodically forced the agents in charge to "flush out the water closets and aisles of the cars with hose."[15] One trainload of immigrants horrified the agent when he "caught them starting a fire for cooking purposes on top of one of the heaters, endangering the whole train."[16] Other incidents included sickness and the birth of children en route.

Not all Ukrainian immigrants travelled the Canadian route. Some came through New York. The port of landing depended on the season of travel — the Canadian ports being closed during winter — and on the steamship line. The cost of passage to a Canadian port included transportation by the Canadian Pacific Railway to Winnipeg. Those disembarking at American ports were charged extra to get to Winnipeg. Few, however, had the money to pay, and the government frequently covered additional expenses. In rare cases, American agents encouraged immigrants to go to Canada in winter, knowing that they would be discouraged from settling there after experiencing winter conditions. In at least one case, immigrants destined for Brazil landed in New York and were advised to go to Canada; presumably they would soon return to the United States.[17]

The immigrants' arrival in Winnipeg signalled the beginning of the last leg of their journey. Few had found an opportunity to rest since leaving the European seaports, and even fewer had been given a chance to wash themselves and their clothes during the month-long trip. Their trip through Canada had not been inspiring. Weary from travel, they had become disenchanted.

In Winnipeg the newcomers were taken to the Immigration Hall. Normally consisting of a large room with a big iron stove in the middle, such halls were located in most cities through which immigrants passed.[18] Pots, pails, axes, brooms, eating utensils, and wood for burning were provided. Along the walls were wooden benches and tables. Soon after arrival, luggage was unpacked so that people could change, and dirty clothes were washed in barrels or pails either outside or in the middle of the hall. The women prepared meals.

> People fill up the place like a swarm of flies. Darkness and commotion engulf all. A very dim light from a small lamp barely illuminates one corner. Everyone chatters at the same time, and their voices blend into one loud confusion. Here, one can find Frenchmen, Swedes, Germans, Russian Jews, Scotsmen, Ruthenians, Poles, and others. Some are undressing and getting ready for bed. One is whistling; one is gabbing away and laughing lustily. In a corner, a religious Frenchman is crossing himself, and right in the middle of the floor is our *muzhyk* [peasant], making himself at home as he repeatedly prostrates himself, forehead to floor, till the room resounds with thuds. Not understanding the meaning of this ritual, the spectators watch his gymnastics, shake with laughter, and assume that perhaps this is the proper thing to do before retiring for the night.[19]

Such scenes were typical in immigration halls. The immigrants slept on tables, benches, and floors — wherever space could be found. Some halls were equipped with bunks, while others had partitioned rooms along the walls to accommodate women and children.

Lice, bed bugs, and grey-backs were plentiful in the halls. One of the women's duties was to pick lice from the hair and clothes of their children: "And there was a lot to hunt for because a lot of them were not very clean at home, and while on the road for a whole month had not changed clothes, so it was not astonishing that these bugs were all over their bodies and clothes."[20] W.F. McCreary, Commissioner of Immigration in Winnipeg, although understanding, was nevertheless quite distressed:

> You can imagine the condition of the Sheds [Immigration Halls] when I tell you that I have discovered gray-backs crawling up my neck-tie after one of these trips [through the Sheds]. Of course with their big blankets and sheepskin coats and coming off the vessel, it cannot be expected otherwise, but it certainly is not pleasant.[21]

In Winnipeg, the halls were used primarily to accommodate immigrants temporarily, pending the choice of settlement location either by or for them. The length of stay was normally limited by the arrival time of the next trainload of immigrants. The immigration officials in Ottawa were usually informed by a telegram from the High Commissioner's Office in London that an immigrant steamship was on its way. In some cases when the London office failed to specify the port of landing and expected date of arrival, confusion reigned supreme.

The hall in Winnipeg was frequented by con-men and shysters who, more often than not, could communicate with "their brethren." The immigrants were subjected to an endless variety of fraudulent "sales" pitches. Some sought to discourage the new arrivals from taking up free homesteads, claiming that land around Winnipeg was more suitable. Of course, they were selling this land at inflated prices and in 20 to 80-acre parcels. Others strove, for a fee, to divert the immigrants to the United States where, it was asserted, conditions were far superior. Still others maintained that the immigrants were better off not leaving Winnipeg, where the government was bound to support them and where they could acquire "cheap" accommodation. A number of visitors sold worthless goods to the settlers for high prices. The disoriented immigrants were easy prey for such schemers.

In May of 1897, a group of Bukovynians refused to vacate the immigration hall because of a rumour that the government intended to cheat them by transporting them to unproductive land without the promised supplies. Requiring the premises for an incoming trainload of settlers, Commissioner McCreary arranged rail transportation for the group to Yorkton. He then tried to eject the immigrants and to board them on the train himself. After a boot was thrown at his head, police were called in. But when the immigrants still refused to board the train, McCreary advised them to speak with their advisors — interpreters who acted as spokesmen — during the course of the night. By morning, the immigrants were on the train, ready to depart.

Such difficulties arose not only because of the immigrants' disenchantment with what they had seen of Canada, but also as a result of the promises made to incite them to emigrate. According to McCreary, this particular group of Bukovynians was told "that the Crown Princess of Austria was in Montreal and that she would see that they got free lands with houses on them, cattle and so forth, and that all they were required to do was to telegraph her in Montreal in case their requests were not granted."[22] Other promises included "not only free land, but that the Canadian Government would further assist them by grants for subsistence and by gifts of cattle and tools."[23] The shattering of the belief in such promises, which had, no doubt, seemed reasonable to the immigrants, created great disaffection. When those who visited the halls turned out to be swindlers, the immigrants lost the last of the pillars that had supported their romantic hopes and dreams. By the time they departed from Winnipeg, most settlers understood the realities of their situation — they were en route to tame the wilderness in an unpopulated land.

After this incident, the government took great pains to run trainloads of immigrants through Winnipeg non-stop, and through other western cities during the night. Immigrants were encouraged to select their destinations en route, to change cars, and to proceed directly to their chosen colonies. However, it was difficult for them to choose a destination, especially when forced to do so in northern Ontario. Most had no idea at that time what lay beyond. One immigration official wrote:

> In connection with the taking up of their destination while on the way west, I must say that it is a very difficult duty, as the people often change their minds not only once but two or three times and many although earnestly declaring themselves bound for a certain part while on the journey do change their mind after arrival in Winnipeg even thus making the statement of the Interpreter or Agent in charge incorrect and the only correct statement as to their final destinations can be obtained from the Commissioner's Office after all have left for the West.[24]

Nevertheless, the efforts to prevent the immigrants from coming into contact with the deceivers in Winnipeg were increasingly successful.

The stop in Winnipeg had provided an opportunity for the immigrants to rest from travel, clean up, and gain their bearings in the new land before proceeding into the wilderness. It had also given them a chance to release the frustrations and disaffection associated with their dislocation. Subsequent groups, which were rushed through to their wilderness locations, were denied this period of adjustment. Accordingly, they arrived at their locations weary, dirty, and even more disheartened at the sight of the vast, empty land.

The Colonies Assemble

Until 1897, the settlement patterns of Ukrainians in western Canada had developed naturally. Influenced by a familiarity with and a need for wooded surroundings and water, the colonies were established in areas where employment was available from earlier German settlers. Due to the rapid climb in the number of arrivals after 1896, the government surveyors were unable to keep up so that immigrants could be located according to their wishes. Furthermore, the government was concerned that the labour market not be overstocked in certain areas and, no doubt, feared large concentrations in a few Ukrainian colonies. Steps were taken to disperse the Ukrainians among a number of colonies.

To 1896, the patterns of settlement were indirectly initiated by Ivan Pillipiw and Wasyl Eleniak, who had come to Canada in 1891, and by subsequent arrivals from their villages. Eleniak had located at Gretna, south of Winnipeg on the Canadian-American border, where he worked as a farmhand for German settlers. Pillipiw had gone back to Galicia, where he was tried and jailed for inciting immigration. Pillipiw's return to Canada was delayed, but a group destined for Gretna left his village in June of 1892. When the families arrived, they could not reach Eleniak because the area in Manitoba was under smallpox quarantine, so they chose to settle in the Beaver Lake district in Alberta (60 miles east of Edmonton). The 20 families that arrived in the next year proceeded directly to Alberta to join their friends. Pillipiw, upon his return to Canada, also settled in that area.[25]

Later immigrants proceeding to Edmonton were boarded onto C.P.R. trains and were transported, free of charge, through Calgary to Edmonton. The Winnipeg to Calgary run was lengthy and monotonous: "When we were travelling through southern Saskatchewan and the cities of Regina, Moose Jaw, Swift Current, Medicine Hat to Calgary, we were again overtaken by fright, that here are bare, endless fields without trees, meadows or bushes, and it became very sad and monotonous."[26] The first glimpses of Indians on the prairies also frightened the immigrants: "In a few places we had the opportunity to see from the train Indians on station platforms. We glared at them, being immediately scared . . . they looked so scary, wild, and dangerous."[27] There was also much flooding on this route in the spring, which caused delays for those travelling during this season as the engine was taken ahead to test the track, leaving the rest of the train behind.

In Edmonton, the immigrants were taken to the immigration hall where they were met by earlier Ukrainian arrivals who had been requested to meet the new settlers, or by those who had come into Edmonton for supplies and were taking advantage of the free accommodation provided by the immigration hall. Here new settlers learned of the advantages for settlement in the various districts around Edmonton, and were offered transportation to their chosen homesteads. Some chose to remain in the immigration hall, while others rented halls or municipal buildings to avoid becoming infested in the crowded surroundings. A large city building which could house ten families cost $5 to rent for a week.[28] Others took advantage of the rooms rented by Ukrainians who owned homes in the city. In the evenings, the homes of Ukrainian immigrants filled with people and one could "find out a lot about different matters and news about all surrounding colonies, as if in a central information bureau."[29]

The immigrants were now on their own. Some remained in the city to earn money to pay for the trip to the homestead — a wagon could be hired for $15 per family to Andrew (90 miles northwest of Edmonton) — or to buy a wagon, horses, and supplies before taking up a homestead. Those with funds hired wagons to look over the country before choosing a homestead, while others chose homesteads on the advice received in Edmonton. Some went out to work with farmers.

The trip to the homestead could be treacherous. There were no roads and there were many rivers and swamps to cross with wagons which were normally laden down with supplies, so the journey could take weeks. In this respect, the men's compulsory two-year experience in the Austrian army came in handy. Not only were they familiar with the German language, but they were also versed in scouting techniques — they could build rafts and bridges, and had other skills which facilitated the cross-country travel by wagon.

Eleniak had returned to Galicia in the fall of 1893. By the spring of 1894, he was back in Gretna with his family, where he spent four years. In 1896, 26 families, encouraged by Kyrylo Genik, the immigration agent, examined the territory and settled near Eleniak at Stuartburn. The proximity to Mennonite settlements was an important consideration, as employment and supplies would be readily available. Thus, the nucleus of the second Ukrainian colony in western Canada was established. Those bound for Stuartburn normally chose representatives who inspected the district before homesteads were selected. Government officials accompanied the scouts on the two–day trip and took special care that survey marks were visible. The immigrant representatives were favourably impressed when shown the progress made by the Mennonites. In addition, temporary employment opportunities in North Dakota attracted many Stuartburn settlers. Once suitable areas were chosen, the representatives returned to Winnipeg, collected their group, and proceeded southward to settle. By 1900, the Stuartburn area was the home of 3,000 Ukrainian settlers.[30]

The large influx of Ukrainian immigrants into this area necessitated a re-examination of titles on vacant land. Some quarter sections had been registered and some adjacent sections preempted with small down-payments by absentee owners. Other odd–numbered sections had been patented by railways. By 1897 the government was able to cancel land sales and open most odd–numbered sections in the area to settlement.[31] Nevertheless, government agents continued to accompany settlers to that area in order to ensure that the immigrants were able to select suitable districts and locate on open homesteads within surveyors' boundaries. Immigration officials also supplied those of limited means with food. The immigrants who settled in the Stuartburn district, and in the Dauphin, Yorkton, and Saskatoon districts, generally received more assistance from agents than those in Edmonton.

On Joseph Oleskiw's advice, the Dauphin area about 200 miles northwest of Winnipeg was recommended to a group of 30 families which arrived in Canada in the spring of 1896. Settlement was postponed in that location until late in the year due to bad roads and because the area was described as "nearly all swamp" with "soil of second and third quality" by government publications.[32] Reports by the initial settlers that the area was in fact suitable, however, confirmed Oleskiw's initiatives. Thereafter, some Ukrainian immigrants from each group of arrivals were directed to the Dauphin area: "by 1901, the Ukrainian colony in the Dauphin district, including Sifton and Ethelbert, numbered 5,500 persons and was still growing."[33]

The settlers bound for Dauphin travelled there by train through Portage la Prairie. The "Caretaker" in Dauphin, June Mouat, was responsible for locating the immigrants on homesteads. He was aided by a local Ukrainian settler who acted as interpreter and who, in some cases, accompanied new arrivals from Thunder Bay. Upon arrival in Dauphin, the immigrants were put up in the immigration hall, in tents, or in empty railroad cars until districts suitable for settlement were located. But, as in Stuartburn, the officials had problems with the lack of surveyed lands. This became especially aggravated when large groups arrived. Early in May of 1897, for example, some 500 immigrants converged on Dauphin at one time. The "Caretaker," although able to find temporary shelters for them, was unable to locate them all.[34]

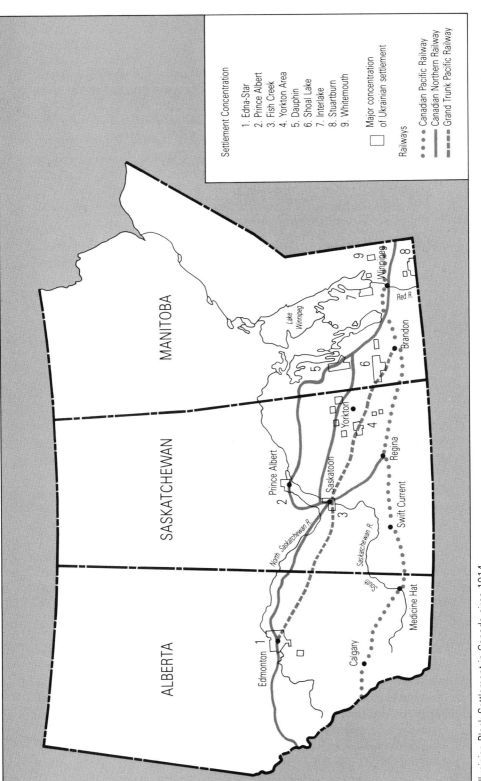

Ukrainian Block Settlement in Canada circa 1914

Settlement Concentration

1. Edna-Star
2. Prince Albert
3. Fish Creek
4. Yorkton Area
5. Dauphin
6. Shoal Lake
7. Interlake
8. Stuartburn
9. Whitemouth

☐ Major concentration of Ukrainian settlement

Railways

• • • • Canadian Pacific Railway
———— Canadian Northern Railway
– – – – Grand Trunk Pacific Railway

ALBERTA

SASKATCHEWAN

MANITOBA

Lake Winnipeg

Edmonton

Calgary

Medicine Hat

Swift Current

Regina

Saskatoon

Prince Albert

North Saskatchewan R.

South Saskatchewan R.

Yorkton

Brandon

Winnipeg

Red R.

One pioneer described the site selection process, which was a prerequisite to settlement experienced by many immigrants in all areas of western Canada:

> We arrived in Dauphin on May 6, 1897. The little town was just beginning to grow. We were put up in tents near the station and next morning, having left the women and children in the tents, we started on foot to look for places available for settlement, north and west of Dauphin, because the land nearer to town was already taken by English and Scottish immigrants who arrived before us. . . .
>
> I being a lad of twenty, was given the task of carrying the heavy bags with provisions for our group of prospectors, while they went ahead with spades and axes, occasionally testing the quality of the soil and cutting a path through the underbrush. We made about 30 miles during the first day, going in a northwesterly direction, inspecting the land which was covered with dense bush, some meadows, and in places with forests. . . . Some ten miles beyond Sifton we stopped for the night in the middle of the woods. . . . The next day our party went further in a northwesterly direction and halted in the bush not far from where the Ukrainian village of Ethelbert is today. We found good black soil and spent several days looking over the district.[35]

Some emigrants, after spending as long as six weeks looking for a suitable location in the Dauphin area, returned to Winnipeg and were redirected to the Pleasant Home area.[36] Others squatted on the government's Permanent Timber Reserve south of Dauphin. Immigration authorities had felt that the Dauphin area would be advantageous because the immigrants would "be able in that neighbourhood to find ready employment in the cordwood camps during the winter season,"[37] but few expected that 19 sections within the Timber Reserve would be settled.[38] After a long period of correspondence, the government agreed to relinquish the even-numbered sections of the Reserve to the squatters and the railway agreed to relinquish its claim to the lands on the understanding "that we may select even-numbered sections of equal value in lieu thereof."[39]

The Pleasant Home colony, located 40 miles north of Winnipeg, was established in 1897 by settlers who were unable to find suitable locations in Dauphin. Because of their depleted resources, Genik suggested that they settle closer to Winnipeg. Settlement in the area, however, was hampered by the confusing classifications placed on quarter sections. Odd-numbered sections were not open to colonization because the release of the timber reserves for settlement had been delayed.[40] In addition, the district had been reserved for Icelandic colonies. Commissioner

McCreary nevertheless urged the Deputy Minister of the Interior to open the area:

> If all those Townships in that district were open I think quite a nice colony of Galicians and Germans from Pennsylvania and Europe might be added to the eleven families who settled there about a month ago. I may say that the six delegates whom I sent out a few days ago to look over this district returned this morning well satisfied. Two of these were Galicians from Pennsylvania who spoke good English and the others were German-speaking Galicians of a superior class.[41]

By settling English and German-speaking immigrants within 40 miles of Winnipeg, the immigration authorities assured themselves an easily available source of interpreters. The Galicians considered the area to be most desirable, as it was densely timbered. In addition, the government devised an employment scheme for the settlers which involved clearing timber and cutting a road 25 feet wide.[42] By 1903, 700 to 800 Ukrainian families had settled in this southern interlake district.

The Bukovynians who had refused to vacate the immigration hall in Winnipeg were sent to the Yorkton district in 1897. McCreary noted the difficulties in establishing a new settlement: "If I had not used force, locked them in the cars, got the Police and so forth, there would not have been one at Yorkton yet."[43] The destitute group was accompanied to Yorkton by an immigration agent who had been instructed to see to it that the settlers were placed on farms and set about ploughing a few acres. Those settlers who had no money were each to be given two sacks of flour and two bushels of potatoes.[44] The Bukovynians had received flour on departing from Winnipeg, and arrangements had been made for the Manitoba and North-Western Railway, which transported the immigrants, to provide employment for them. Upon arrival in Yorkton, the immigrants were detained to build an immigrant reception hall, while surveyors located homestead boundaries.[45]

Residents of the Yorkton area welcomed the immigrants. Federation Day celebrations on 1 July 1897 saw active immigrant participation, and the local Board of Trade passed a resolution recommending the district for further settlement. The businessmen from nearby Saltcoats were also anxious that their area be settled. By 1899, 175 Ukrainian families had settled in the three colonies in the vicinity of Yorkton — Saltcoats, Crooked Lakes, and Beaver Hills.[46] By 1901, Yorkton and Saltcoats had attracted 4,500 Ukrainian settlers.[47]

The 4,000 Ukrainian immigrants who arrived in western Canada prior to the late spring of 1898 had their choice of settlement districts: Edmonton, Stuartburn, Dauphin, Pleasant Home, and Yorkton. But in April of 1898, immigration agents were instructed that Clifford Sifton,

Minister of the Interior, wished to have Galicians settled in the Fish Creek area on the Prince Albert Route of the Canadian Northern Railway.[48] The task of establishing a new colony was not easy. McCreary found it impossible to convince immigrants to go to a new settlement, so he simply sent a trainload through Regina to Fish Creek, some 50 miles north of Saskatoon. He noted that "they do not know they are going there, however, and think they are bound for Edmonton or Dauphin."[49]

When the Galicians arrived at Fish Creek, they refused to settle. A group which had originally been destined for Edmonton set out on foot to Regina and was intercepted by police. The minor rebellion was finally quashed when some 50 families were allowed to proceed to Edmonton. But the 12 families that remained established the nucleus of Ukrainian colonies in the Saskatoon district. Thereafter, McCreary instructed immigration agents that "those having close relatives, such as brothers, fathers, sisters, and mothers in any one of the present colonies, send them there; those having no relatives, or distant relatives, in any of the colonies, send them to Fish Creek or some new settlement."[50] The second group sent to the Saskatoon district, in June of 1898, refused to locate when a heavy frost which enveloped the area scared them off. The immigration agent reported:

> On arriving at Duck Lake, I found the Galicians all camped around the Station, determined to return. A heavy frost which occurred on Monday night, also Sunday night, previous had so frightened them that they decided to leave the district. I may say the frost was unprecedented, even old settlers told me that in twenty years they had never seen its equal. Ice was formed three quarters of an inch thick; many of the small trees were blighted, the foliage entirely black.[51]

The immigrants were finally persuaded to return to the settlement and within one week were locating on homesteads. By 1901, the population of the Ukrainian colonies in the Saskatoon district reached 1,000.[52]

A new settlement was established in the Strathclair and Shoal Lake region of Manitoba (150 miles west and north of Winnipeg) in May of 1899, after a Ukrainian scouting expedition was satisfied that the area was suitable. Although the growth of the colony was initially stumped by a scarlet fever epidemic, by 1903 some 3,000 Ukrainians had settled in the district. In the years 1898 to 1900, the immigration authorities also diverted Ukrainian immigrants to the interlake region in Manitoba. The general patterns of Ukrainian settlement in the Canadian west had been established by 1900. By 1905, 55,042 Ukrainian immigrants had made Canada their new home.

In the process of settlement, both the immigration authorities and the Ukrainian immigrants had a number of concerns that affected choice of location. Initial Ukrainian settlers sought proximity to German colonists; a number of Ukrainians spoke German and employment and supplies were available in established settlements. The Ukrainians also sought land rich with a resource that had been scarce and dear in Galicia and Bukovyna — trees. One farmer, for example, proudly wrote home that "I have here enough forest that I could provide firewood for winter for the whole village."[53] But this attitude puzzled immigration authorities:

> The Galicians are a peculiar people; they will not accept as a gift 160 acres of what we should consider the best land in Manitoba, that is first class wheat growing prairie land; what they particularly want is wood, and they care but little whether the land is heavy soil or light gravel; but each man must have some wood on his place.[54]

Nevertheless, the immigration agents complied with the Ukrainians' wishes and settled them on sub-marginal lands.

Ukrainians also wished to remain together, and the government agreed that they would have a greater chance of success in colonies. However, there were a number of difficulties the immigration officials faced in satisfying the immigrants in this regard. Among the practical considerations was that the government could send settlers to a colony only after the group sent there previously had been located on homesteads. Problems arose in choosing property that suited the settlers' needs, and many homesteads were either unsurveyed or the surveyors' marks had been obliterated. These factors prolonged the settlement process, and other immigrants had to be delayed or diverted elsewhere. Furthermore, settlement on even-numbered sections proved insufficient — the immigrants complained of the distance to their neighbours and that the available districts were filled up too quickly — and permission had to be sought from Ottawa to open the odd-numbered sections for settlement. In some colonies, the good lands were taken up by the initial waves of settlement and the remaining lands were of inferior quality. Many Ukrainians sacrificed land quality to be near friends or relatives.

The government had its own concerns. The labour market had to be considered. For the benefit of both the immigrants and the established farmers who employed them, the newcomers had to be evenly dispersed. It was also important that railways be equally favoured with sources of business and labour. And finally, the government was concerned that the colonies not grow too large to withstand British-Canadian influences. For practical as well as political reasons, the compromise between the Ukrainians and the government was characterized by scattered colonies. One geographer aptly noted that "fragmentation of Ukrainian block settlement did not prevent the immigrants from attaining their objectives in settlement but it provided an effective counterbalance to their tendency to live together."[55]

Establishing the Homestead

By the time the immigrants reached the homesteads they had, of necessity, already begun to adjust to the Canadian environment. Although they preferred a landscape similar to the one they had left behind, they nevertheless chose land which had resources they had lacked in the old country. Their unfamiliarity with things Canadian extended from mosquitoes to white bread, but the most severe difference between Canada and Europe was the organization of townships.

The expectations of community development that the Ukrainians brought with them are most vividly exemplified in one pioneer's plans for a colony:

> I showed him [Kyrylo Genik] on a map, my detailed plan, about how our little village would look, which would be called Kolomyia. In the centre of the township, I selected the 16th section and through its centre I planned a road; and on each side I divided the land into 32 parcels, 10 acres for a garden and lot for each settler. In the middle was to be a church, school, post office, store, at first a wind and later a steam mill. Nearby was to be the reading hall, the carpenter, tailor, and everything that was possibly required for a self-sufficient community.[56]

To Genik's observation that the tavern, police station, and jail were missing, the immigrant replied, "We are fleeing from bars, Jews, Poles, and police, so we don't want them there."[57] To Genik's further comment that "one section is for four families and you want 64," the pioneer answered: "Each would have 10 acres for his garden, and besides each deserves the 160 acres where he would have his grain field . . . and where he would drive out to work, but the family would live in the village, so they would not feel lonely and would have all comforts, like in the old land."[58] As one scholar has explained, "most of the incoming Ukrainian settlers, initially anticipating subsistence farming in the peasant tradition, viewed the quarter section homestead as being in excess of their requirements."[59] Having lived in compact village communities in Galicia and Bukovyna, the immigrants naturally had similar expectations in Canada. The notion of owning and working a field at some distance from their home was not uncommon. Lands, often acquired through intermarriage, were rarely situated adjacently. Adjusting to life on a quarter section meant adjusting to a life of isolation.

Encountering mosquitoes for the first time was another new and startling experience. Incidents were often recalled by pioneers:

> There were such masses of them [mosquitoes] that they obstructed the view to work. . . . They once attacked our father so badly, in spite of the heavy sheepskin coat he was wearing for protection, that his neck and throat were badly swollen and his face and ears were a shapeless mass.[60]

Veterans soon became accustomed to the insects, but the new arrivals felt persecuted: "These poor people suffered great pain and some of them almost went mad from the pain; it was so difficult for them to endure these tortures."[61] The immigrants learned quickly that burning dry dung and other materials that produced clouds of smoke kept the mosquitoes away.

Harnessing horses became quite a chore for those who were loaned or possessed horses. Stories abounded about farmers who proudly rode atop their newly acquired wagons, but could not let the horses to pasture, not knowing how to approach the harness. If they were accidentally successful in removing the harness, they surely failed in trying to re-harness the animals.

Immigrants were even surprised by the white bread eaten in Canada on a regular basis — a delicacy in Galicia and Bukovyna where rye bread was the staple. Genik explained the situation to one disappointed immigrant who was expecting traditional Easter celebrations upon arrival in Canada: "In Canada people eat paska [Easter bread] every day, because the bread here is better and whiter than in the old country. Meat, butter, and eggs are eaten here every day of the year. As you see Easter here lasts all year, not like in the old country for only three days."[62]

The immediate concerns of the settlers, however, were simply to keep themselves fed and sheltered. The first contact with the reality of homestead life was often traumatic. One farmer described the sense of helplessness:

> When he first came out here . . . there was not a living soul for miles and miles around. He and his wife were brought in a wagon to a certain spot on the vast prairies by a C.N.R. agent who with a wide sweep of his hand indicated to them the land which was now theirs and then drove off, leaving them standing there like children seemingly abandoned by both God and Man.[63]

Nevertheless, most homesteaders came prepared with experience at subsistence living and with the basic tools — axe and shovel.

The first task was to construct a temporary shelter, referred to as a *burdy, kurnyk,* or *zemlianka* — a simple dug-out. A pit was sunk a few feet below ground level and covered with an inverted "V" pole-roof overlaid with sod. The structure, as described by observers, was a low hovel "not unlike the dwellings you may still see in backward parts of Ireland or in the Scottish highlands."[64] The shack was meant to offer some protection from the elements. It was not always successful, as one pioneer recalls:

> My earliest memories are the old sod shack, the loud, crashing prairie thunderstorms, as my poor mother huddled in the corner of our rough home with her brood and asked us to pray aloud with her for Divine protection; the earth trembled with peals of thunder and the rain water poured in bucketfuls through the sod roof of the shack. We had to rush around in the shack, using all available pails, tubs and utensils to catch the rain water which was pouring through the roof. Usually our efforts to protect ourselves and our few belongings weren't too successful. The hard packed clay floor would turn to slippery goo. The bedcovers and clothing would be streaked and spotted with the muddy rain water which dribbled through the roof. What a clean-up job after the rain.[65]

Frequently, more than one family lived in these dwellings.

Once the temporary shelters were constructed, the more destitute men left the homestead to seek work. The women and children were left to fend for themselves. The wife began clearing the land for a garden, and frequently, with the accumulation of logs, undertook the construction of a permanent house. Men, in those families with sufficient funds to supply food for a longer period of time, normally delayed leaving for work until a permanent shelter had been constructed for their families.

The construction of the house was a major undertaking, involving long months of hard manual labour. Cooperation from all available family members was essential and, when possible, neighbours helped with the work. Men normally cut and put up the logs to form the walls and frame for the roof, whereas women did most of the work involving clay — plastering the walls, glossing the floors. Both men and women also hired themselves out to do such work, for which they were paid with small quantities of food. For the immigrants, it was indeed a joyful occasion when the house had been constructed.

The house was "fundamentally a south-facing, rectangular, single-storey, two-room, mud-plastered" structure,[66] whose size was determined by the length of available timber. Its furnishings "approximated that of the average peasant household in Ukraine during the same period"[67] — wide rough lumber bunks, a small table, a stationary bench, and a large mud stove on which children slept to keep warm. The floors were packed earth smoothed over with clay; their glossiness was maintained by a weekly washing with a solution of cow dung and water."[68] Walls were made of corner-notched or dovetailed horizontal logs covered with clay: "We dug a round pit in the ground about 5 yards in diameter, just deep enough to scrape the black earth off the top and reach the clay underneath. We mixed hay and water with the clay and kneaded it with our bare feet. With this clay we plastered our house."[69] Where oxen were available, they were led through the pit to mix the clay underfoot. Many settlers added horse or cow dung to the mixture. The house was whitewashed inside and out to protect the clay plaster from eroding and also to repel insects from windows. To make whitewash, an "ash-clay found under the surface of the ground cover in swampy areas" was dug, pressed into flat cakes, dried, then dissolved.[70] Later, active lime and water with skim milk was used for whitewashing. The roof was either thatched with slough grass, necessitating a high pitch to shed water rapidly, or covered with turf or sod, with a low pitch to prevent sod from eroding. Thatched roofs often rose "in a series of steps at the corners."[71]

The building accommodated the family and, in the first years, fowl were also offered protection under the same roof. Often, oxen and a milk cow lived on one side of the house. The house also afforded shelter to those newcomers — family or friends — who had arrived later and who had not yet had a chance to construct their own dwellings. One government observer was astounded by the overcrowded conditions. Among the Galicians about 15 miles north of Neepawa, he "found 25 individuals, all women and children, cooking, living, and sleeping in a one-roomed, one storey house, 14' × 20' × 7½'. . . . There were 10 men in the party. Nine of these slept in a cow byre 12' × 14' × 5½', in which all their spare household goods were also stored. . . . The tenth man slept under some brush outside."[72]

Such was the fate of the pioneers. Once their circumstances improved, frame buildings were constructed in the Anglo-Canadian style. Often poorly insulated, they "were found to be poor substitutes for the tested traditional variants. Some families underwent considerable hardship in their new 'improved' Anglicized and modernized dwelling and in the words of one 'many near froze to death'."[73] It was by relying on only a few tools and available materials — logs, clay, straw, slough grass, cow or horse dung, and lime (when accessible) — that the pioneers were able to construct the most practical permanent dwellings.

Clearing land for a garden was another major undertaking, which normally coincided with the building of the house. Trees were cut, stumps rooted, stones removed, and the land ploughed: "At times the wife and husband harnessed themselves to the plough. Having ploughed a few acres, the Ukrainian farmer sowed rye [and] planted potatoes to survive the winter on his own food. It was great luck for a family when all was harvested successfully."[74] Others planted cabbages, turnips, garlic, poppies, and hemp. Staples included bread, potatoes, and vegetables. Mushrooms, fish, and rabbit completed the diet. When supplies were depleted, grass prepared with fungus kept the pioneers alive.

Methods of eking a living from the soil were primitive. Wheat grinders were a luxurious commodity. The hand-made and hand-operated machine for pressing oil was a "farm implement widely sought by housewives."[75] With it, cooking oil was squeezed from flax and hemp seeds. Cloth was woven on looms. Rope was made by stripping fibre from hemp plants and spinning it on a spinning wheel. Socks were made from rabbit skins. For tobacco, pipe smokers used the bark scraped from the red willow, trying to "console themselves with the delusion that the smokes were, in fact, quite delightful."[76] Grains were reaped with a primitive scythe, called a cradle because it caught the falling stalks on three or four prongs attached to its long handle. Women and children were kept gainfully employed digging seneca or snake root which, when dried, was sold for 13 cents a pound.[77]

Obtaining supplies meant trekking to the nearest village, which in most cases was located 40 to 60 miles away. Under such conditions, shopping became a "carefully planned procedure, recurring at necessarily frequent intervals, and gone through with as methodically as the spring plowing."[78] In the winter, supplies were hauled on hand sleighs. In summer, they were carried on the pioneers' backs. Many times, when men were away working, women carried the 50-pound bags of flour or potatoes from the general store to the homestead. One pioneer recalls the distance covered in the acquisition of firewood, flour, and mail:

One had to walk two miles almost every second or third day to get wood which I carried on my back. Also one had to go every second or third day two miles to the neighbour to mill the wheat into flour for bread, and every two weeks 16 miles to the post office for letters. Mail between Edmonton and the farms was delivered only every two weeks.[79]

When cattle were acquired, there was great joy in the family. Oxen eased the burdens of working the land, horses alleviated the strains of walking long distances, and cows provided a new variety of food to the menu — milk, cream, cheese, and butter. Settlers often used cows to plough fields when only one large animal could be afforded. But keeping the cattle fed in winter was quite a chore. Snow had to be dug to find old dry grass, and river ice had to be melted for water. When the settlers reached the cattle-owning stage, the acquisition of poultry followed, and then the goal of subsistence farming was achieved. The initial three to five years of settlement were the hardest. Once established, the settlers took great pride in what they had done with their own hands. Subsequent immigrants were able to get help and borrow supplies from these "established" settlers, alleviating some of the initial hardships.

Fate Does Not Ask

Hardships on the prairies involved more than isolation and hard manual labour. They included coping with unforeseeable developments: illness and a troublesome climate. Lack of proper medical attention in Galicia and Bukovyna, faulty medical examinations at point of departure and at port of entry, confinement on trains, ships, and in quarantine, and unhealthy, unsanitary conditions and incomplete diets on the homesteads contributed to the incidence of illness among Ukrainian immigrants.

Stuartburn had been quarantined in 1892 due to an outbreak of smallpox. In 1897, scarlet fever claimed several lives at Gonor, Yorkton, and Stuartburn. W.F. McCreary noted that "one splendid man at Gonor . . . lost his entire family of three within a week from the disease."[80] The most government and health officials could do was set up quarantines in areas where contagious diseases did exist, and vaccinate the population.

About 1,000 Galician passengers who arrived in Canada in mid-May of 1898 were quarantined at Halifax due to an outbreak of smallpox. The state of health among the group was dubious: "650 left [Halifax] by train this morning. 150 held being families in which were measles and non-contagious diseases. Have had three deaths pneumonia and infantile diseases. Two born, twins. All well when on train. No new cases smallpox. Everything disinfected."[81] After a month's delay, most of the group were sent westward, but smallpox broke out again on the train. At the end of June, immigration authorities set up a quarantine for the passengers in Winnipeg. The immigrants were accommodated in tents. Their condition was described by McCreary:

So far there are only three cases of smallpox: one child of eight months old died. . . . In addition to the smallpox we have 28 cases of measles, now isolated, and one family with whooping cough. There have also been three births and of course these required a little extra care on account of having to sleep on the damp ground.[82]

When a long and heavy rain came, McCreary was forced to report that after 48 hours of the downpour, the quarantine area was a disaster:

The ground as you know is low and wet, and I have been moving the tents every few hours to keep the people out of the wet as much as possible; but there is great disaffection. . . . There are now about 58 cases of Measles, and I regret to say one death, and one or two children have contracted Pneumonia, from the effects of sleeping in the wet tents, I suppose.[83]

Early in July, McCreary reported that "some seven or eight children had died from Pneumonia contracted from the wet."[84] By this time, McCreary was ready to send the majority of the immigrants off to their destinations, but not without disinfecting them first:

Prior to despatching them to their destinations we in the first place had a strong solution of formaline in which we bathed their heads and the upper portion of their bodies. We then made them go to the deep ditch along the railway track and everyone took a bath, clothing themselves in their clothing which had been washed in the meantime; and were all started to their destinations in grand shape.[85]

It took this group of immigrants two months and some ten deaths to complete the Halifax to Winnipeg leg of the trip. This kind of experience was common with subsequent large shiploads. The quarantine depot at Winnipeg was moved, however, to Stoney Mountain, fifteen miles from the city and one mile from the penitentiary. The total number of deaths due to disease during the time of passage reached 20 in the summer of 1898, and averaged 5 to 7 per group of 500 people. Illnesses included scarlet fever, smallpox, measles, chicken pox, pneumonia, whooping cough, and deaths from exposure.

Notwithstanding the precautions in Winnipeg, some groups were sent on to the colonies without prior medical attention. Measles broke out undetected among a group of 46 Ukrainians who went to Neepawa in early July of 1898. During their 24-hour stay in that town, they were visited by curious citizens. Thereafter, a measles epidemic broke out in the district.[86] A serious scarlet fever epidemic erupted among the 80 families who moved to Strathclair in May of 1899. The deaths were the worst possible shock to the already miserable families. As one official wrote: "I buried four in one Waggon yesterday and could scarcely restrain the Bereaved Mothers who followed the Waggons kissing the Crude Coffins and had to be turned back."[87] Six children died en route from Winnipeg. Four more passed away at the colony. For the 197 arrivals in this, the first group of Ukrainians to settle in the Shoal Lake and Strathclair district, the number of deaths was high, and the experience a tragic one.

Medical assistance during childbirth along the route or on the homesteads was rarely available. Many women were experienced mid-wives who helped and treated one another, but in the isolated environment of the homestead, babies were frequently born before the mid-wife could arrive. The frequent deaths of mothers and infants added to the trauma of pioneer life. Nevertheless, one Canadian observer felt that Ukrainian mothers handled childbirth rather bravely, as a fact of life: "the women as a rule are very healthy. They have plenty of children — whose arrival gives them little trouble. A Galician matron who has had an addition to her family in the morning may often be seen out and about by the evening, though more commonly she will take two or three days' rest."[88] Notwithstanding such feats, the consciousness of isolation on the farms was only aggravated when serious illness struck.

Ukrainians were able to cope with uncontrollable forces such as illness, and even family death, with the help of their strong supernatural, mystical, and religious beliefs in which dreams, folk medicine, witches, and spirits played significant roles. Beliefs and medicinal practices were handed down from generation to generation, together with the legends and tales of the ancestors. In addition to making vows, which entailed the sacrifice of some pleasantry of life in return for good health, Ukrainians had faith in cures. Cures could be assured by the use of amulets, incantations, and concoctions. Concoctions could be a strange mixture of ingredients from the animal, plant, and mineral worlds, or they could be as simple as easing swelling by applying a hot white onion and cooling a fever by drinking whisky spiked with garlic.[89] In times of tragedy, a belief in the forces of good and evil — manifested through witches — offered explanations and consolation. The folklorist, Samuel Koenig, noted that "the fields of activity of the various witches embrace practically everything of concern to man, from personal affliction to bad luck with cattle and extremes in weather, and the means they employ are equally varied."[90] As an example, the peasants believed that illness would strike a person traversing a path on which an evil witch had sprinkled thorns or ashes. Evil witches were attributed with the Devil's power to cause illness and famine, and were blamed for hail, storms, floods, and droughts. But the black evils had counterparts in white magic which could be summoned for protection in a variety of ways, most dealing with a strong belief in God and strict Christian observances. Evil was, literally, exorcised.

A multitude of proverbs also eased and explained incomprehensible events or tragedies. Fatalism, resignation, and misery — appropriate not only in the Galician and Bukovynian settings, but also in the early years of settlement in Canada — were topics of a number of sayings:

> Rusyna Pan sotvoryv na bidu ta na nuzhdu (The landlord created the Ruthenian for poverty and destitution); Tak bude iak Boh dast (It will be as God wills); Dolia ne pytaie: schcho khoche te i daie (Fate does not ask: what it wills it gives); De nema boliu tam nema i zhyttia (Without pain there is no life).[91]

This belief in fate and supernatural forces was sometimes carried to extremes, causing a few immigrants to refuse to work or to defy hazards. One woman in Alberta refused to abide by diphtheria quarantine regulations, and when five of her children died, she replied, "God will punish who he will."[92] Other Ukrainians, familiar with "higher" scientific explanations, sought to discard these vestiges of their peasant culture. But there is no question that initially these explanations helped the immigrants to survive despair.

The Ukrainians had left Galicia and Bukovyna hoping to perpetrate their traditional lifestyle in a land of greater opportunity. Their behaviour aboard the trains, their definitions of suitable settlement areas, their goals on the homestead, and their means of coping were, naturally, typical of their background. But circumstances in Canada required some immediate adjustments. Although insulating themselves from the foreignness of the new land, they were nevertheless hampered by the unmanageable forces of disease and climate. To counter these, they invoked traditional remedies. Economically, they were achieving their goal of subsistence agriculture. Socially, they had transplanted into Canada their own society. In order for all Canadians to reap the economic benefits — in Stuartburn, non-Ukrainian storekeepers became fluent in Ukrainian[93] — cultural differences had to be tolerated.

CHAPTER 6

THE ADVISORS

The intelligentsia and clergy did not accompany the immigrants in significant numbers; as a result, leadership roles were assumed by those educated Ukrainians who offered an effective liaison with the host society. Ukrainian agents employed by the Canadian authorities were especially prominent for practical reasons. They were able to advise and aid their fellow countrymen. In the 1890s, a triumvirate of men arose, constituting whatever leadership and sense of direction existed among the peasants on arrival in the new land. They were the overseers, dedicated to the immigrants' well-being in Canada.

Joseph Oleskiw: Pioneer Advisor

The community spokesmen who became prominent as godfathers to the Ukrainians in Canada were Dr. Joseph Oleskiw, Kyrylo Genik, and Reverend Nestor Dmytriw. Their guardianship extended from the moment the peasants departed the old country until the time they settled on their homesteads. All three were representatives of the Ukrainian "radical" intelligentsia.

Like the Austrian government, the Ukrainian intelligentsia believed that emigration could not be stopped. But whereas the Austrian administration (plagued by landowners losing their manpower supply and citizens worried about the disorganized exodus) remained inactive, the Ukrainian intelligentsia sought to organize the emigration. In the forefront of this endeavour was Oleskiw.

Oleskiw, however, laboured under a handicap. To retain his position as Imperial and Royal Professor at the teachers' seminary in Lviv, he could not openly advocate emigration for fear of arrest. Nevertheless, he undertook an investigative trip to Canada and the United States in the fall of 1895 and was accorded access to Canadian government officials: Sir Charles Tupper, High Commissioner in London; T. Mayne Daly, Minister of the Interior; and Edward Schultze, Austrian Consul-General in Canada.

Upon his return he unobtrusively set about organizing emigration. He reported his findings to a meeting of "leading Ukrainians from the capitol and various districts of the province held on November 14, 1895" in Lviv.[1] From the meeting, an emigrants' aid committee was formed "to assist emigrating peasants and to protect them against exploitation."[2] An impressive list, consisting of an economist, an architect, a lawyer, a newspaper editor, and a number of priests made up the directorship. Oleskiw, however, remained the linchpin of the committee and all prospective emigrants were encouraged to seek his advice.

Oleskiw's role as advisor rested on the publication of two of his pamphlets: *Pro Vilni Zemli* and *O Emigratsii*. The national populists of the Prosvita Society, committed to redirecting the stream of Ukrainian emigrants bound for Brazil, published *Pro Vilni Zemli*, which depicted the horrors of Brazil. After Oleskiw's return from North America, the Russophile Kachkovsky Society published *O Emigratsii*, Oleskiw's description of Canada and what it had to offer newcomers.[3]

Peasants did seek out Oleskiw, as illustrated by the case of one Tymko Hawryliuk from the village of Lakhmanivka. He had heard of Canada but desired more information. First he sought out his priest, who offered no advice but scolded him for his excessively worldly concerns; next he tried the village lawyer, who knew about Canada but being opposed to emigration in principle would not advise him. Nevertheless, the lawyer did refer Hawryliuk to Oleskiw in Lviv. The peasant then borrowed funds for train fare and managed to locate the Narodni Dim (National Hall). There he made enquiries as to where he might find "the professor" who knew about Canada. The secretary of the Narodni Dim, although not particularly interested in emigration, gave directions to the professor's house. Ultimately, the peasant arrived and was cordially greeted. The two men chatted for several hours, Oleskiw describing the conditions to be encountered in Canada and asking pointed questions about the peasant's means. Hawryliuk was pleased to have found someone who was willing to help him but was distressed to learn that the good professor advised him not to emigrate because he did not have sufficient funds. Hawryliuk decided to go to Canada anyway.[4]

Such, then, was the chain of events that haphazardly led many peasants to Oleskiw. While his two booklets, published by the two most influential Ukrainian reading societies in Galicia, were ensured wide distribution, they did not guarantee an orderly flow of emigrants under the direction of the intelligentsia. Indeed, problems arose with the Kachkovsky Society's translated edition of *O Emigratsii*. Oleskiw's daughter, for example, lamented that "it is a shame that the language in the book released by the Kachkovsky Society is very bad and I fear that a bad impression was made on Father by his own thoughts, translated into 'iazychie' [a mixture of Old Slavonic and Russian] at the proof stage."[5] Claims were made that Oleskiw's cautions and warnings were misrepresented to the point of discouraging emigration to Canada altogether. Thus, although Oleskiw was able to inspire a stream of prospective emigrants to seek his advice, his success was circumscribed.

Indeed, the efforts of the intelligentsia were, on the whole, limited. First, their energies were often diverted by the Russophile-Ukrainophile debates of the period. Second, some adamantly opposed emigration on the grounds that problems in Galicia and Bukovyna would be solved and "that the peasants too must do their share, rather than flee to other lands."[6] One lectured a peasant by telling him "that once the 'Eastern Question' [Ukrainians in Russia] is resolved, Galicia will have its own Tsar. Then the Polish dominance over our lands will end, and there will be no need to emigrate."[7] Third, although a network of reading societies did exist, they were restricted to an advisory role only. Oleskiw never realized his most important and practical goal, a steamship concession, which would have put the venture on some sort of professional or institutional footing. And finally, the intelligentsia could not compete with unscrupulous agents, who roamed about the Galician and Bukovynian countryside promising great riches overseas — for a price.

It is difficult to ascertain precisely how many Ukrainians came to Canada as a result of Oleskiw's activities. He was directly responsible for only a few hundred. However, his publications, his constant stream of articles in the local Galician press, his correspondence advocating emigration to Canada, his work on the Emigration Committee, and his lectures to Prosvita societies probably influenced thousands. Yet the Canadian government questioned Oleskiw's effectiveness as only a small percentage of the total Ukrainian immigration to Canada could be directly ascribed to him. Oleskiw blamed his failure to receive proper recognition on his approach to Canadian authorities:

I deeply regret that I initially approached the Canadian government on humanitarian rather than business grounds. They do not understand the former. However, they have a point — such a stand is window-dressing and not saleable. I have been humanitarianizing for an entire year and now see that nothing can be done in this manner. It has no strength, no power of persuasion, and my entire effort is being dragged in the mud. Nowadays steamship agents are storming through Galicia, and our peasants are going from Winnipeg to the swamps of Beausejour and Brokenhead, or buying 10-30 acres in St. Norbert.[8]

By the latter half of 1896, Oleskiw was discouraged. He had launched but one successful colony (Genik's) and a second group did not reach the destination he had chosen for them — private agents had gotten hold of them first.[9] Despite the setbacks, Oleskiw continued to act as advisor to emigrants until his death in 1903.

Oleskiw's main advice was that only emigrants with capital should seek out Canadian prospects. He directed poor emigrants to the United States to earn money before settling. He recommended areas for homesteading and endlessly issued warnings against swindlers along the route. Finally, at his urging, Kyrylo Genik was appointed as an immigration agent in Winnipeg.

Kyrylo Genik: "Tsar of Canada"

Born in 1857, Kyrylo Genik-Berezowsky graduated from the Gymnasium in Lviv. He first became an elementary school teacher and then a store owner. His affiliation with the Radical Party brought him into contact with leading members of the intelligentsia, including Ivan Franko, the prominent historian, and Oleskiw, who encouraged him to emigrate to Canada. After attending the meeting which saw the creation of the emigrant aid society, he left Galicia in 1896 as a group leader for Oleskiw's Stuartburn colony. On 25 July, he arrived in Winnipeg with his wife and four children.[10]

From the beginning, it was recognized that Genik would be a great aid in organizing the Ukrainians in Canada. He turned his minor appointment as translator for the Immigration Branch into an overworked, full-time position. Genik would be Oleskiw's counterpart in Canada — the advisor. He articulated to the peasants the realities of the Canadian environment. He also provided, however tenuously, a symbol of the old world intelligentsia in the new land.

Genik kept a regular correspondence with *Svoboda*, the Ukrainian newspaper first published in New Jersey but later in Pennsylvania, and with *Narod* (People), the Galician Radical Party organ, as well as an interchange of letters with Franko and Oleskiw. He shared completely Oleskiw's sentiments about how the emigration should be run; in fact, Oleskiw's recommendation, along with his linguistic capabilities (he knew German as well as English) secured him his job. The Ministry of the Interior contacted him to use his "influence" in stemming unseasonal emigration.[11]

The major forum through which Genik expressed his views was *Svoboda*. Prior to the establishment of *Kanadiiskyi Farmer* (Canadian Farmer) in Winnipeg in 1903, it was the only Ukrainian-language newspaper of any note in North America. Ukrainians not only in the United States and Canada, but also those in Brazil, Galicia, and Bukovyna, subscribed and contributed to it. Indeed, *Svoboda* provided a channel of communication for those of the intelligentsia concerned with peasant emigration and life in the new world. Oleskiw, for example, retained very good ties with the newspaper; his letters often appeared in its pages. On his first trip to North America, he visited its headquarters in Pennsylvania. Meanwhile, an editorial described Oleskiw as an "honest and intelligent" Galician patriot.[12]

Svoboda, from the beginning, had a radical tinge. Its editors never lost sight of the intelligentsia's ideals of improving the condition of the peasants. In North America, however, new perspectives and new definitions articulated those ideals. The backwardness of the peasants was measured against the "civilized" characteristics of Americans and Canadians. Most of the obstacles erected by the class structure in Galicia and Bukovyna had to be toppled to be rectified, but such obstacles were absent in the new world. Canada and the United States promised egalitarianism. Consequently, the intelligentsia, through *Svoboda*, sought to prepare the peasants for an improved lifestyle; they took great pains to identify the pitfalls of the peasant character, to criticize them, and to offer advice in regard to breaking out of the peasant mold.

Editorials, for example, abhorred the "selfish individualism" of the Ukrainian peasant, citing this characteristic as the main restraining force in setting up organizations.[13] Drinking was a major problem,[14] and fisticuffs were denounced as a useless means of settling disputes.[15] Ukrainians were accused of being their own worst enemies due to their ignorance and lack of desire to break away from it.[16] Their servility was said to be a result of weak character.[17] Although immigrants in the Yorkton area, for example, were hard-working and thrifty, an editoral nevertheless declared that they would do well to exorcise old country "sins."[18] Ukrainians were compared unfavourably to Doukhobors; indeed, it was thought that the peasant way of life resembled the condition of Indians and Inuit. The peasants were berated for not conforming to the ideals of European civilization.[19] In a moment of despair, one editorial stated: "Either here or in the old country we always hope for better things for our people, but we say there is little hope for the future because the root of our problem is us ourselves."[20]

Through letters and editorials, *Svoboda* promoted a program for enlightenment, urging the establishment of Ukrainian schools, the teaching of native language and history, the acquisition of Ukrainian books and newspapers, and the organization of reading halls. Using a "carrot and stick" approach, it pointed to other "enlightened" nationalities as providing the example.[21] *Svoboda* also constantly warned against non-Ukrainian priests and impostors invading Ukrainian colonies, called for an end to the lawsuit epidemic, "a Galician disease which only the Canadian climate might cure — but only with the younger generation,"[22] and praised Ukrainian women domestics, who had gained a favourable reputation in Canada. *Svoboda's* contributors were imbued with the imperative to retain and foster a distinctive Ukrainian identity, yet make it appropriate to the North American environment.

Genik personified this newspaper's point of view. As immigration agent and interpreter, the majority of his time was spent accompanying newly arrived immigrants to their homesteads and advising them on practical matters — long winters, early frost, wheat prices, and the dangers of travel.[23] Like Oleskiw, he issued warnings that only those with money should come, that they should not arrive in fall or winter, and that they should proceed directly to their destinations to avoid contact with shysters.[24] He also did not hesitate to respond to what he thought were slights in Anglo-Canadian newspapers on the value of the emigration or of the Ukrainians. By many peasants he "was considered . . . something of a tsar of Canada"[25] — a trusted confrere, much like Oleskiw in Galicia. Indeed, he had an advantage over Oleskiw; his government position gave him stature, whereas Oleskiw floundered before the officially recognized emigration agents.

Yet desirous that the peasants present a favourable image in the new land, he was highly critical of his countrymen. He believed that the "khlops" were faltering under bad habits and nefarious influences. Illiteracy, lack of hygiene, syphilis, and just plain ignorance were but some of the attributes that disturbed Genik.[26] To improve their appearance, for example, he strongly recommended that they discard the garments of the old country and arrive in Canada dressed in western clothes.[27]

Genik was an old world radical but a new world liberal. Responsible for the fate of thousands of peasants in Canada, he was gratified by the Laurier administration's concern for his people. Governmental care for the peasants was one of the elements lacking in Galicia and Bukovyna. Indeed, it was an essential aim of the radicals that authorities respond to the distress of Galicians and Bukovynians. Genik had frequently accused Vienna of negligence, of "treating us like a step-mother and giving us no help."[28] In this respect, the goals of the Ukrainian radical intelligentsia in Galicia and Bukovyna were redefined in the Canadian context. Until 1905, what was radical in the old country was merely liberal in Canada. Genik, while retaining his radical tinge and socialist beliefs, was a strong supporter of the Liberal Party.[29]

As a spokesman for Ukrainians in Canada, Genik had difficulty in translating their nationality into terms Canadians would readily understand and respect:

> . . . it is difficult to translate the word "rusyn" into one English word, because it comes out Russian and we are not Russians. The Roman Catholics take good care of the Poles but Ruthenians or "rusyny" are overlooked. From that point of view, I side with Russia, because of its fame. And Canadians understand clearly what that is. A "rusyn" cannot clearly explain his nationality and that is why they are called Galicians. But there is no such country on earth. If one says he is Austrian, then there is respect. But then when someone speaks to our man in German (because a lot of Canadians speak German) our man does not understand, and is viewed as a nationless liar. We must rid ourselves of this lack of nomenclature and our responsibility is to do this as soon as possible.[30]

At the same time, he was an internationalist in outlook; this stemmed from his socialist perspective. For him, it was the ill effects of the capitalist system that had led to the emigration in the first place.[31] On one occasion he wrote:

> Workers need no longer console themselves with the hope that perhaps some day things will get better — rather they should boldly and openly join in the struggle against capitalism and exploitation and demand absolute social justice, justice to which they are entitled as human beings. How is one to adapt to this struggle? The answer is: through unification, by forming associations of workingmen of all nationalities.[32]

Genik's international viewpoint was developed along economic and class lines rather than national ones. It was a conception that many Anglo-Canadians, preoccupied with theories of British racial superiority, could not comprehend.

Indeed, Genik exemplified an international *Weltanschauung* that was prevalent not only among the intelligentsia but among many Ukrainian settlers. It was a product of the old world experience. First, the peasants' nationality was not readily identifiable; its definition was still developing in Galicia and Bukovyna. Second, the Austro-Hungarian Empire was the home of many nationalities with whom Ukrainians had to interact and co-exist. The compulsory two years' army service also brought them into working relationships with a multitude of peoples and languages. And third, the teachings of socialism, to which a large number adhered, sought to differentiate humanity along class rather than national lines.

Of course, this international outlook did not necessarily imply a lack of prejudice. Those groups, especially Poles and Jews, who were blamed for the Ukrainians' economic woes, were despised, and many of the Ukrainians in Canada reacted negatively to any perceived economic or religious intrusion by them. On the other hand, the Germans, who had become synonymous with economic opportunity to Ukrainians in the Austro-Hungarian Empire, were well-liked and trusted as employers and neighbours in Canada.

Anglo-Canadians also provided economic opportunities, and being accepted by them was important to the Ukrainians. In part, this desire for acceptance explained Genik's chagrin at the negative impression of Galicians and Bukovynians often announced in the Anglo-Canadian press. Although he knew that the peasants needed "improving," they were nevertheless economically necessary and beneficial to Canada.[33] Genik saw no legitimate reason for the hostile attitude exhibited in some quarters. There was, for example, little justification for the actions of English settlers in Brokenhead, Manitoba, who sold their farms cheaply and moved out when a Ukrainian colony was established nearby.[34] Or why should the report of a mixed marriage in the Dauphin area, between a Frederick Nex, of London, and Carolina Zavivna, outrage the English press; what was this nonsense about racial purity being blemished as a result? It was a reminder of old world chauvinism and discrimination which angered and, at the same time, perplexed Genik and other Ukrainian spokesmen because it was inconsistent with new world egalitarianism.[35] As one *Svoboda* contributor succinctly put it: "the English boast about freedom but this is a lie if they do not recognize the right of all people to freedom."[36]

It was precisely the apparent egalitarianism in North America that appealed to Genik the most. A recognition of freedoms new to Ukrainians would lead to equality. Genik maintained, for example, that "our fate depends upon ourselves; we have to prove that we are men to shape our destiny."[37] For Genik, this was a statement of faith. On the basis of this faith, he encouraged the establishment of reading halls so that "every person would recognize himself as a free man in a free land and know both his responsibilities and privileges, as well as who he should believe and who he should not."[38] To Genik, emigration was a necessity because the peasants required freedom of opportunity in order to mature.[39] His conviction that it was the lack of opportunities in Galicia and

Bukovyna which stunted the peasants' development was based on the notion that Ukrainians were capable of breaking out of their peasant traditions. In the initial stages, it was his task to ensure that the primary economic opportunities, a necessary prerequisite to social, cultural, and political development, were available.

While Genik did not idealize the peasants, he was harsh on the intelligentsia. He doubted whether the old country intelligentsia fully understood what a blessing emigration was to the peasant. Consequently, he lambasted the intelligentsia who did not emigrate until the peasants had first done the work in the new land. He cited the example of a Mr. Velychko, an acquaintance, who lasted eight days in Canada and returned home without even seeing all of Winnipeg.[40] He warned the intelligentsia that if they emigrated they must be prepared for everything, even hard physical labour. In fact, in one of his more dour moments, he wrote that mass emigration was "the people's way of spitting on Ruthenian intelligentsia."[41] He noted that emigration would continue with or without the aid of the intelligentsia, and that the flow of peasants was the visible sign of the intelligentsia's uselessness.[42]

A complex individual, Genik never really completely adapted his political views to Canada. A practical advisor on one level, a utopian dreamer on another, he considered Russophilism (although rejecting Pan-Slavism)[43] and was stimulated by the writings of Tolstoy.[44] Genik's attitudes were representative of the ideological disorientation that many of the radical intelligentsia experienced on their arrival in Canada. This disorientation is best exemplified by the Ukrainian Brotherhood experiment. Genik corresponded with Ahapii Honcharenko, "an aging Ukrainian religious dissenter and political fugitive from the Russian Empire" who lived on a 60-acre farm in Hayway, California.[45] Finding the "battle with nature" difficult during Canadian winters, Genik entertained thoughts of moving to California to join Honcharenko, who was willing to share his farm.[46] But after persuading a handful of young radicals to go south, Genik himself changed his mind about leaving Canada. The Ukrainian Brotherhood struggled through the winter of 1902-03 and, by the fall of 1903, had disbanded. A participant analyzed the reasons for failure:

> While one imagined the Ukrainian Brotherhood to be a matter of living a real Christian life in accordance with the principles of Tolstoy, another thought of the Brotherhood as the modern equivalent of the Zaporoshka [Dnieper Cossack] Sich, a third saw it as a colony, with good, selected neighbors.[47]

But the failure of the commune can be attributed to more than the lack of a unified ideology among Ukrainian radicals. The lack of "evil forces" (wrongs such as restricted freedoms, economic debasement, and social repression) against which the ideologies could rally created a vacuum which rendered the ideologies ineffective when applied to reality. There wasn't enough negative stimulation to force the radicals to work out their ideals practically. Ukrainian radicals in North America, to 1905, had no common enemy. With the primarily agricultural character of immigration and the Canadian government's efforts to ease the difficulties of the settlement process, there was little to criticize. Success depended largely on the peasants themselves. Some Ukrainians were part of the labour force before 1905, but the unions, in their struggle for recognition, had served more as an injurious and disruptive force to the peasants than as protectors. But after 1905, conditions would change.

Reverend Dmytriw: Pastor of his People

Along with Genik, Reverend Nestor Dmytriw expressed the general attitude of early Ukrainian spokesmen in Canada. He arrived in Canada via the United States. In September of 1895, Oleskiw visited Dmytriw in Mt. Carmel, Pennsylvania, where Dmytriw was heavily involved with *Svoboda*. They continued a correspondence and eventually Oleskiw recommended Dmytriw for a position with the Immigration Branch. This cleared the way for Dmytriw to reside in Canada from April of 1897 to August of 1898, until his health failed him and he returned to the United States.

In this short time, Dmytriw produced a considerable body of writing. Included were travelogues — the eight-part *Kanadyska Rus* (Canadian Ruthenians) and the short *From Halifax to Winnipeg* — as well as a series of fictional pieces. However, like Oleskiw and Genik, he is best remembered for his role in the immigration and settlement process. He offered advice to prospective emigrants and reported (often under the pseudonym of "Korrespondent") on peasant homesteads in Canada. He retained a position as government interpreter for a time and, like Genik, accompanied Ukrainian arrivals on their trans-Canada trek. As a priest, he frequently visited peasant colonies, ministered to their religious needs, and encouraged the building of churches. Genik described him as a "son of his people."[48] Oleskiw referred to him as "superintendent of Galician Emigration."[49]

A product of the Galician radical tradition, Dmytriw was very much the dedicated pastor of his people. He did not hesitate to criticize either the church or the intelligentsia if he felt they were neglecting their duties to their countrymen. Nor did he spare the peasants in informing them of how they should act in order to lift themselves into the ranks of "people of this world." Indeed, his criticism of the peasants was most harsh. "Canadians," he stated, "view them as worse than Indians; some even talk of sending them to the latter for civilizing."[50] The men especially were a case in point: "years of Galician upbringing have made them boorish, brutal and lazy — unfit for the demands North America places on them."[51]

Yet there was hope. Dmytriw praised the progress of young females who were serving as domestics, some of whom were so "civilized" that they were ashamed of the filth and squalor of their parents. Young men working on English or German farms were a source of pride for Dmytriw because they were able to learn the English language very quickly.[52] He placed his hopes in the Ukrainian children and fully expected that, with time, they would be wealthier than their English neighbours.[53]

Dmytriw's advice to the immigrants was similar to that offered by Genik and Oleskiw. In one article he summarized it:

1. Canada is a good land with a future if you have the $400–$500 to set up;
2. Seek advice from Dr. Oleskiw and not from Carlsburg or Hamburg agents;
3. Before leaving change to western clothes. Englishmen do not tolerate sheepskins and regard those dressed in such as nothing more than cattle;
4. When arriving in Winnipeg do not listen to the misleading advice of Jews or other shysters; go to Genik or myself;
5. Buy all the necessary goods in Winnipeg as Edmonton and Dauphin prices are two to three times higher;
6. Do not buy in Jewish stores but in those certified by the Immigration House. You will get better quality at a lower price;
7. Do not buy land. Much good free land is still available and if one is selling, it likely will not be good land;
8. If one is able to live in Galicia or Bukovyna, do not come to Canada, because the best land cannot replace your own, just as a step-mother can never be a real mother.[54]

Like Oleskiw and Genik, Dmytriw saw his role in terms of setting guidelines immediately attainable by the peasants in Canada. Criticism was strong, but the advice was practical and born out of their Galician and Bukovynian experience and the conditions for pioneers in Canada. Whether their advice was often followed, however, is doubtful.

CHAPTER 7

VIEWS FROM THE OTHER BRIDGE

The arrival of Galicians and Bukovynians in Canada evoked a strong response from both the English and French. Initially repulsed by the alien style of dress, habits, language, and standard of living, Canadians sought ways to cope with the newcomers. For some, the aversion dissipated quickly. They rationalized that the immigrants were facilitating economic growth, which was more important than the temporary "social stir" they caused. Others believed that the immigrants were detrimental to Canada; racially impure, they would blight the country's development both within the Empire and the world community of nations. These people advocated segregation from foreign contamination and urged a cessation of "undesirable" immigration. Still others attempted to assimilate the East Europeans to their particular norms. The "Anglicizers," for example, endeavoured to mold the Ukrainians into British subjects by imbuing them with the language, ideas, and religion of Anglo-Saxondom. Both Protestants and Catholics, from their divergent perspectives, made up the front ranks of the assimilators.

The Preachers of Social Darwinism

Subscribing to racial definitions which were "conventional as well as respectable within the cultural milieu of the nineteenth century,"[1] Anglo-Canadians were convinced of their inherent superiority. Evidence of this rested on their origins; they were a product of the Northern European race. And the superiority of the British was evident in their ability to create and maintain democratic institutions. In addition, they were tempered by the vigorous Canadian climate. The Dominion's good showing in athletic competitions, for example, proved "that Canada is producing a race of men which is physically the best in the world — strength backed by nerve, common sense, science, and intellect."[2] Anglo-Canadians became distressed that their "genius" would be blemished by the inferior races. Although some believed that the northern climate would temper the immigrants' unappealing characteristics, the combination of repulsion and fear permeated the reaction to them for generations. Eastern and Southern Europeans were considered a lower form of humanity.

The concept of one race being superior to another had irresistable appeal: many Imperialists, for instance, preached "social Darwinism," accepting the theories of Sir Francis Galton, who in 1883 "concluded that the advancement of race and, consequently, society could only be accomplished with the propagation of the fit and the elimination of the unfit."[3] Echoing these sentiments, one Canadian commentator wrote: "It is a people's duty to set their face toward a high ideal of national life, to conserve such elements as are in harmony with this ideal, and to eliminate whatever is opposed to it. The higher civilization has a moral right to displace the lower."[4] Imperialists believed that Canada's future rested on its ability to attain and maintain the role of a senior partner in the British Empire. This would be achieved when the Dominion had grown in population and economic status to a level that would rival the United Kingdom. Therein lay the significance of the North-West to Confederation. Ontario institutions were transplanted to the prairies. With Manitoba "reborn in the image of Ontario," the road was clear "to advance that Anglo-Saxon civilization which seems destined to dominate the world."[5]

Such rhetoric was a forecast of Imperialist reaction to mass Ukrainian immigration into the Canadian west. An *a priori* assumption had been that immigrants possess, or readily acquire, the English language and assume British social and political ideals. But could "dirty" Galicians and "backward" Bukovynians be made into acceptable British subjects? Throughout the last decade of the nineteenth century and the early years of the twentieth, the issue was hotly debated.

The Hostile Reception

Imperialists feared the foreigners not only because they could not be relied upon to uphold Canada's British character, but also because they threatened to destroy the precious links that the Dominion had with the

British Empire. Archibald Hurd, a Canadian journalist, wrote:

> The newcomers from America and Europe may make good enough
> Canadians, but will they become loyal subjects of the British Empire?
> The two terms are not synonymous. . . . Will not the present feeble
> separatist movement gather strength when the time is ripe, when the
> Dominion has increased in prosperity, and the population has been
> further swollen by foreign peoples, and particularly Americans, who
> are never weary of pointing to the progess of the United States as an
> independent power.[6]

The non-American immigrants were cast as pawns capable of holding
the balance of power in the struggle between supporters of Imperial
connections and those advocating closer union with the United States.

A great many politicians shared Hurd's views. E.G. Prior, for example, Member of Parliament from Victoria, believed that "the aim should
be to people Canada with those who have the courage and the wish to
build up the British Empire and perpetuate British institutions."[7] Ad-
mitting that he had never met a Galician ("but I have heard a great deal
about them"), he was, nonetheless, one of their strongest critics in the
House of Commons. He considered the situation to be hopeless:

> How can we expect Canadians to welcome these people? We have
> nothing in common with them. They cannot assimilate with us in
> any way, and the settlers around them say they do not wish their
> young people to have any communication with them whatever. Are
> such people likely to make good citizens and contribute to building
> up the British Empire?[8]

Prior's definition of Canada's character and destiny as a member of the
British Empire brooked no exceptions.

Other misgivings about the Ukrainians were also based on the hope
that Canada would become an Imperial power. The *Daily Evening Review* of Peterborough, Ontario seconded Prior's opinion. While conced-
ing that "Glacians [sic], Doukhobors, and now Huns" — who were referred to as "spirit wrestlers" — might be industrious, the newspaper
doubted that they could be transformed into "good Britishers when
imported en bloc."[9] The *Halifax Herald* outlined its perception of Canada's long-term goals: "What Canada greatly needs is population — immigrants; not immigrants just of any sort, but immigrants fit for the
developing and up building of a British country of great mineral and agricultural resources."[10] In an article entitled "British Institutions in
Danger," the *Montreal Daily Star* expressed fear that Canada would lose

its British character if it continued to promote immigration of "Galician and other foreigners" who are "opposed to British customs, lazy and vicious."[11]

The immensity of Canada's task in preserving its British character was discussed by Clive Phillips Wolley in the *Ottawa Anglo-Saxon:*

> the whole world is at present ringing with rumours of a federation the greatest that the centuries have seen, a federation of the Anglo-Saxons of the world. . . . We must build a British race with British bricks. You cannot make Anglo-Saxondom of Doukhobors, Galicians, and Fins. . . . It is or should be the principal object of all good Canadians is [sic] to build up a race which shall hold and develop Canada for the Empire.[12]

According to Wolley, Canada was failing in this monumental task. Employing rhetorical questions, he criticized Clifford Sifton's open immigration policy:

> What do you think of Mr. Sifton's policy, brother Anglo-Saxons? Is it a policy of preference to Great Britain or of discrimination against Britons? Is it a policy which will unite the Empire and her colonies or one which will sow in the greatest of them a seed of division more dangerous to Canada than the Negro element is to the States today?[13]

It is noteworthy that for many Imperialists the only genuinely suitable immigrants were red-blooded Englishmen. The *Morden Chronicle,* for example, used this criterion to assess the Ukrainians:

> The Galicians are not approved settlers as they come to us, and there is not yet any assurance that they will eventually assimilate with our people and develope [sic] into Canadian citizens of the high standard that obtains in this Dominion. . . . The doubt in regard to the Galicians is the fact that they have no kinship with us in blood.[14]

That racial purity was seen by many as necessary to the achievement of a British world federation cannot be doubted. According to Wolley:

> It is not too much to affirm that in the Anglo-Saxon type, man has reached to the highest point of excellence to which he has hitherto attained and whilst it is our duty to do what we can to bring mankind as a whole up to our level, it is at least fair to ask whether it is wise to spoil THE BEST by reckless admixture of the SCUM.

The dogs may pick up the crumbs which fall from the children's table, but there is no reason why they should be asked to sit at that table, mix blood with and share the heritage of the children.

And that is just what is being done to-day. Into Manitoba and the Northwest Territories we are pouring Mennonites, Doukhobors, Galicians, Finns and heaven knows what besides.

Why? They are not of our race. . . .[15]

Vitriol displayed at the influx of Ukrainians into Canada was intertwined with another phenomenon — the large exodus of Canadians, both English and French, to the United States. Politicians were expressing grave concern long before the mass immigration of East Europeans commenced. In 1891, a Member of Parliament described the causes of emigration: "Our education is so well organized, we educate our young men so highly, that they become discontented with the plough, and we have more men of education and professional ability at the present moment in Canada than Canada can support. That is the reason those men of professional ability go elsewhere."[16] Another parliamentarian lamented the fact that "the best part of our population is going away; our young men are leaving, only the old people remain behind who are not able to work the farm."[17] Many Canadians faulted the federal government for failing to divert the emigration to the Canadian west. The arrival of the Ukrainians when the "cream" of the Canadian population was leaving the country made the situation that much more serious: "Far better is it for Manitoba to be filled up with Canadians from Ontario or with ex-Canadians from Dakota, than with the miserable Galicians Mr. Sifton seems determined to pour into that portion of our fair domain. Let us think of the welfare of the Dominion as a whole."[18] Ukrainian immigration at a time of Canadian emigration was for some an inconceivable inversion of events:

What is the matter with expending some of the money of this country in settling some of our own people out west in comfortable homes? Why go across the water to get the offscourings of the world, to Galicia, or some other point, and pick on the remnants of humanity, which have got to be made into people.[19]

But unlike some other critics of Ukrainian immigration, those who emphasized the problem as being coupled with Canadian emigration had a solution. Canadians should be financially encouraged to move west rather than south, and the immigrants should be repatriated.

French-Canadian spokesmen also emphasized the seriousness of the loss of Canadians to the United States. In 1893, Louis-Philippe Brodeur, M.P. for Rouville, underlined the fact that "during the past ten years the emigration from this country, especially from the province of Quebec, has been very large."[20] He, too, offered a financial solution:

> How is it . . . that the Government, in their wisdom, have never offered our own people, our French-Canadian compatriots, the same advantages they offer strangers brought from Europe? How is it that we have given money, passage, fares, board, etc., to strangers who are an inferior class of settlers, while our own compatriots are forced into exile? Why has not the same encouragement been offered to French-Canadians as was accorded to Europeans, under the shape of transportation fares and money bonuses?[21]

However, the objectives of French Canadians, especially those already living on the prairies, were to maintain and strengthen the French presence in the North-West. They feared that if the prairies were populated with foreigners susceptible to Anglo-Celtic proselytizing pressures, the Francophone element would be swamped.

If political ambitions weren't enough to aggravate the issue, the peasants' lifestyle itself posed a problem. The Canadian standard of living was high compared to that of Ukrainians. Because racial explanations underpinned their observations, Canadians could not conceive that the Galician or Bukovynian peasant could ever improve to their level. Many Canadians were, quite simply, repulsed by the East European "muzhik" (peasant). Even Clifford Sifton, their staunchest supporter, conceded that "of course there are some things in connection with their social habits which are more or less distasteful to the Canadians."[22] Critics argued that when "a large number of people are content to live in squalor and ignorance, they tend to lower the standard of the whole population."[23] Ukrainian dress was the most obvious object of ridicule. In 1897, the *Edmonton Bulletin* speculated that "if only Clifford Sifton could see a photograph of a newly arrived Ukrainian 'in all the glory of' its [sic] ultra negligee attire as it [sic] parades through our streets, he would have a violent and nauseating feeling in the region of his watch pocket."[24] Commentators, obviously, found peasant attire quite unfashionable. They also objected to women and children walking around barefoot. Frank Oliver, editor of the *Edmonton Bulletin*, delineated the appearance of Galicians:

> There began to appear on the platforms and in the waiting rooms of the old C.P.R. station in Winnipeg strange men and women wearing sheep-skin coats with the wool turned inside, either very large boots

or often no boots at all, the women with shawls or scarfs on their heads and hemp skirts extending not quite to the ankle.[25]

In pointing out the characteristic guise of Ukrainians, Oliver stressed the basic lack of similarity between them and "respectable" Canadians.

Ukrainian raiment often provoked comparisons of the immigrants to animals. The editor of the *Belleville Intelligencer*, for instance, wrote:

> The Galicians, they of the sheepskin coats, the filth and the vermin, do not make splendid material for the building of a great nation. One look at the disgusting creatures as they pass through over the C.P.R. on their way west has caused many to marvel that beings bearing the human form could have sunk to such a bestial level.[26]

The *Quebec Mercury* agreed: "Of the Galicians, there is another story to tell. They are described as being bestial in their habits, dirty and unkempt, poor in pocket and criminal in their antecedents.[27] Such descriptions of Ukrainians were used as strong and tangible weapons against them. Basic dissimilarities were assumed to be obvious by newspaper writers:

> Mr. Sifton's Galicians have not parted with any of the usages which mark them off from the rest of mankind. They herd together, and live in the same state of social depravity here as they did in the country they came from. They profess godliness, but they are as stubborn in their adherence to uncleanliness as the Doukhobors are to the doctrine of non-resistance. There are some Indians in the Northwest who are pretty low down in the scale of humanity, but they appear to be above associating with the kind of Galicians Mr. Sifton has introduced.[28]

The most common indictment of the Ukrainians was based on their appearance and their alleged uncleanliness. The implication, of course, was that Canadians were an exceptionally clean people.

It is interesting to note that while the protests made against Ukrainians were most often published and reprinted by eastern Canadian papers, the experience of the majority of Ontarians with Ukrainians was second-hand. Newspaper reporters may have caught glimpses of trainloads of Ukrainians travelling west from Atlantic seaports which would have enabled them to report accurately, but the intentions of their descriptions were obvious. They were meant to appeal to the fears of Canadians and to inspire criticism of the newcomers.

It was easy for the critics to go one step further in their condemnation of the Ukrainians. Surely the presence of such creatures would discourage desirable settlers from going to western Canada. The *Halifax Herald* concluded just that: "Their presence in our Northwest tends strongly to disgust and keep away, or drive away, persons who are really desirable settlers."[29] This message was repeated in a later issue: "Every batch of Galicians put into the Northwest reduces the value of the country and tends to deter useful immigrants from going there."[30] Ample evidence for such conclusions was provided by reports of English settlers moving out of Ukrainian districts. The *Toronto Mail and Empire* reported that "the Brandon Independent says that respectable settlers on the Edmonton road are moving away from good farms because there are Galicians in the neighbourhood."[31]

The reception accorded Ukrainians in the early years of immigration no doubt dampened their aspirations in the new land. When they found that acceptance was not forthcoming, many withdrew into the colonies, emerging from these enclaves only when necessary. Others met the hostility head on. But in their efforts to be admitted to the Anglo-Canadian milieu, they "frequently absorbed more of its weaknesses and evils . . . than the virtues."[75] Whatever the Ukrainian response, however, the need for tolerant, broad-minded treatment was not fulfilled.

The Assimilation Debate

There were those Canadians, however, who did not endeavour to solve the Ukrainian problem by curtailing immigration. Whether motivated by political party loyalties or by economic considerations, they maintained a welcoming attitude. Revelling in incidents that illustrated ways in which Ukrainians were good for Canada, they comprised the ranks of the assimilationists.

Foremost among the defenders of the Ukrainians was Clifford Sifton. Through public statements and the *Manitoba Free Press*, which he owned, Sifton expressed his firm belief that Ukrainian settlers would be successful because they had emigrated to Canada to better their position. Given the opportunity, they would continue to do so until they were indistinguishable from Canadians. Sifton recognized that criticisms stemmed from the external appearance of the Ukrainians:

> Now, with reference to the Galicians, I wish to say a few words. When I first saw these people I was not favorably impressed with them. I do not think that any one would be favorably impressed with people who have come across in an immigrant ship and an immigrant car, seeing them near the end of their journey. Their costume is peculiar and their appearance strange.[33]

But he pointed out that "after only a few months' residence in the country it is wonderful to see the change in their dress and customs."[34]

Sifton was able to maintain a positive approach to Ukrainians for two reasons. As the architect of the policy that favoured them, it was only politically sensible that he and his staff be their staunchest supporters. In addition, he did not set very high goals for them. He was satisfied that "the Galician is anxious to assimilate, the Galician is anxious to be independent, the Galician wants to be a Canadian, he wants his children to go to a public school."[35] Sifton was confident that the Ukrainians would perform the economic function for which they were imported.

Sifton's rebuttals of those who criticized Ukrainians were based on economic arguments. Economic deprivation, for example, was not a crime in Sifton's eyes:

> So far as their general habits are concerned, I may say that they are people who have lived in poverty. That is no crime on their part. I do not think that we as members of the House of Commons are prepared to say that we would not allow people to come into Canada because they have been unfortunate enough to live in poverty in the countries from which they come. I venture to say that the ancestors of many prominent citizens of Canada were poor in the country whence they came, and nobody thinks less of them on that account.[36]

Sifton was not alone in fighting socially oriented arguments with economic ones. Other parliamentarians supported his view that Ukrainians should be judged by their industry and earning power:

> The Galician, when he came out, had not very much coin in his pocket, and he asked the government, as he had the right to, for a small advance. The advance was given, and what was the result? Out of the very first money he earned, he paid the government back the money he had borrowed. . . . I submit that a man who does that in a new country, and who does not try to live off the government, is not a bad citizen.[37]

Indeed, after 1900, the initial repulsion had worn off and many more politicians sided with Ukrainians — all of them pointing to their economic advancement: "A few years ago a howl went up against the Galicians . . . but to-day there is no person in the west who will say a word against the Galicians. They are thrifty hard-working people and they are helping us to build up that country."[38] Ukrainian successes even caused some wonder:

> The Galicians have taught the people of Canada to know the value of

our poor lands . . . along the south shore of the North Saskatchewan River are regions that no person, even the most enthusiastic and optimistic Canadian ever imagined were fit for settlement; yet these people have gone in there among those hills and have shown us that a rolling hill country, which most of us thought to be useless for settlement, can be converted into a prosperous country.[39]

Many pro-Ukrainian arguments were aimed at Frank Oliver. As a Liberal renegade and editor of the *Edmonton Bulletin,* he sought to discredit the Ukrainians. His ignorance of the reasons for emigration were exhibited when he repeatedly argued:

The Germans have increased so much, that they and the native Galicians crowded each other, and it became a question for the Austrian government whether the Germans or the Galicians should leave the country. The Germans began first to leave, and some of them came to Canada, but the Austrian government, taking alarm at this movement, took measures to stop it and replace it by a movement of Galicians. That is why I used in this connection the word "deportation" instead of "immigration". It is a movement of population urged by the Austrian government for the purpose of actually getting rid of these people, and it is only fair that the House should understand these facts.[40]

Sifton attempted to put the attacks of his caucus colleague in perspective: "There seems to be something about my hon. friend's [Oliver's] constitution which while it does not affect the keenness of his intellect prevents him from expressing a favourable opinion about either men or things."[41] Another House member criticized Oliver for claiming to represent the opinions of all westerners:

The hon. member for Alberta has taken some dislike to these people, but he has no right to say that in expressing his dislike he is voicing the sentiment of the whole North-west. He has no right to speak for the people of the west but only for those of his own constituency. In my own district I have a lot of Galicians. And if the minister of Interior can send us more Galicians they will be welcome. If my hon. friend from Alberta is not satisfied with these in his district, let him send them to my district and I will be very glad.[42]

Oliver was free to criticize the Ukrainians until 1905. Thereafter, he assumed the post of Minister of the Interior and became responsible for Ukrainian immigration.

Assimilation meant different things to different people; to some, it was rather distasteful. As one politician stated:

Do you know what that word "assimilate" means? It is a nice sounding word. Do you know that it means that if you settle on a farm on the prairies amongst them or in their neighbourhood you must depend for the schooling of your children on the tax-paying willingness and power of people who neither know nor care anything about schools? Do you know it means the intermarriage of your sons or daughters with those who are of an alien race and alien ideas? That is assimilation, or else there is no assimilation. There is no assimilation, and there will be no assimilation for many, many years, and the whole country will suffer a drawback to that extent for a number of years.[43]

Unlike Sifton, who felt that assimilation would be accomplished as soon as Ukrainians discarded their old country clothing, became part of Canada's agricultural economy, and expressed a willingness to learn the English language, others set much higher standards for assimilation — standards which seemed unattainable:

We also want people with whom our young folks can associate and assimilate. Do we find these qualities in the Galicians and Doukhobors? In my opinion, both of these races are very far indeed from coming within that category. They are physically strong, I believe, but is that all that is expected of them. . .? As for physical strength we know that some of the lowest types of humanity are physically strong.[44]

Most of those who did offer advice on how best to achieve assimilation agreed that settlement of immigrants in distinct colonies was not advisable: "It is held out as one of the inducements to immigrants coming into the North West that they will be allowed to settle in distinct colonies. This policy seems fatal to any hope of assimilation."[45] The settlement of immigrants in colonies, however, was not the only problem facing assimilators.

Western British-Canadians were saddled with the responsibility of assimilating the foreigners. It was easy for eastern Canadians to maintain that "the future of our country would be better assured if there was a liberal sprinkling of Canadian and British people among the foreigners."[46] Many westerners preferred to segregate themselves from immigrant settlers. Manitoba journalist J.R. Conn noted that "while there are obstacles to assimilation presented by the aliens, there are also decided objections on the part of those Canadians who are, to vary a war phrase, not on the fighting line, but on the assimilating line."[47] The problem of westerners associating with Galicians was presented in terms very sympathetic to the English:

First an attempt was made to settle them [Galicians] in colonies by themselves, but it was found that it would be injudicious to do that; for fear many of them might die of starvation. Therefore it was decided to distribute them amongst the English-speaking people of the country: and they have been a great burden to these people, who with their humane instincts, will not allow them to die of starvation. But it is a great mistake to impose that burden upon our people.[48]

One politician commiserated with the English-Canadian westerners:

The flooding of western Canada with people who are not used to the duties of citizenship is a serious question for the west and for all Canada. It is said that these strange people will assimilate with the English-speaking settlers, possibly to some extent and at great length of time. But the work of their assimilation is that much of a drag and burden upon those with whom they are expected to assimilate.[49]

But there were those who thought such resentment unbecoming. One Member of Parliament made it clear that shirking the duties of assimilation was un-Canadian:

Well, in this country, with its millions and millions of acres, are you to be afraid of a few Galicians. . . . It is because I believe in Canadian civilization that I do not fear a few Doukhobors or Galicians. . . . If I lived in the North West, I would not be afraid of 17,000 Galicians, I would feel humiliated if I could not take my place against ten or twenty or 50 people that could not speak my language.[50]

Such confidence was certainly heroic, especially expressed by those not forced to deal with Ukrainians on a day to day basis.

Arguments for and against the Galicians were more or less related to party allegiances and were thus reflected in party newspapers such as the Liberal *Manitoba Free Press*. Isolated criticism of Ukrainians in Liberal papers, as well as praise of Ukrainians in Conservative papers, were given much attention by opponents and supporters of Ukrainians. The Ukrainians had added another issue, an emotional one, to the normal disagreements of the political parties. It was, after all, Canada's future that was being shaped. Some newspapers sought to define the criticism and its sources:

A great deal of prejudice has been excited against the Galicians, partly through the efforts of ignorant writers . . . partly also through the deliberate misrepresentation of party organs. . . . The prejudice has been confirmed and aggravated in many instances by our observation of them as they arrive in the country uncouthly clad and tired, dirty, and dejected after a journey of six or seven thousand miles. They are strange to our eyes. . . .[51]

Other newspapers based their conclusions on incidents:

The statement has been frequently made, both on the platform and in the press that the foreign element that was being brought to Canada would not assimilate with the people or become familiar with the genius of our institutions. That in the case of war the country could not count on their services. But a most effectual answer to the latter statements was made on Monday when L. Cohen, on behalf of twenty able-bodied Galicians, came to the *Press* office to state that these men were anxious to serve the Queen in the Transvaal War, and were ready for enlistment at any time. It is facts like these that reveal the true character of the foreign settler and the material he is composed of.[52]

Many politicians were quick to cite incidents which they found significant. One noted the example of a little girl who when asked whether she was a Galician answered, "No, I am a Canadian."[53]

Many Canadians had never heard of Ukrainians before their mass exodus from Galicia and Bukovynia, and they were naturally curious. They relied on the information that could be garnered from reports of isolated incidents, and drew conclusions which depended on the newspaper they read: either the Ukrainians were perceived as hard-working, thrifty, and anxious to assimilate, or they were considered dirty, murderous, and poor. Canadians generally knew next to nothing about the conditions that had prompted the Ukrainians to seek a home in Canada. As one parliamentarian asserted:

These people have never shown themselves in their native country, Russia, to be thrifty and able to make a good living on the lands on which they were established. The lands on which many of them who have come here were settled, are, I am told, even finer than the lands in the North West Territories, and the climate is good, if not better. Yet with all these advantages, they have been found going off to the cities and turning out anything but desirable citizens.[54]

W.T.R. Preston, the government immigration officer stationed in London, England, did visit Galicia in 1899. Accompanied by Professor James Mavor of the University of Toronto, he toured small villages and major cities in Galicia "for the purpose of inquiring into the manner of life of this people in their native country." Preston's report was favourable:

> I am fully aware that the Galician whom I have seen here, neat and tidy in his attire, although somewhat quaint to the Anglo-Saxon eyes, cheerful in his demeanour, and deferential to a marked degree, does not bear a strong resemblance to the Galician whom I have seen arrive in Canada, haggard and tired after four weeks' travel by land and sea. But I have seen his home, the village from whence he has come, the farm he has cultivated, and I have no difficulty in arriving at the conclusion that given a chance in our country, and its free institutions, he will quickly become Anglicized, and through his natural thrift and industry, will develop in a few years into a citizen of whom the most sensitive Canadian will not be ashamed.[55]

To what extent Preston's position as a Liberal appointee affected his conclusions cannot be determined precisely.

The effects of the initial hostile reaction permeated Ukrainian-English relationships for generations. Ukrainians continued to question the legitimacy of their existence in Canada, wavering between outward resentment when times were safe to demonstrations of their loyalty when threatened by the host society. The clash in cultures at the turn of the century resulted in a lamentable period in Canadian social history.

Significantly, the Anglo-Canadians, especially the Imperialists, basing their analyses on external differences and caught up in their own rhetoric, did not realize that Ukrainians fulfilled two crucial tenets of their doctrine. First, in the age of rapid industrialization, Imperialists had romanticized the agricultural way of life; it was the immigrants who gave it substance. Second, while preaching the Protestant work ethic, they failed to recognize this quality in the newcomers. On the homesteads, settlers could not survive without long hours of diligent, self-sacrificing toil.

Party Politics and the Ukrainian Citizen

Ukrainians were not only an issue, but also a weapon that provincial and federal parties sought to wield against their opponents at election time. Federal Liberals had a foothold in the Ukrainian community through immigration agents. Kyrylo Genik, Reverend Nestor Dmytriw, Ivan Bodrug, and Ivan Negrych were all employed by the Liberal administration at various times. As leaders among their countrymen, their political advice was accepted readily. In addition, the Liberal Party, along with the Presbyterian Church, lent its support to the *Kanadiiskyi Farmer*, first edited by Ivan Negrych:

> Our Galician paper has at last made its appearance. J. Obed/Smith and John Appleton with the assistance of a Galician interpreter are keeping an eye on the matter that goes into it. It has been thought desirable to keep contentious matter out of the first few issues; later on we shall give a few knocks to the Tories.[56]

Conservatives followed the lead of the Liberals by lending their support to *Slovo*, published in Winnipeg in 1904, but this newspaper soon folded.

Both parties sought to tap the Ukrainian block vote. Ukrainians were encouraged with liquor and tobacco to apply for naturalization papers, which were a prerequisite for registration on voters' lists. It was stressed that naturalization was necessary to obtain letters patent for homesteads. On voters' lists, a Ukrainian was often included under two or three different misspellings of his name, a devious practice which expanded the lists considerably. In the Manitoba election of 1903, some 1,500 Ukrainians were naturalized by Conservative Party organizers. They were listed as having met the language requirement — a knowledge of English, French, or German — because they responded to military orders given in German. The endorsement of a Ukrainian Training School for teachers by Conservative candidates was designed to ensure the Ukrainian vote.

Yet the Ukrainian vote prior to 1905 had not been mobilized in sufficient numbers to tip the scale in favour of one or another of the political parties. Nevertheless, the encouragement of Ukrainians to vote caused much concern among English-Canadians. The issue ran deeper than the underhanded buying of electoral support. At the heart of the problem was the question of whether Ukrainians were to be given citizenship and all its rights and privileges. As one Canadian senator stated:

> Just what makes a resident a citizen is not always clear. The extension of the suffrage to an individual is perhaps the truest test of the citizen, because when he attains to that privilege he commences to bear a share in the legislating and in the administration of justice in this country. He possesses the power to vote on all public issues as presented in municipal, provincial, or federal elections, or in by-laws and plebescites. This privilege distinguishes him from the Chinaman, the Italian, the Galician and others of foreign birth and education who are unable to understand or take an interest in issues which appear to him to be vital.

Canada, like the United States, has erred very grievously in the unjustifiable extension of the suffrage to the uneducated.[57]

Some Canadians believed that the maintenance of the democratic system of government and free institutions was at stake. Citizenship was not considered an automatic right; it carried with it certain responsibilities. Senator Lougheed of Alberta, for example, maintained that naturalization qualifications should be made stricter:

> . . . take for instance the Doukhobors and the Galicians and that class of aliens. I think it is not desirable at all that simply three years' residence should give such men a right to vote, except they identify themselves in some way with the institutions of the country by being able to read and write English or such other desirable qualification.[58]

Lougheed was particularly disturbed by the fact that some 60,000 to 75,000 Doukhobors, Ukrainians, and others "who do not understand the English language . . . might be easily approached with a view to signing a declaration as to qualification" to vote:

> They know nothing about it, and they sign. I have seen immediately before an election a great number of declarations being forwarded to the clerk of the court from distant points signed by all kinds of persons. I am reasonably satisfied that in many cases those people were not aware in the slightest degree of what they signed.[59]

It is impossible to know whether Lougheed was expressing real concern about the need to educate immigrants about institutions, or whether party politics and jealousies underpinned his criticism. Certainly some Canadians used the issue of Ukrainian enfranchisement to inspire fear:

> The Galicians are being put on the lists whether they are qualified to be there or not. It must be a pleasant reflection for those British and Canadian-born citizens, who by the Greenway [leader of the provincial Liberal party] registration clerks, have been disfranchised by wholesale, and prevented from exercising their natural right of having a voice in the government of their country, to find the right of which they are deprived being widely and illegally accorded to these ignorant aliens. It must be almost equally galling to those free and independent subjects of native birth who have succeeded in getting on the lists, to find that their votes can be cancelled by the wholesale stuffing of the lists with these unqualified foreigners, who, besides owing allegiance to a foreign state, know nothing of the constitution and laws of this country, and will record their votes at the dictation of the

officials of the Administration by whom they have been imported
and fed and from whom they are securing special privileges which
are denied to Britons and Canadians.[60]

But the real fear was not based solely on a notion of the Ukrainians'
ignorance. It was rooted in the view of Ukrainians as an interest group
which could be motivated to vote en bloc in favour of those who supported its demands. Canadians, not knowing what Ukrainian interests
were, naturally feared that they would run counter to Canadian concep-
tions of the future character of their country. The safest course, then,
was to demand a complete indoctrination into the British-Canadian
way of life prior to enfranchisement. "If large communities of foreigners are to be enfranchised without being assimilated the result will be
the creation of innumerable sectional interests which will prevent any
national question being decided on its merits," declared J.R. Conn.[61]
The apprehension that immigrants would take over Canada was serious. An Edmontonian expressed alarm: "They were not fit for the free
institutions of this country and the time will come when they will hold
the balance of political power here unless a damper is put on them very
soon, and when they become our legislators God help us."[62]
    Legally, Canada generously extended its freedoms and opportunities
to all new immigrants. But in reality, a fierce debate raged over such a
carte blanche approach. In day to day dealings, the belief in the superior
race undermined legal niceties. The egalitarian host society could not
justify fully extending its liberties to those who, it believed, would
abuse them. Ironically, while expecting the immigrants to pay homage
to the superior character of Anglo-Saxondom and to emulate it, they
were reluctant to allow participation in its freedoms and responsibilities.

Catholic vs. Protestant: Missionary Fervour

The task of assimilation was left to institutions that were willing to assume social roles. The churches were among the most active. The
Roman Catholic Church, seeking jurisdiction over the Catholic Slavic
immigrants, built hospitals and schools, as well as churches, in Ukrainian communities. Protestant churches, meanwhile, appealed to Orthodox Ukrainians. They too established medical facilities and schools
in colonies. The missionary role of churches was aptly described in the
Montreal Witness:

Talk of foreign missions! Canada seems likely before a year or more
is gone by to have upon her own domain a foreign mission work a

hundred-fold greater than any she has ever done, in the task of Canadianizing the masses of continentals being poured on her shores at a rate that must sensibly affect the abundance of her public domain and very seriously influence her future.[63]

Missionary work was indeed required. Both churches realized the need for non-religious work and assumed the responsibilities. Protestants explained social work through interpretations of the Bible — that the kingdom of God must be established on earth. English in allegiance and imbued with social gospel teachings, which stressed that to save a man's soul, one had to improve his socio-economic position, the Protestant churches sought, if not to convert individuals, then at least to win the Ukrainians as allies. The Protestant churches, at this time, represented more than a religious faith in the Canadian west; they symbolized the presence and interests of British-Canadians on the new frontier. The provincial and territorial governments relied on local initiative for the establishment of schools, and the Protestant churches naturally planned their local initiatives to extend Protestant influence. The Roman Catholic Church, identified with the French, also concentrated its local initiatives on schools, which would help to maintain its presence in the west. It is interesting to note that Catholics approached social work with as much zeal as the Protestants. The Protestant social gospel movement provided a justification for the social role of the Protestant Church. The Catholic Church, although without a comparable rationalization, did not hesitate to play a similar role.

This quest for immigrant souls added to the contest between Catholics and Protestants. Ukrainians provided the battlefield and the ammunition. Catholics used Ukrainians to oppose alterations in the language rights of the French in the North-West. At a mass meeting in Winnipeg on 2 January 1902, for example, Archbishop Langevin voiced French-Canadian concerns when he protested that "the Protestants were more interested in converting rather than educating." Maintaining that "all Ukrainians were Catholic," he aroused a great deal of enthusiasm.[64]

But the attempts of Roman Catholics to gain the support of Ukrainians were hampered. They were unable to maintain an alliance with Catholic Ukrainians because they did not understand the Greek Catholic rite. Their imposition of Roman Catholicism on Ukrainians disenchanted many supporters. In addition, the church had to concede that one of the primary needs of Ukrainians was to learn English. But there was no English Catholic church, and the Roman Catholics were unable to cater, simultaneously, to the linguistic and religious needs of Ukrainians. As preservers of the French tradition in the North-West, their work with foreigners could not be all-encompassing. They were left with trying to gain maximum mileage from separate but English-language schools and from the support of bilingual education.

Furthermore, Roman Catholic efforts were stifled by the reactions of French-Canadians to Ukrainians. Maintaining that the immigrants were a threat to the institutions of Canada, French-Canadians sided with English-Canadians in criticizing Ukrainian habits and standards of living. The French were also imbued with theories of racial superiority and feared assimilation. Their chagrin went further. Even Catholics conceded that the Ukrainians had to be Anglicized, and as such their numbers would be a threat to the French in the North-West and Confederation.

English Protestants, on the other hand, were able to assume all aspects of social work. The only effective Roman Catholic criticism of Protestants was directed at their opposition to bilingual schools — the only argument the Roman Catholics had that assured them of Ukrainian support. Nonetheless, Protestant efforts in education were subject to the bilingual laws of the land, and Protestants did abide by them. They went so far as to train teachers. They supported a newspaper and the Independent Greek Church. The Protestant churches appealed to Bukovynian Ukrainians, who were not Catholic but Orthodox. They solicited those who, disgruntled by the enormous powers of the church in the old country, sought a Ukrainian religious reformation. Most importantly, they appealed to the progressive ideas of Ukrainian leaders and offered financial support. In return, they were able to attract the allegiance of large numbers of Ukrainians. Their cooperation with the federal Liberal Party, as evidenced by their co-support of *Kanadiiskyi Farmer*, eliminated, in large part, any disapproval on political grounds.

Well armed, the Protestants made their attack on the Catholics. Infused with social gospel teachings and confidence in their social role among foreigners, they disparaged the basic organization of the Catholic Church: "Roman Catholics did not know individual liberty. They were not taught to read the Bible and think for themselves; instead they obeyed the instructions of their priests. Such as system was destructive not only of individual freedom but also of the democratic state."[65] In fact, "the hierarchical structure of the Roman Catholic church was considered antithetical to true democracy."[66] Protestants interpreted the religious beliefs of Ukrainians as not being God-inspired but church-controlled. They objected to the influence of the church and clergy in the lives of Catholics. In the spirit of the social gospel which supported individual actions and freedoms, the Catholic Church was accused of impeding individual religious development. Individual faith in Christ was encouraged by the Protestants, and honouring the church and its personnel was discouraged. "There was a widely spread belief that

Catholics were fanatical, autocratic, and superstitious, while the Protestants were supposed to have such virtues as initiative, industry, freedom, and democracy."[67] Protestants went so far as to blame the Catholic Church for the unacceptable condition of Ukrainians — their poverty, drunkenness, dirtiness, laziness, and strange habits:

> Like many of the other people of Europe, the Galicians are yoked to an ignorant and none too scrupulous clergy. Their religious forms have become soul-less. Tithes and fees loom large in the eyes of the priesthood, and press heavily upon the people. Ignorance and superstition are not only tolerated but are encouraged by precept and example.[68]

Although Protestants perceived the immense power that the church had in Ukrainian life, they, like the Roman Catholics, did not understand that it was also a cultural institution steeped with tradition, a preserver of heritage and identity.

Apparent differences in faiths, although used as weapons, were not the truly contentious issues. The two churches had been relatively tolerant of one another until the immigration boom. The influx of Europeans prompted a power struggle which was largely a question of numbers (in 1902, Archibald Hurd calculated from census statistics that the Canadian population was 41 per cent Catholic). To 1905, both churches were able to claim at least partial victory with the Ukrainians because of the split between Catholic and Orthodox among the Ukrainians themselves. The battle was a serious one for the churches, but it did not escalate, as neither side could claim total defeat of the other. In the end, most Ukrainians deserted both Roman Catholics and Protestants to establish their own churches. They continued to support both public and separate schools with bilingual education.

CHAPTER 8

THE LABOURING FRONTIER

For the Ukrainians who had suffered the consequences of unemployment in Galicia and Bukovyna, opportunities to work meant a substantial step forward in their quest for economic welfare. Their need for money was urgent. Unskilled, in large part illiterate, they were not particular, initially, about the character and quality of their jobs. Familiar with seasonal labour and having to migrate temporarily for employment, they suited the requirements of the western-Canadian job market. Many worked on railways, some worked in the mines, others found various employment opportunities in the cities or created their own. The attainment of personal economic stability — at a subsistence level — was the immediate goal.

The Immigrant Work Force

Although Ukrainian immigration in Canada prior to 1905 was agricultural in character, at least 80 per cent of the new arrivals entered the labour market for varying periods of time. Those immigrants who arrived penniless at Winnipeg or Edmonton naturally had to seek work to pay for supplies and passage to the homestead. Once on the homestead, whether their arrival was government-assisted or not, they needed money to sustain themselves until enough land could be cleared for a garden. Stocking the farm with cattle, poultry, and implements also required funds. The men who emigrated ahead of their families needed money to bring them to Canada, so they entered the work force immediately. Debts and needy families in Galicia and Bukovyna were also a motivation. And because women assumed the major responsibilities on homesteads, the men were free to seek employment elsewhere.

Another factor accounts for the high number of Ukrainians who took jobs off the homesteads. The dimensions of Canadian farming were utterly foreign to them. They had expected to practise subsistence farming on perhaps 10 productive acres. Prior to 1905, the immigrants were still adjusting to the notion that one could work 10 times as much land and earn a living by selling the crops. They had believed that hard cash could only be earned through employment off the homestead.

In Galicia and Bukovyna, the Ukrainians had held a variety of jobs, both temporary and permanent. They were familiar with work on the farms of large landowners, in the homes of the wealthy, in oil and gas fields, and on road construction and repair sites. They had also taken advantage of better opportunities for employment through temporary emigration to Germany or other neighbouring countries. (The Canadian equivalent did not require emigration outside the country, but places of employment were located up to 600 miles from the labourers' homesteads.) In Canada, they would find similar employment opportunities, beginning with agricultural and domestic labour.

Ukrainian men quickly found work on established farms. The tasks were varied, from rooting trees and cutting wood to harvesting. Payment also varied. Some workers "received room and board if they cut ten cords of wood a month."[1] Wasyl Eleniak, one of the first immigrants, is reported to have received $100 for a year and, later, $120.[2] Luckier workers got $15 per month, while others had to settle for $15 dollars for an entire harvest season.[3] With room and board provided, salaries fell as low as 25 cents a day ($7.50 a month)[4] and, for boys, $3 a month.[5] Free room and board was an important consideration, however, especially for younger labourers whose families had difficulty supporting them. Farmers who had promised cash salaries often sent workers away with supplies instead. One pioneer recalls that instead of the $15 owed him for working during the harvest season, he received a rifle and two buckets full of milk from the cash-poor farmer.[6] Eggs, potatoes, and other farm products were common means of payment. More fortunate workers received a cow or a horse in lieu of cash as payment for prolonged work periods. Needless to say, payments in the form of cash substitutes limited the manner in which workers could spend their earnings.

The dismissal of labourers a short time prior to the date of payment was not uncommon. Stories abounded about "rascals who will hire a man 'on trial' for a month, pick a quarrel with him just before the month is out, send him off without a dollar of wages, and repeat the operation on the next newcomer."[7] Although this "ridiculous legend . . .

that the Canadian farmer is a sort of slave-driver or sweater" was claimed to be "started by the 'slacker' and spread by the credulous," the Salvation Army, nevertheless, prepared a black list of such employers.[8]

Immigrants working on farms had to rely solely on the good graces of their employers. Working conditions varied greatly, but the distance between employers limited any effective comparisons by the labourers. Ukrainians preferred to work for fellow countrymen or Germans, with whom they could communicate, but many worked for Swedes or Englishmen as well as others. Regardless of conditions of work, location of employment, salary, or the character of employers, the Ukrainian farm labourer was able to return to his homestead with at least a little something to show for his efforts. Under the circumstances, that was enough to make him a proud man and the occasion of his return a joyous one for his family.

Women whose primary responsibilities did not involve clearing land, building a house, or looking after children on the homestead — generally those young and single — sought work under conditions similar to those faced by male farm labourers. They worked as domestics. Women had little difficulty in securing jobs, as "the English always wanted a Ukrainian girl because they are harder workers."[9] Although places of work for females were generally concentrated in towns and cities, many worked for farmers. Their duties included preparing or helping to prepare meals, washing dishes, cleaning the house, washing floors, washing and ironing clothes, combing hair, and helping with children. In short, they solved "the servant problem" in the west.[10] Most domestics received room and board. Their salaries varied greatly, but were generally much lower than men's. Like the male farm labourer, they had little or no time off, and payment in kind was not unusual. Employers often gave women and girls dresses, shoes, and other items to "improve" their appearances. Employers, of course, felt that they were doing Canada a great service by encouraging the girls to adopt the manners, customs, and language of their new land. Many Ukrainian domestics did find it necessary to learn English quickly.

Some Ukrainians used their ingenuity to become self-employed. Those who had acquired horses and a wagon, for example, met their newly arrived countrymen in Edmonton or Winnipeg and offered them transportation to homesteads — for a price. One Ukrainian transported travellers on a raft across the river on his land for 25 cents per person, grossing $2 to $3 a day.[11] Others went from house to house selling cut wood, earning 50 to 75 cents per day.[12] Women plastered houses for those able to pay. Such self-employment was limited by the Ukrainians' means and skills and the opportunities available to sell goods and services. It usually served to provide supplementary or contingency funds.

Generally temporary in nature and dependent on the mobility of the labourer, the work available to immigrants was menial. But farm and domestic labour did allow a one-to-one relationship between employer and employee. When employers were reasonable, the relationship could prove rewarding. Conditions were often negotiable.

Industrial Labour and Working Conditions

Work in mines, on railroads, or in urban centres usually took the immigrant far from home. Opportunities to negotiate conditions and salaries were all but non-existent, but at first Ukrainian labourers were concerned only with securing a position and earning whatever they could. The fact that they were hired along with many of their countrymen helped to compensate for the severity of their dislocation. In fact, at this stage the Ukrainian labourer was pleased with his good fortune.

Opportunities were many. In response to the influx of immigrants, Canadian financial interests embarked on massive and rapid development to serve new markets and to take advantage of new sources of labour. Railway companies spearheaded this expansion in the pursuit of prosperity. The Mackenzie and Mann interests, for example, constructed a second transcontinental, the Canadian Northern Railway. This venture, because of its proximity to Ukrainian settlements (running from Winnipeg through Yorkton and Saskatoon to Edmonton), was especially important to the Ukrainians. The Canadian Pacific Railway Company also increased its service by adding a number of branch lines, the most important of which was the Crow's Nest Pass Railway from Lethbridge, Alberta to the mining regions of southeastern British Columbia.

Most Ukrainian men who came to Canada before 1905 worked temporarily on the railways or in the mines. Many Ukrainian farmers from Manitoba and the eastern part of the North-West Territories (the future province of Saskatchewan) trekked to Winnipeg in search of jobs, and the majority was sent to various points of railway construction in those two districts. Ukrainian settlers in the vicinity of Edmonton were normally sent to work on railways in the southwestern portion of what would become the province of Alberta or to the mines in southeastern British Columbia. Although most tried to secure work close to their homesteads, few succeeded.

Immigrants often received their jobs through the employment agencies located in major cities. These privately owned enterprises served the interests of railway, mining, and other companies. One writer noted that, "unpretentious and modestly located, perhaps at a corner adjacent to the station or in a nearby lane, these places . . . had always an enticing display of ad-heads plastering the walls and windows. Notices were paraded to advantage on bulletins."[13] The employment agency was a lucrative business: "a lawyer has been known to divert his efforts for a time to this remunerative trade."[14] Fees were collected from companies for each labourer sent to them and often labourers were required to pay for information. Labourers were willing to pay because jobs offered through agencies — although far from home — paid 25 to 50 cents more a day than similar jobs in areas close to urban centres.[15] Other inducements included an advance on railway fares to the place of work, the promise of a refund for railway fare after six months' employment, housing and food en route, and sometimes even tobacco. The work of the agencies paralleled that of the emigration agents in Europe. Both made promises that raised the hopes of their victims, and both knew that the promises would be shattered by reality.

One unsuspecting Ukrainian immigrant, upon entering an employment agency, was advised to sign up for a C.P.R. extra gang. Pleased with the opportunity to work, he "registered, gave them $1, but did not know what the C.P.R. or an extra gang was."[16] From the people standing around the agency — mostly Ukrainians — he learned "that it is a large railroad company in Canada and that in Canada railroads are not government-owned but private companies." He concluded, "I was going then to build a railroad." But before he left for work he was warned that it was not only miserable, but brought no money.[17]

Large numbers of Ukrainians, who were often hired in groups, worked on extra gangs. Labourers were transported by train to the designated work areas where they were housed and fed in railway cars. The gangs of 60 to 100 men undertook "track renewal, ballasting and needed improvements for switches, abutments and other structures."[18] Working with basic tools — the grub hoe, picaroon, and crowbar — the labourers required little skill, but a great deal of strength. Accidents often occurred. Burial costs were paid with the labourer's outstanding wages, and the deceased was soon forgotten as workers moved on.

The extra gangs were often on the move; rarely did a group stay at one location for more than a month. Their wages were among the lowest in railway construction. The cost of room and board, supplies (working gloves, boots), and medical and postal services was deducted from the $1.35 average wage for a ten-hour day.[19] When inclement weather prevented work, the men were not paid. Frequently, after two or three months' work, the immigrant labourer had barely enough money to pay for the return trip to the nearest city.

Normally, good food was provided for extra-gang workers. One pleasantly surprised Ukrainian labourer compared a dinner meal to that which King Franz Joseph in Vienna would have. He noted that "on the table there was lots of everything: meat, cheese, butter, some kind of rolls with raisins, others with cream, milk, coffee, and some kind of cookies."[20] For breakfast the next day the worker recalls receiving "a whole tin frying pan full of fried eggs, thin pancakes, liquid honey, oatmeal, milk, bread, butter, and coffee."[21] One observer explained that "due to the competition in the labour market . . . campmen will go where the chuck is best."[22] For the Ukrainian, the reasoning was simple: "They are feeding us well. I think they will demand good work from us in return."[23]

But the mosquitoes and lice were difficult to cope with, especially when extra gangs were located some distance from a stream or river and water was in short supply. There was little, if any, opportunity to wash oneself. A Ukrainian labourer described his experience:

> At night something crawled on the face and did not allow sleep. I heard during the night people tossing and turning, scratching, and ripping their skin. With horror I concluded these were lice that crawled on the bodies, like sheep on a meadow. . . . There was nowhere to wash one's clothes — there was no water at the place, the company was not about to dig a well, and the workers had enough to do all day, to take to digging a well themselves. Water for cooking was gotten by cooks from the locomotive's boiler when a train came. Otherwise one had to do something else.[24]

The labourers tried to cope with the pests as best as they could.

> They dug a ditch in the ground, deep enough to reach dampness. There they put their shirts and covered them with soil, leaving a tiny piece of shirt uncovered. In half an hour the lice crawled on top, as if people from a theatre. Such lice-hunting was done frequently. Some workers awaited for an ointment for which they wrote home. But to completely get rid of lice was impossible.[25]

Mosquitoes were most bothersome during the necessary visits to the bush.

It is difficult to determine whether, after a season of work on an extra gang, Ukrainian labourers returned or sought better-paying railway construction jobs. Employment agencies played important roles in determining the work assigned. A labourer registered for railway work could be sent to any stage of the construction. Ukrainians did, however, work as station men — a job that required more skill than work on extra gangs.

Station men prepared the road bed (a station being 100 feet of right of way) for the laying of tracks after the bush had been cleared from the proposed roadway area. Small groups of men were sub-contracted to engage in such work. Two men, for example, could undertake 5 stations, whereas 8 to 14 men could undertake 20 stations.[26] Although labourers were often hired individually by a sub-contractor who had already undertaken a number of stations, many Ukrainians formed their own station groups. Responsible for their own food and shelter, they erected *burdeys* or *kurnyky* (dug-outs) and built outdoor ovens. Food and supplies were bought from the sub-contractor, who paid them for their work. Their diet consisted of fat pork, beans, bread, and tea, varied with sauerkraut, syrup, and canned tomatoes. Station men were allotted "a minimum amount per cubic yard for the material they hep-up to form a road bed."[27] Although they were given the opportunity to negotiate their price, incidents where "Slavs [were] paid by contractors whose loaded revolvers were on the table" were not uncommon.[28]

Keeping a job depended on obedience. In one group of about 100 workers building the Canadian Northern Railway from Fort William to Winnipeg in 1901, the 50 or so Ukrainians decided to celebrate their Christmas (7 January) by taking the day off. All but the most skilled were dismissed on the spot and had no choice but to walk the 20 miles through the bitter cold to Fort William.[29] Ukrainians who were fired or who were unable to cope with the working conditions lost their earning power, as they had few other skills. In some cases, workers were sent away without wages. Some of those working on the Crow's Nest Pass Railway, for example, "were told to go to Edmonton to collect their money, but after waiting around for months, they could not persuade anyone to pay them."[30] The Ukrainians who knew German or English were more fortunate. Translators for railway bosses could earn $200 in three months ($2.50 per day plus food).[31]

Ukrainian immigrants seeking work in Winnipeg could sometimes choose between railway work and lumbering. Workers lived in bunkhouses under conditions similar to those of railway workers. Aside from selling cordwood or cutting trees privately, few Ukrainians worked in the winter lumber camps of southwestern Ontario prior to 1902.[32] The few who did had tasks that required little skill. Later in the decade as Ukrainians gained experience and expertise, they worked as fellers and logmakers. However, the bankruptcy rate of lumber companies and sawmills was so high that Ukrainians feared this work. Some companies actually feigned bankruptcy, leaving the workers behind when the operations moved elsewhere.

Ukrainians seeking work in Edmonton had a choice of railway or mining labour. Whereas labourers based in Winnipeg toiled mostly on the Canadian Northern Railway, Edmonton funnelled workers to the Canadian Pacific Railway. Sometimes workers were assigned to jobs against their wills, which taught them valuable lessons. One group, for example, taken from Edmonton to Calgary to work, deserted the train after learning they were to dig ditches. When they returned to the train, the cars had been switched and they found themselves in coaches bound for British Columbia, where they were to repair washed-out railroad grades.[33]

After suffering the treacheries of railway work, many Ukrainians looked for more stable work in the mines of British Columbia. And they had learned enough about railways to turn the tables. It became a common practice for labourers to sign "up for work on extra gangs, and when they got free transportation to their destination, they took off for some other job."[34] One worker explained his reasoning and sentiments:

> If I could only get to British Columbia, I'd wave good-bye to the C.P.R. . . . I'm not crazy about roasting in the sun tamping ties or carrying a lining bar for eighty-five cents a day. Gone are the days when sweat flooded my eyes on the track. I can work in the shade of a roof at a sawmill, or in the bush. If I can't get a job in the mine at Frank, I can get one at Coleman or at Michel. Or at Fernie, for sure, because ever since they had an explosion there they are short of men.[35]

Mining and its supportive industries in British Columbia provided better pay and working conditions than railway labour.

The Ukrainian colonies in the Edmonton district were closer to the mines and were also older and larger than those in Manitoba or Saskatchewan. As the settlers near Edmonton began to look higher than the subsistence level, they turned away from railway jobs to mining. Mining in the Kootenay region of British Columbia had developed rapidly after the completion in 1898 of the Crow's Nest Pass Railway, which tied the area to markets. Discoveries of rich metallic ore in the region between 1890 and 1895 had brought an influx of individual prospectors. In the boom of 1896, large companies undertook the mining operations:

> Silver, copper, lead, quartz, and zinc were all discovered in ample quantities, camps constructed, and towns grew up adjacent to the mines. Nelson, Rossland, Trail, New Denver, Slocan City, Sandon, Kaslo, Grand Forks, Phoenix, Greenwood, emerged overnight as boom towns. . . . Silver, lead and quartz were mined in the Slocan

district. . . . The most famous of the east Kootenay mines, the Sulli-
van at Kimberley, discovered in 1892, soon became a leading world
producer of lead, zinc, and silver. Fernie, in the east Kootenay area,
emerged around the turn of the century as a major coal-producing
centre.[36]

The development of mining was accompanied by a large increase in
population and the growth of smelting, lumbering, and hydro-electric
enterprises. In 1890, there were about 2,000 people in the Kootenay region; by 1901 there were 31,962.[37] The railways built a network of
branch lines to integrate the mines and various supporting industries.

Getting to this prosperous area was of paramount importance to the
upwardly mobile immigrant. Not only were jobs all but ensured, but
the labourer had the choice of a variety of industries: lumbering, mining, smelting, sawmills, railroads, and hydro plants. Although as
hazardous as railroad work, employment in the mines and support industries was more remunerative. One worker recalls that "First I got a
job in a coal mine, cutting timber for props. There were a lot of other
Ukrainians working in that mine. I was paid $2 a day. That was a very
good wage. Later I worked on railroads. They gave me $1.25 for a
nine-hour day."[38] Another worker noted that in a Rossland, B.C. gold
mine in 1901, "a common laborer was paid fifty cents an hour, while
wages for sectionmen [on railroads] were only 12½ to fifteen cents an
hour."[39] A working day in British Columbia was eight hours long in
accordance with the 1 May 1899 provincial law.[40] On railroads, however, workers were usually expected to work a minimum of ten hours
per day. Miners could also try their hand at individual prospecting, and
generally the work in mines was more permanent than on railways. But
mining offered as few opportunities for advancement as railway work
did. On the railroad, a Ukrainian section-gang worker with a knowledge of German or English and the equivalent of a college education
could become "a section foreman in a year or two and a roadmaster in
about ten years, and that's it."[41] In the mines:

> Day men (paid a flat daily wage) might become contract miners (paid
> by the amount of coal dug, graded as suitable and weighed at the pit
> head) but this was as far as they could go. In the hardrock mines a
> mucker might become a miner, an even less important promotion
> than that from day man to contract miner in the coal fields.[42]

Mining areas attracted, primarily, single Ukrainian workers who
could stay for a year or two and then return to their relatives or take up
homesteads. Most married men with families on homesteads could af-

ford to work in the mines only seasonally. When families did come to the region, the women took odd jobs such as washing clothes and cooking for miners. "Some spent two years digging coal on their knees, their families housed, if at all, in a two-room company shack. While the family lived in one room, the other was given over to three or four male workers for whom the mother cooked."[43] Because the majority of towns were company-owned, the cost of food and supplies was high. But many Ukrainians shared company shacks or constructed their own and were generally able to keep costs down. Not all, however, were able to avoid the vices. Gambling, prostitution, and liquor were lucrative businesses in the boom towns, and there were Ukrainians who were unable to withstand these diversions — in many cases, the only available diversions — and became tied to labour in the mines to support their habits.

Labourers who worked as contract miners set their own hours and rate of work and generally worked with partners. Each could gross $80 to $120 in two weeks.[44] Their payment was calculated either by the amount of suitably graded ore dug or "on the basis of a price per foot of hole drilled — this being possible with the homogeneous character of the ore body."[45] The day men were paid on the basis of an eight-hour shift, receiving anywhere from two to four dollars per day depending on the location and the value of the ore being extracted. The eight-hour law forced mines to divide the working day into shifts.

Miners worked the horizontal veins located on mountain sides by extracting the ore from exposed veins or by tunnelling into the mountain to reach it and then transporting it down on rawhides pulled by horses:

> About 15 sacks of ore (100 to 150 pounds) were wrapped in raw cowhide and slid down the mountain . . . the thick mantel of snow with which the ground is covered throughout the long winter making it possible to form a trail for use in this way at a cost little exceeding that necessary to remove the underbrush and a few large trees that cannot be avoided along the selected route.[46]

On return trips the same horses carried provisions and supplies to the mine.

Ores located in vertical veins (such as coal) were extracted in underground mines. The Frank coal mine, for example, had 300 feet of underground rooms "one above the other" to facilitate working the coal seam.[47] Tunnels and underground mine shafts were supported by wooden props. Accidents were frequently caused by cave-ins and by the explosive gas in the shaft. In the east Kootenay region, "it was not discovered until after several major disasters, in which hundreds of miners were killed, that the coal . . . was 15 times more gaseous and therefore much more likely to cause explosions than comparably-graded bituminous in Pennsylvania.[48]

Growing Pains in the Labour Market

Winnipeg and Edmonton were major meeting centres for immigrant Ukrainians. During the spring exodus from homesteads and the return to them in fall, Ukrainians passing through urban centres were able to share news, compare experiences, and offer advice to each other on various aspects of farming and working life in Canada.

Although exact numbers are difficult to ascertain, there was a good number of Ukrainians who became permanent residents in the cities. Some found more stable and better-paying employment in urban centres than on railways or in mines. Others, who had fully intended to take up farms after earning sufficient funds, for a variety of reasons never left the cities. This was particularly true of unmarried men.

The distribution of Ukrainian immigrants before 1905 is indicated by shifting population figures, although the numbers may not be exact because of the confusion over ethnic designation. In Winnipeg in 1901, for example, the immigrants born in Austria-Hungary, Russia, Poland, Galicia, and Bukovyna (many of whom were Ukrainians) numbered only 2,741, or 17.14 per cent of a total 15,989 foreign-born immigrants. By 1911, the number had increased to 18,673 or 24.55 per cent of the 76,068 immigrants in Winnipeg.[49] Austro-Hungarians, Russians, and Poles (among whom Ukrainians were included) comprised 4.2 per cent of Winnipeg's total population in 1901. The rapid increase of the urban labour population toward the end of the decade boosted the percentage to 9.8 in 1911.[50]

The employment secured by these immigrants in urban centres was varied: digging ditches and sewers, shovelling snow, constructing buildings, bridges, roads, and railway yards, laying streetcar tracks, delivering coal or wood, and washing dishes. Women worked in restaurants, hotels, or as domestics. Few Ukrainians were highly skilled, but those with a knowledge of English or German, and especially those who had emigrated from the United States, were able to secure better-paying positions as store clerks or translators. Wages and conditions depended on the job and its location. Winnipeg, the Gateway City to the West, home of 43,340 people in 1901,[51] offered greater and more diverse opportunities than Edmonton, where in 1901 "there were only about ten stores on main street, two lumberyards, two hotels, three butcher shops, two restaurants, and a few boarding houses,"[52] to serve the population of 5,547.[53]

It was a struggle for immigrants in these cities to live within their means. With rents in the booming centres high — in Winnipeg the average rent for a house was $20 a month — and cheap accommodation scarce, the immigrants were forced to share their dwellings, often having four or five families in one house.⁵⁴ Accommodation affordable to immigrants was normally concentrated in an area near the city's train station. In Winnipeg, it was in the North End. In Fort William the immigrant district developed as a "cohesive community sandwiched between the C.P.R. tracks and freight sheds, coal docks, railway yards and grain elevators then lining the Kaministikwia River."⁵⁵ In Winnipeg, the construction of "the longest railway yards in the world" — 120 miles of track to accommodate 10,000 cars — through the North End and the development of industry adjacent to the yards provided employment for Ukrainians. But it also "effectively cut off the North End from the rest of the city."⁵⁶ The North End developed rapidly during the housing construction boom in Winnipeg after 1896, but with average lots 25 or 32 feet wide and houses "built to the very edge of the property," the area developed a "terribly cramped appearance."⁵⁷ In addition, "lack of sanitary installations, dirty back-yards, muddy, foul-smelling streets, and poor lighting conditions," caused in part by the general neglect of immigrant areas by civic authorities, turned these districts into ghettos.⁵⁸

Urban centres were used as a place of refuge during strikes, the most obvious example being the 1901 strike of maintenance-of-way employees on the C.P.R. in Alberta. Strikes were crippling to the immigrants who desperately needed money to get established; Ukrainians, although "satisfied with the pay . . . were forced to quit their jobs because the strikers harassed them as scabs."⁵⁹ Stranded in Medicine Hat and without any pay, several hundred Ukrainian railroad workers walked to Edmonton, "begging bread from farmers and ranchers along the way."⁶⁰ This group housed itself in Edmonton in caves dug into the hill at the present site of the Macdonald Hotel. Their quarters were dubbed the "Galician Hotel."

> On the slope at the foot of the bank, we improvised kitchen ranges and heaters. We collected tin cans from bacon and conserves and used these as utensils for cooking, frying, and drinking. We baked flat cakes and biscuits, and cooked pyrohy and noodles which we greased with lard and greaves. We enjoyed our meals which we usually topped off with tea without milk and, at times, without sugar.⁶¹

In order to earn the $10 a day needed to feed their group, the men went from door to door looking for work. They did chores around houses or stores "for a dollar or two," cleaned toilets, moved outdoor toilets to new sites, built and mended fences, dug and cleaned wells, cut or trimmed trees, grubbed stumps, plastered stables or cowsheds, repaired roofs, or sawed and split loads of wood. One participant noted that "as long as the townspeople took advantage of our low rates and hired us, we were not idle and did not go hungry." Any cash earned was handed over to the sympathetic merchant "from whom we bought everything."[62]

The Ukrainian workers were "disappointed, to say the least, as the strike dragged on throughout the entire summer."[63] Regardless of their capacity for survival, the primary concern of the Ukrainian labourers was their families on the farms: "If we managed to earn more than we needed for our provisions, we would divide sacks of flour in two and send a half bag to the wives and children of each of the unemployed, out in the country."[64] By the time the strike was settled at the end of August, many of the workers had dispersed. For the Brotherhood of Railway Trackmen, the strike was a success — achieving union recognition and an increased wage for its members. But for the Ukrainians the strike was all but disastrous, undercutting their means of life support.

In British Columbia by the turn of the century, the Western Federation of Miners was making headway in forming union locals. Its strike, called early in 1899 in support of legislation for an eight-hour day, affected almost 4,000 workers in the west Kootenay.[65] The Rossland strike of 1901 was called in reaction to "anti-union discrimination by companies,"[66] but was crushed when owners imported miners from the United States to assure themselves of "an abundant supply of labour."[67] Many displaced strikers lost their jobs. In Winnipeg, a two-month strike by trackmen against the C.P.R. in 1901 affected railway operations across Canada.[68] A strike in Winnipeg in 1902 on the Canadian Northern Railway resulted in the United Brotherhood of Railway Employees, "a radical western-oriented industrial union," reaching a settlement which covered only skilled workers.[69]

The recognition of unions by companies meant little to the Ukrainians, who depended on their wages to support their newly established farms — employment not being an end in itself. The unions, fighting to achieve recognition, obviously could not understand the immigrant's position. In the period to 1905, the unions were only partially successful in alleviating the burdens of those whose livelihood depended on employment. The unskilled workers, especially those like the Ukrainians, paid the price in the unions' quest for legitimacy. Few benefits, if any at all, were garnered by labourers before 1905 who supported the recognition of labour organizations.

At first, Ukrainian immigrant labour in western Canada was an extension of agricultural settlement. The railroad workers from eastern settlement colonies and the railroad and mine workers from western colonies filled only part of the need for unskilled labour, while earning whatever meagre funds they could to ensure some economic stability on their homesteads. To 1905, the labour force was dominated by Orientals in British Columbia and Italians from the United States. But by 1905, most industrial and financial enterprises were enlarging their operations with unprecedented speed. Pressure was exerted on the government to permit the entry of unskilled Ukrainian workers to fill the vacuum created by the enforcement of the Alien Labour Law, which limited the employment of Orientals and Italians. Ukrainian immigration after 1905 was of a significantly different character than the earlier immigration. Most of the new arrivals were bound for the labour market and many had socialist leanings. Augmenting the already established unions, this new wave of Ukrainian immigrants would be a potent weapon against business interests in western Canada.

CHAPTER 9

THE SOCIAL AND INSTITUTIONAL FRONTIER

Ukrainian immigrants in the period to 1905 were preoccupied with the quest for economic stability, but the adjustment and establishment of basic Ukrainian institutions was also a primary concern. Immigrants needed the security offered by familiar institutions to counteract the trauma of dealing with the foreign social organization of the new land. Although the early years of settlement witnessed economic considerations taking up the major portion of the immigrants' total existence, cultural and social institutions were inextricably intertwined with the well-being of the Ukrainian settlers.

The church was a basic Ukrainian institution. In Galicia, the Greek Catholic Church played a particularly significant role; it was a preserver of historical tradition, an educational institution, and it protected Ukrainians from Russophile and Polonizing pressures. In Canada, its role was severely restricted. Lack of clergy, the fact that only celibate priests were recognized in Canada, jurisdictional questions of Eastern vs. Latin rites, and the competition of other denominations — Russian Orthodox, Methodist, Presbyterian, and even Baptist — caused bitterness and confusion. Further difficulties arose between Bukovynian Orthodox and Galician Uniate Ukrainians living within the same colonies, difficulties which often resulted in factionalism.

Once churches were constructed and priests were attracted, schools were established. But schools, too, were fraught with problems: these included language of instruction, lack of teachers, lack of compulsory education regulations, and the need to retain as much manpower as possible on the homesteads. Still, immigrants were concerned that their children not grow up like "wild animals." After 1905, the Ukrainians were assisted by provincial governments, which built Ukrainian-English training schools for teachers.

The Search for Religious Leadership

Religious communities among Ukrainians in Canada developed without established leadership. Immigrants set about building their own churches and seeking out priests to serve them; the impulse for religious institutional growth was spontaneous. But a large number of religious faiths sent their missionaries to save Ukrainians, forcing a redefinition of the specific church they wanted to preserve in Canada. Ukrainian religious leadership was closely connected with Ukrainian secular leadership and provided a liaison with the religious and secular institutions of the host society.

Reverend Nestor Dmytriw was concerned that the Ukrainian Catholic Church be fostered in Canada. During his trip through the Dominion in 1897, he established a number of church-building committees. He also reserved 160 acres of land "ad personam" for priests, and the 40-acre government church grant wherever he could. Most Ukrainian immigrants supported his efforts, and the building of churches was generally the first expression of community life. On 13 September 1897, Dmytriw blessed a chapel at Lake Dauphin.[1] The Star colony had also erected a church by 1897.[2] An Orthodox church in Gardenton, Manitoba was completed in the same year.[3] By 1898, churches were standing in Beaver Creek[4] and Gonar[5] in Alberta and at Stuartburn[6] in Manitoba. A second church was completed in Stuartburn in 1900.[7] By 1901, an Orthodox church at Wostock, Alberta,[8] and another in Winnipeg, were constructed.[9] Churches in Chipman, Alberta[10] and at Yaroslav, near Yorkton, Saskatchewan, were completed in 1903.[11] And a second Ukrainian church was completed in Winnipeg in 1904.[12] By 1905, most Ukrainian colonies had erected churches.

To construct a church, settlers normally first organized a building committee, whose task was to collect donations and solicit volunteer labour. Wood was cut and gathered, using whatever implements were available in the colony; anyone who owned oxen was conscripted to transport materials. Experienced carpenters lent their expertise to the undertaking. All available manpower, even that of the children, was harnessed. Construction rarely went smoothly. Some settlers complained that the church building began too early, before some colonists had constructed their homes.[13] The issue of whether to accept funds and materials offered by non-Ukrainian missionaries became contentious.[14]

Some committee treasurers spent building funds indiscriminately[15] and, in other cases, contractors disappeared with the money.[16]

Serious difficulties were caused by the denominational differences within the Ukrainian community. Ukrainians from Galicia were Catholic, belonging to the "Ruthenian" or Uniate Church. The Ukrainians from Bukovyna, on the other hand, were Orthodox, and were associated with the Orthodox Church in Russia. In the old country, the two Ukrainian churches were based in different regions. In Canada, the two faiths were thrown together. In some areas, the difference was resolved by the construction of two churches. In other colonies, even though Ukrainians of different faiths joined together to build one church, they continued to argue over which faith owned and had the right to use the church. Normal recourse for such arguments was the courts.

The case of the church in Star, Alberta gained notoriety because of the persistence of each faction in its attempts to prove the other wrong. Trouble escalated during the Easter celebrations in 1901, when both Catholic and Orthodox Masses were planned for Easter morning in the one church. Fighting broke out and police prevented both groups of celebrants from entering the church. The Catholics took the matter to the justice of the peace in Star for a ruling. He decided that the issue was too serious for his consideration and passed it on to the Higher Court in Edmonton. Hearings commenced 16 May 1902 and on 15 March 1904 the judge ruled that the church belonged to the Catholics. The Orthodox faction appealed to the Higher Court of the North-West Territories, where the case was dismissed. The Orthodox group then took its appeal to the Supreme Court of Canada which, on 2 February 1906, gave them ownership of the church. The Catholics decided to appeal to the highest court of the British Empire, the Judicial Committee of the Privy Council. The ruling of 3 December 1907 read: "Held, upon the evidence, that the purpose for which the land was vested in the trustees was for building a Greek Orthodox Church and not a Greek Church in communion with the Church of Rome."[17] The six-year battle illustrates well the extent and severity of religious differences within the community. In most other Ukrainian colonies, such difficulties were solved locally, but not without a lot of bickering.

Before 1905, the Catholics suffered from a shortage of priests. The arrival of married Ukrainian Catholic clergy in the United States in earlier decades had caused such a stir in the Roman Catholic population that the married priests were not only denied recognition but were ordered to leave the country.[18] By 1890, a ban had been placed on married Catholic priests in North America.[19] The problem was a serious one for Ukrainians because in Galicia only missionary priests, making up three per cent of all the clergy, were celibate.[20] The monastic order of St. Basil the Great was the only Ukrainian order which met the requirement and, to complicate matters further, it had just undergone major reforms and did not have a sufficient number of priests.[21] There was also a problem of jurisdiction. In Galicia, both Latin (Polish) and Greek (Ukrainian) rites were practised, but both of these rites were under the jurisdiction of Catholic bishops.[22] The assumption was made in Canada that all Catholics were of the Latin rite, and difficulties arose in understanding and fulfilling the needs of non-Latin rite Catholics.

Few Ukrainians understood or were even aware of the rulings and jurisdictional matters of the church hierarchy which underpinned the shortage of priests. The church was simply an important part of their lives. In their new, foreign environment, it was the only link with their past and homeland, and it served as an easily identifiable base for Ukrainian social and cultural development in Canada. Moreover, the Ukrainian churches in Galicia and Bukovyna, although state-controlled, protected the Ukrainian identity, however ill-defined, against Polonizing influences. In Canada, where that identity seemed to be threatened by foreign religious influences, the churches served as a safeguard. Prodded by people such as Dmytriw and the *Svoboda* editors, the churches assumed importance beyond spiritual and moral leadership. They became the means of national expression.

Ukrainians dealt with the lack of priests and the abundance of churches as best they could. Even before churches were constructed, the peasants met in homes: "On Sundays, early in the morning, everyone hurried, as if to church,"[23] and then, led by a cantor, they sang the customary parts of the Mass.[24] Carollers roamed the countryside at Christmas, and Easter was celebrated with all the traditions. On occasion, non-Ukrainian priests were engaged. One group of immigrants, stranded at the Calgary Immigration Hall, decided to have their Easter baskets blessed. They virtually dragged a much confused, French, Roman Catholic priest to the hall. After a while, the priest understood — he had thought it was a picnic. Pandemonium had broken out when he started eating the food.[25]

Occasional tours were taken through Canada by Ukrainian Catholic priests from the United States. Reverend Dmytriw visited the colonies in 1897. Reverend Pavlo Tymkevych concentrated his efforts in the Edmonton-area settlements in the spring of 1898, as did Reverend Ivan Zaklynsky in the summer of 1899. Reverend Damaskian Polivka served Ukrainians in Winnipeg in 1899, and was succeeded by Reverend Zaklynsky.[26] Meanwhile, the Roman Catholic hierarchy in Canada was attempting to encourage the arrival of Basilian monastic priests, who were celibate. In 1898 and 1900, representatives were sent to Europe —

Rome, Vienna, and Lviv — but they had little immediate success. After the investigative visit to Canada in 1901 by Reverend V. Zholdak, secretary to Metropolitan Andrij Sheptytsky, Ukrainian bishop of Galicia, a handful of missionaries was dispatched.[27] In 1902, three Basilian priests, one brother, and four Sister Servants of Mary Immaculate arrived in Canada.[28] They made their headquarters in the Ukrainian settlements of the Edmonton district.

In 1900, Reverend Dmytriw had estimated that it would take five priests three months to visit all the Ukrainian settlements in Canada once.[29] But by 1903, Ukrainian churches were still far from having regular services; fewer than ten Ukrainian Catholic priests were working in Canada. Although later arrivals supplemented their ranks, the lack of religious personnel would plague Ukrainians throughout the decade.

In the meantime, the Roman Catholic Church sought to minister to the Ukrainians of the Uniate Church. But most of the immigrants, unable to understand Latin services, did not respond favourably. In Winnipeg, the Roman Catholic Archbishop, Langevin, built "a costly stone church, residence for six priests, and a proper stone elementary school with the capacity to Grade VI, in 1899."[30] A young Polish priest from Montreal, Reverend Kiliawy, was engaged to serve all Catholic Slavs there. However, many Ukrainian Catholics saw the appointment as an attempt to Polonize them and, encouraged in their rebellion by *Svoboda* and by Ukrainian Catholic priests from the United States, they broke away from the Church of the Holy Ghost and built their own "small" church of Sts. Volodymyr and Olga in Winnipeg in 1901.[31] Father Polivka came from the United States to serve the new parish. However, after being denied permission by the French Archbishop to serve Masses in the Ukrainian church, he left Winnipeg and was succeeded by Father Zaklynsky.

Intolerance on both sides was based on a number of misunderstandings, primarily concerning the jurisdictional regulations of the Catholic Church in Canada. Because Catholic bishops in Canada practised only Latin rites, the Roman Catholics — who in the west were French — assumed leadership and responsibility over all Catholic immigrants, even those who practised Greek rites. French Catholics offered aid in the building of churches, sought out priests, and attempted to draw new arrivals into their fold. French Catholics did not understand that the Eastern rite of the Ukrainian Catholic church underpinned the distinction between the Ukrainians and the Poles, that the Ukrainian Eastern rite was an expression of a fiercely guarded national identity. When the French Catholics showed their ignorance of the historical animosity by sending a Polish priest to serve Ukrainians, the Ukrainians were convinced that the French Catholics had devious plans for them.

1. Ukrainian immigrants arrive in Montreal after a journey of more than 6,000 miles. For many of these peasants, emigration presented the only hope of survival.

2. Galician immigrants at the Immigration Sheds in Quebec. "How can we expect Canadians to welcome these people?" asked a Member of Parliament, "We have nothing in common with them."

3. The luxury of the Canadian trains was a gratifying surprise. Bound for Winnipeg in the C.P.R. Colonist cars, immigrants often remarked that it seemed as though they were not travelling to homesteads but enjoying a "holiday trip."

4. Ukrainian dress caused some Canadians to compare the immigrants to animals. But Clifford Sifton, Minister of the Interior, defended the "stalwart peasant in a sheepskin coat" as the sturdiest sort of pioneer.

5. The first permanent home of the Ukrainians usually had a thatched roof and two rooms. The floors were packed clay, washed every week with a solution of cow dung and water. This home was built in Saskatchewan about 1903.

6. The celebration of a successful harvest was long in coming. The dimensions of Canadian agriculture were foreign to the Ukrainian peasants, to whom 100 acres was a vast estate.

7. Ukrainians dedicate a new church near Foley, Manitoba in 1906. The church was a cultural and educational institution, the guardian of heritage and identity.

8. Delegates to the second conference of Ukrainian Orthodox priests in Winnipeg, 1905. The Orthodox Church in Canada competed fiercely with the Greek Catholic Church for immigrant converts.

9. Inside the Presbyterian Mission Boys' Home in Teulon, Manitoba, 1911. Presbyterians attracted Ukrainians to Protestantism by establishing residence schools.

10. Plum Ridge School in Manitoba, 1908. Built in the town of Pleasant Home in 1898, it was the first school for Ukrainians in the province. Teachers became a potent intellectual force in the immigrant community.

11.   Band members from the
Crowsnest Pass area in Alberta.

12.   A Ukrainian wedding celebration in Samburg, Saskatchewan,
1914.

13. Dr. Joseph Oleskiw, Canada's unofficial representative of Ukrainian immigrants. Oleskiw left his position as Imperial and Royal Professor in Lviv to investigate and promote emigration to North America.

14. Ukrainians on a C.P.R. construction site, Crowsnest Pass. Struggling to earn money to maintain his homestead, the railway worker often found after three months' work that he had barely enough to get home.

15. Coal miners in Nordegg, Alberta. Mining offered better pay and working conditions than the railway. Wages were $2 a day in the mines and $1.25 on the railway.

16. Andrew Shandro, the first Ukrainian M.L.A. in Canada, with his cousin, William (right). Elected in 1913, Shandro was involved in shady electoral practices and was considered a pawn of the Liberal Party in the battle for Ukrainian rights.

17. Nykyta Budka, the first Ukrainian bishop of the Greek Catholic Church in Canada. An ambitious man, his goal was to establish church control over the Ukrainian immigrants. This portrait hangs in the Archbishop's Chancery in Winnipeg.

18. A Catholic congregation in Borschiw, Alberta, 1916. Bishop Budka (in rear at door of church) battled with Ukrainian nationalists who demanded independence from Roman Catholicism. The nationalists established the Ukrainian Greek Orthodox Church in 1918.

Unaware that the church was separate from the state in Canada, Ukrainians saw the Roman Catholic ministerings as attempts to "put them into the bondage of darkness and ignorance."[32] When the Roman Catholics attempted to gain ownership of all Catholic church land and buildings, Ukrainians accused them of having purely monetary motives — of robbing the riches of the Ukrainian church. In many cases, Ukrainians refused to sign over church property to the Roman Catholic church. In communities such as Brokenhead, two Catholic churches — Roman and Ukrainian — were built. Nevertheless, some Ukrainians did join the Roman Catholic Church and some communities welcomed Roman Catholic efforts to fill the religious void.

The greatest successes of the Roman Catholics were in social work. They had, for example, "a monopoly on the hospital business" in northern Alberta.[33] They were also instrumental in setting up schools. It was students of the Catholic evening school for working girls in Edmonton who met the Basilian missionaries with a concert on their arrival.[34] The Belgian Redemptorist priests also gained acceptability. One Belgian missionary preacher, Father Delaere, began work in Brandon in 1899. In 1904, he took charge of the Ukrainian colonies in the Yorkton district. In 1906, Delaere transferred to the Ukrainian rite and, thereafter, was joined by other Redemptorists.[35]

Obviously, the Ukrainian Catholic Church of Galicia could not be transplanted intact. It had to adjust itself to the religious leadership available in Canada. Whereas in Galicia the density of population allowed priests to reside within each community, in the Canadian west the communities were spread far and wide apart and required travelling missionary priests who were able to cope with all the hazards of pioneer life. In addition, many Ukrainian Catholics in Canada broke away from the political and social control exercised by the church in Galicia. Their adaptation to Canadian conditions would cause problems with priests arriving later, who would seek to impose the Galician clerical control over their congregations.

The Orthodox Ukrainians from Bukovyna also had difficulties acquiring priests. Russian clerics from the San Francisco eparchy, home of Bishop Nikolai, Russian Bishop of the Aleutians and Alaska, undertook missionary work among the Ukrainians in Canada. Armed with financial inducements, Reverend Dmitriv Kannev and Deacon V. Alexandrov worked in 1898 to establish Orthodox churches in the Edmonton area.[36] They supplied, for example, $500 for a church east of Edna and $200 for a chapel west of Edna.[37] Reverend John Maliarevsky, from the Russian Missionary Church of St. Mary in Minneapolis, visited Orthodox Ukrainians in the Stuartburn district in 1897.[38] Reverend Popff arrived in the area in 1899.[39] Their success depended on their willingness to offer funds, to support independent, unincorporated parishes, and to accommodate the Ukrainians by using *rusyn* (Ukrainian) rather than *russki* (Russian) terminology and by using the familiar Church Slavonic for services.[40] Their efforts were susceptible to political criticism, and they were accused of fostering a "Muscophile plot to praise the tsar and rip the remaining flesh off the Rusyns."[41] They also became embroiled in the bickering between the Ukrainian Orthodox and Catholic churches. In the Russian Orthodox newspaper, *Svit*, published in San Francisco, Russophiles made persistent attacks on the work of Ukrainian Catholics or Ukrainophiles, such as Dmytriw and Genik.[42] Representing not only the Orthodox faith but also the Russophile political orientation, the Russian Orthodox priests were able to maintain their influence until funds ran out after the Bolshevik Revolution.

In 1903, the self-proclaimed "Bishop and Metropolitan of the Orthodox Russian Church for the whole of America," the notorious imposter, Seraphim, made his appearance in Winnipeg. As head of the All-Russian Patriarchal Orthodox Church, he came from New York. His grandiose scheme to establish independent Orthodoxy appealed to those Ukrainians of the Orthodox faith who were disenchanted with Russian Orthodoxy, and many "local farmers, workers, school teachers, and deacons"[43] were ordained as priests of his church. In 1904, Seraphim built the Cathedral of the Saviour in Winnipeg.[44] Some 50 priests were sent into the Ukrainian colonies "preaching Orthodoxy independent of any patriarch and trustee ownership of property."[45] The movement attracted 60,000 East European followers in two years. Seraphim was persuaded by his supporters to go to Russia "to seek sanction and support" for his church from the Holy Synod in St. Petersburg. Managing only to be excommunicated by Metropolitan Pobedonostsev, he found on his return that a number of priests had seceded. With the encouragement and support of the Presbyterian Church, the mass movement was transformed into the Independent Greek Church in 1904. Retaining the Orthodox vestments, it reflected Presbyterian teachings in the sermons. Former Seraphimite clergy assumed its leadership, among whom were Ivan Negrych and Ivan Bodrug.

Negrych and Bodrug emerged as influential leaders in the period from 1900 to 1905. Originally from Bereziv Nyzhnyi, a village in the Kolomyia district of Galicia, Negrych and Bodrug had both been schoolteachers. Fluent in German and Polish and with some knowledge of English, they espoused radical concepts of "religious nonconformity, liberalism, egalitarianism and socialism."[46] In Canada, Negrych and Bodrug studied theology at the Presbyterian Manitoba College in 1898 before being employed as teachers in Ukrainian communities in Manitoba. Also engaged as interpreters for the immigration branch of the federal government, they accompanied immigrants from Winnipeg to their homesteads and ensured that they were settled. In 1903, they were ordained by Seraphim. Assuming the leadership of the Independent Greek Church allowed them to crystallize their views of a progressive church. Negrych and Bodrug were able to maintain mass support because of their non-religious social roles as teachers and interpreters; they could explain the ways of the new land and acted as a link between the immigrant and the establishment.

Among immigrants to Canada from the Russian-occupied territory of Ukraine were Baptist-Stundists fleeing religious persecution. The first group, from the Kiev district, arrived in 1900 and was followed by other families in 1901 and 1902.[47] A Baptist community was formed in Winnipeg in 1902. Missionaries were picked and they set out to preach the word of God to Ukrainian colonists. Mykhailo Nikifor and Choma Tvardovsky travelled throughout the Canora district of future Saskatchewan. Vasyl Bubys worked in the Edmonton-district settlements. Ivan Shakotko joined his brothers in Canora and, after organizing a small community there, proceeded to Radisson, in Saskatchewan. Mykyta Kryvetsky, a former student for the priesthood in the Greek Orthodox Church, preached in the Stuartburn area in Manitoba, where "the First Ruthenian Baptist Church in Manitoba, and indeed the world," was built, later to be known as the Overstone Church.[48] Another church was organized in Winnipeg, with Shakotko as preacher, and a Baptist community was established near Edmonton.

Small in number, the Baptists had limited success among the Ukrainians. They received the full support of the English and German Baptist Church in Canada, but were short of funds and never stimulated mass support. One writer noted that the Baptists "in free Canada got rid of the Russian-Orthodox persecution, but did not rid themselves of its influence or its language."[49] Therein lay their greatest handicap. And the evangelical approach, no doubt, had little appeal for most Ukrainians, whose religious observances were steeped with elaborate ceremonies.

The Methodists of Canada also sent missionaries to work among the Ukrainians. They were handicapped by linguistic problems and their evangelical approach. Their success lay, however, in social work and education. One Methodist missionary, Reverend Charles H. Lawford, operated a mission northeast of Edmonton, but found himself involved to a large extent in secular work — advising the immigrants "on a wide variety of secular matters such as the assembling of machinery, arranging for the payment of bills and dispensing information concerning land laws and the formation of school districts." As a doctor, he also tended to the medical needs in the surrounding community.[50]

It was only after 1905 that a uniquely Ukrainian religious leadership became evident. Until then, some Ukrainians who sought religion for its moral teachings consoled themselves with membership in other progressive or evangelical faiths. However, the majority of Ukrainians sought to preserve the cultural and traditional aspects of church life, and therefore joined whichever faith came closest to their previous experience. But their new-found independence from Polonizing influences and from social control by the church made them regard the clergy who arrived later in Canada with intolerance and impatience. As the church building-spree suggests, Ukrainian immigrants were quite willing to take control of their own religious destiny.

First Accomplishments in Education

The role of religious institutions involved more than moral teachings and cultural preservation. In many villages in Galicia and Bukovyna, the priest and cantor were the two literate individuals who ensured the existence of Ukrainian schools. The priest also spearheaded reading societies. In Canada, the void of religious personnel delayed the development of social and educational institutions. Whereas in the homeland priests and cantors complemented the work of secular teachers, in Canada there were too few religious leaders to supplement the work of the handful of Ukrainian-English teachers effectively. Non-Ukrainian religious, social, and political interests were free to assume the role of educating Ukrainians. And by 1905, educational responsibility was placed squarely on the doorstep of provincial governments.

A small number of Ukrainians made attempts to start schools. These activists, faced with the general apathy of immigrants concerned more about economic survival on the homesteads and the building of a local church, had a further difficulty in resolving the question of language instruction. Some felt that instruction should be in Ukrainian because it was more pleasant and Ukrainian-speaking children would be ashamed of their disadvantage in English schools.[51] Aside from isolated instances, such as the working girls' evening school in Edmonton begun by Roman Catholics and continued by Basilians, educational development made little headway before 1900. A school district called Galicia was formed near Gimli in 1899.[52] In Vermillion River, with Presbyterian support, a school was operational in 1900, and another was established seven miles south of Ethelbert soon after. But they were few and far between.

Canadian churches were willing to aid the development of schools "until such time as the province takes over the school."[53] They were handicapped by their inability to procure Ukrainian-speaking instructors. The Manitoba government had committed itself to second-language education: "where ten of the pupils speak French (or any language other than English) as their native language, the teaching of such pupils shall be conducted in French (or such other language) and English upon the bilingual system."[54] Provincial activity in stimulating education had little success: "there was no compulsory education act; but if there had been such an Act its provisions could not have been enforced when we could not furnish bilingual instruction."[55] In the North-West Territories, similar provisions existed for bilingual education. A Territorial Ordinance of 1901 empowered "the board of any district . . . to employ one or more competent persons to give instruction in languages other than English to the pupils whose parents so desire, on condition that such instruction shall not supersede or in any way interfere with the instruction required by the general regulations and provided that the cost of such instruction shall be met by a special levy on the parents of the pupils concerned."[56]

In the early period, the impetus for education lay with the people:

The development of the school system had been hit or miss, go as you please. Wherever there were ten children of school age, and settlers bestirred themselves to organize, a school district could be set up. The Education Branch gave it a number, a corporate status, and its blessing. The rest was up to the people. Buildings were secured in any possible way and no particular plan or size was demanded. Some districts borrowed a few hundred dollars and built by volunteer labour, others took out logs and built without a loan. Sod construction was used where logs and lumber could not be obtained. Abandoned farm shacks, a spare room of a larger house, or an unused granary was pressed into use. Teachers were secured from any possible source and paid about $30 a month. If a country school managed to stay open six full months a year, it was a triumph of local enterprise. The government grant was 75¢ a teaching day.[57]

The Manitoba government, pressured by high-ranking Presbyterians concerned with making Galicians into "good Canadians," was finally compelled to act in 1903. But the appointment of school organizers who were poorly qualified as both teachers and administrators resulted in the organization of "practically nothing but the foreign vote."[58]

Ukrainian churches remained virtually powerless to change the situation until after 1905, when Manitoba, Saskatchewan, and Alberta tackled the problem seriously by appointing more school organizers and establishing training schools for Ukrainian teachers. But almost a whole generation of Ukrainians growing up in Canada would remain illiterate.

The Beginnings of Social Organization

To 1905, organized cultural meetings depended solely on the ability of active religious and secular leaders to encourage participation. Reverend Tymkevych, for example, acquired 80 books from Lviv in 1898 for a Prosvita Society in Edna.[59] Genik spearheaded a Taras Shevchenko Prosvita in Winnipeg which was organized in 1900. Meetings were held in Genik's home at 109 Euclid Avenue.[60] But with the church preserving and protecting cultural and traditional elements, and the Ukrainian immigrants living in the peasant manner with which they were well acquainted, such volunteer cultural and educational institutions were not viewed as essential preservers of the Ukrainian character. They were merely social gatherings of individuals committed to whatever progressive or educational motives may have brought them together. Such groups were admirable, but they were seen as something of a luxury at the time.

Economic cooperatives and organizations were also slow in developing. Although prodded by those of the radical persuasion, most Ukrainians still felt comfortable dealing with old world merchants — even if they were the Jews, a group that the Ukrainians had historically regarded as their adversary.[61] It seemed an ingrained habit. Indeed, one enterprising Ukrainian complained to *Svoboda* that he could not get a store going because the people preferred to go to a Jewish merchant. Non-Ukrainian store owners would quickly provide service when no alternative existed. Some even learned to speak Ukrainian. Genik attempted to get government backing for a Ukrainian cooperative, but the proposal was rejected.[62] The short-lived Ukrainian "Austro-Hungarian Company" was organized in Winnipeg in 1903, but it folded after an argument so serious that its manager shot a director.[63]

The Ukrainians' involvement in Canadian politics was limited. Heated opinions were voiced, however, as to which parties ought to be supported. Some favoured the Conservatives, who they believed "would block entry to the completely impoverished" immigrants.[64] But Dmytriw, Genik, Negrych, and Bodrug, all one-time employees of the federal Liberal administration, were quick to answer. Calling the Conservatives "self-serving aristocrats who would do nothing for the immigration," Genik maintained that the Liberals should get the credit: "the immigration is proof of their merit and democratic tendencies."[65] Genik, Negrych, and Bodrug published the *Kanadiiskyi Farmer* through the North-West Publishing Company, with funds supplied by the Liberal party, the *Manitoba Free Press,* and the Presbyterian Church. With Negrych as editor, the first four-page issue was released on 3 November 1903. Ukrainians reacted favourably and the paper would grow to exert a great influence in the development of social and cultural institutions.

PART III

STEADYING THE FOUNDATION, 1905–1914

CHAPTER 10

CANADIAN IMMIGRATION POLICY AFTER 1905

The year 1905 marks a watershed in Ukrainian-Canadian history. Prior to 1905, Ukrainians headed for their allotted homesteads, their role in the labour market being only an extension of agricultural settlement — a source of temporary employment in order that they might procure capital to improve their financial position on the farms. Between 1905 and 1914, however, the pace of Canada's "golden era" quickened dramatically. Canadian entrepreneurs suddenly cried out desperately for cheap, unskilled labourers. A response was readily forthcoming from the Department of the Interior, a response which ensured that Ukrainian immigration after 1905 would be significantly different in character than earlier immigration.

Although theoretically the official immigration policy adhered to the Siftonian principle of accepting agricultural settlers above all others, the economic boom dictated that a large proportion of the Ukrainians streaming into Canada would be general labourers. Indeed, this period saw the creation of a Ukrainian-Canadian proletariat — a proletariat that became evident not only on the prairies and in British Columbia, but in the mining and urban regions of Ontario, Quebec, and Nova Scotia.

Presiding over the Department of the Interior for most of this period was Frank Oliver. Until his appointment, he had argued tirelessly against the importation of Galicians, Bukovynians, and others from central and eastern Europe. Ironically, during his tenure in charge of immigration, more Ukrainians entered Canada than when Sifton was Minister of the Interior.

Immigration and Canadian Industrialization

As the first five years of the twentieth century rolled by, it seemed that Laurier's remark about the twentieth century belonging to Canada was more than just political rhetoric. It was demonstrated by the freshly broken soil of the prairies, by the feverish activity to exploit new-found mineral resources and, most of all, in the mad rush to build more transcontinental railway lines. By 1901, the C.P.R. was having difficulty hauling out the bumper crops of prairie wheat. Optimistic entrepreneurs argued that more railways were needed, especially if western settlement was to expand beyond the confines of the C.P.R.'s main line. Two railroad companies were eager to oblige. In 1902, the Grand Trunk offered to build a second transcontinental line from North Bay, Ontario to the Pacific — if the government would guarantee a subsidy for construction costs. A year later an agreement was reached between the Grand Trunk and the Laurier administration. The primary contracts were awarded in 1906 and 1907 in the form of a number of large (75 to 245 mile) sections to a series of contractors.[1] At the same time, William Mackenzie and Donald Mann of the Canadian Northern announced their intention to expand operations to include still another transcontinental. Another heyday of Canadian railway building had begun.

The significance of this — its magnitude unparalleled in Canada — cannot be underestimated: between 1904 and 1914, railway construction added approximately $775 million to the economy in wages, and another $825 million was spent for materials and equipment.[2] Most of the money came from British capital investment; of the $5.5 billion that Great Britain invested abroad between 1907 and 1913, more than one quarter came to Canada.[3]

Canada also began a new era of timber, pulpwood, and mineral exploitation, especially with the development of northern mining frontiers. Ontario led the way. Nickel and copper had been discovered in the early 1880s in Sudbury, but it was not until after 1900 that full-scale mining began. With the discoveries of silver in Cobalt in 1903 and gold in the Porcupine District in 1909, Ontario surpassed British Columbia as the leading mining province, "producing in 1913 over $59,000,000 of minerals, 41 per cent of the Dominion's total."[4] Ontario's mining industry accelerated the growth of other kinds of activity through its demands for transportation, hydro-electric power, the products of farm and forest, and urban amenities for its instant communities.[5] It ensured the development of Ontario's northern frontier into a largely industrial, urban-centred area. By 1911, the six northern districts of Ontario, which had been virtually unsettled in the latter half of the nineteenth century, had acquired a total population of 218,777.[6]

Across the rest of the country, established regions turned to industrialism at a rate that out-distanced development in the primary industries. While between 1903 and 1913 agricultural capital went up 140 per cent and mining capital by 100 per cent, manufacturing capital rose by 150 per cent.[7] Measured by productivity, agriculture increased 40 per cent and mine production 65 per cent, but there was a doubling of manufacturing output, a trebling of transportation activities, and general merchandising and banking shot up 200 per cent.[8]

This unprecedented boom in the Canadian economy had major implications for Canada's immigration policy. Canadian industrialists wanted a large continuous stream of immigrants who would work long hard hours for low pay. Labour was expensive; in the mining industry, for example, it accounted for an estimated 40 to 50 per cent of total expenditures. To minimize such costs in a raw capitalistic market, a proletariat had to be created — a large proletariat, in view of the rapid turnover of unskilled labour, which was docile and difficult to unionize.[10]

The nation's captains of industry set about achieving their goal in a determined fashion, through employment offices and steamship agents engaged in the business of recruiting immigrants, and through political pressure exerted on both the Laurier and Borden administrations for an open-door immigration policy. The percentage of unskilled labourers entering the country increased from 31 in 1907 to 43 in 1914; in contrast, the percentage of agriculturalists decreased from 38 in 1907 to 28 in 1914.[11] Included in this swelling proletariat were eastern European immigrants who were encouraged to remain in the labour-intensive industries of eastern Canada rather than proceed to rural settlements in the west.

Frank Oliver's Immigration Policy

After 1905, Ukrainians and eastern Europeans in general became the most eligible candidates for the labour market in Canada. The preference for these immigrants was a compromise between the industrialists, who considered Asiatics and southern Europeans (notably the Italians) as the ideal navvies, miners, and general labourers, and the Department of the Interior, which had grave reservations about the "quality" and "cultural acceptability" of Asiatics and southern Europeans. The man who found himself in the unenviable position of directing this compromise was Frank Oliver, Minister of the Interior from 1905 to 1911.

Oliver, by the time he replaced Clifford Sifton, had a richly partisan career behind him. Born to parents of Irish and English descent on 9 September 1853, near Brampton, Ontario, he began his career with the

Toronto Globe, coming under the influence of George Brown and the Clear Grits (progenitors of the Liberals). In the 1870s he moved west to Winnipeg, where he found employment on the *Manitoba Free Press*. Investing his savings in a small freighting outfit, he joined an ox-cart brigade bound for Fort Edmonton. Edmonton became his home and in 1880 he founded the *Edmonton Bulletin*. He was a self-righteous individual who never really shed the moral earnestness which characterized dour Ontario Grits,[12] yet he became a true westerner, a staunch defender of the North-West's right to challenge policies from Ottawa and an advocate of the agricultural and industrial potential of the prairies.[13] Elected to the House of Commons in 1896 after a turbulent career in the North-West Territorial Assembly, he became a tenacious critic of Sifton's policy of "indiscriminate immigration." The Galicians and Bukovynians became favourite targets. At every opportunity, he thundered against these "undesirable" peasants who would be a "drag on our civilization and progress."[14]

Throughout his term as Minister of the Interior, Oliver pursued a more restrictive immigration policy in accordance with his own prejudices, but not without due regard for the demands of the powerful industrialists. The Laurier government, after all, was inescapably bound to the railway companies in particular, having committed itself to railway construction. An unpublicized recruitment program was initiated and at least tacitly supported by Oliver, who accepted the view that the prosperity of Canada depended upon the influx of thousands of labourers. In 1907 he stated, rather hesitantly:

> It is true that in Canada to-day there never was such a demand for unskilled labour as there is at the present moment. As a matter of fact the great railroad projects which are in hand for the development of Canada are largely handicapped if not at an actual standstill because of a lack of necessary unskilled labour. It seemed to us therefore that although we are getting immigrants to settle our land . . . there was also room for immigrants . . . for employment of thousands and thousands of unskilled labourers.[15]

Although he had denounced Sifton's policy of paying booking agents for recruiting immigrants, this policy not only remained intact but was extended. "We should," he declared, "take means to utilize the services of booking agents in any country in continental Europe from which we might think it desirable . . . to secure suitable immigrants to meet the present urgent requirements of this country."[16] Accordingly, in 1907 an order-in-council was passed which permitted the direct payment of bonuses (10 shillings per head for adults and 5 shillings per head for children) to booking agents. These extended payments covered not only farmers, farm labourers, and female domestic servants, but also "gardeners, stablemen, casters, railway surfacemen, navvies or miners who had signified their intention of following such occupations."[17] The wording was deceptive, but the intention was plain.

Oliver, however, still had his qualms about the compromise. Clearly, the most culturally acceptable immigrants came from the United Kingdom, but they did not fit the industrialists' ideal of malleable labourers. They were not prepared to tolerate the low wages or the sordid working conditions of railway construction, for example. Moreover, they were familiar with unions, which could prove very troublesome. Thomas Shaughnessy, president of the C.P.R., reflected the attitude of many businessmen:

> Men who seek employment on railway construction are, as a rule, a class accustomed to roughing it. They know when they go to work that they must put up with the most primitive kind of camp accommodation. . . . I feel very strongly that it would be a huge mistake to send out any more of these men from Wales, Scotland or England. . . . It is only prejudicial to the course of immigration to import men who come here expecting to get high wages, a feather bed and a bath tub.[18]

Asiatics, on the other hand, were ideal labourers; they were "living machines." But from the point of view of both Canadian workers and Canadian nationalists, Asiatics in large doses were culturally unacceptable.[19] Oliver, certainly no less public spirited, summarized his opposition to wholesale importation:

> Possibly a Chinaman is a better man than an Englishman . . . a Japanese may be a better man . . . than the Englishman; I say nothing about that, he may be a much better man, but he is not one of us, and in as much as he is not one of us he is not helping us to develop along those lines that Providence has chosen for us or that we have chosen for ourselves. His presence is a hindrance and not a help.[20]

Anti-Asiatic feelings were particularly strong in British Columbia because of the large numbers of Asians there, and resulted in riots and the formation of the Asiatic Exclusion League in Vancouver in 1907. For political as well as cultural reasons, the Laurier government moved to restrict Asiatic immigration severely. In the case of Japan, a gentleman's agreement was reached in 1907, whereby Japan undertook to restrict emigration to Canada. In 1908, Oliver enacted restrictive legislation against various immigrant groups with two orders-in-council: "the first excluded immigrants from coming to Canada other than by continuous journey from their country of birth, or citizenship; the second stipulated that immigrants from India had to have $200 in their possession upon landing in Canada."[21]

Canadian industrialists, while still agitating for an open-door policy, had no choice but to turn increasingly toward central and southern Europe for their "coolie" labour.[22] Yet southern Europeans, especially Italians, were also considered of "inferior stock," prone to crime and immorality.[23] One parliamentarian summarized the prevalent attitude:

I know for a fact that over 60 per cent of the Italians that come to this country are convicted criminals. When a man gets into trouble in Italy and is convicted, he generally leaves the country after having served his sentence, as he finds that he is not wanted at home. For years Canada has been the dumping ground of these criminals. It used to be the United States, but owing to the enforcement of stricter laws, the United States [is] not so popular . . . as [it] used to be. Canada is now their goal because it is so easy of access. . . . Their own country has grown too warm for them and Canada offers ample shelter. . . .[24]

Oliver moved to adopt a tough line against the indiscriminate entry of Italians, and he did have a rational justification: the department was still interested in agricultural immigrants who could be temporarily utilized in railway work and other labour-intensive industries, but then directed back to farming. Southern Europeans tended to join the permanent urban proletariat.

Oliver attempted to balance the short-term demands of industrialists with the long-term objectives of the Department of the Interior. Railway and mining companies were able to circumvent many of the obstacles set up by the department and backed by public opinion, but they still suffered from a shortage of cheap labour. They too had to settle for East Europeans. These immigrants had one drawback as far as industrialists were concerned. Prior to 1905, before the full economic boom was evident, these immigrants had proved to be part-time labourers, available during late spring and summer but quitting in August to go back to the homesteads to harvest their crops.[25] Moreover, once they had accumulated enough capital, they had quickly established themselves full-time on the land, causing a disturbance of the labour market.[26] Conversely, these labourers suited the purposes of the Department of the Interior just because they were temporary.

Of the continental Europeans, the Ukrainians were the most acceptable both to the industrialists and the Immigration Branch. They were poor and degraded enough to work for wages and in conditions that other nationalities would rebel against; they were successful enough as agriculturalists to indicate their worth to the Department of the Interior; and they were already streaming into Canada. Between 1891 and 1905, an estimated 63,425 Ukrainians had entered Canada.[27] During Oliver's term as Minister of the Interior, the gates were opened to 58,676 more.[28]

The unexpected defeat of the Laurier government by the Borden Conservatives in the election of 1911 produced no significant alterations to Canada's immigration policy. Both Robert Rogers (Minister of the Interior from October 1911 to October 1912) and his successor, William James Roche, (October 1912 to October 1917), admitted that, in the main, they had not changed the Liberals' policy.[29] Although the Conservatives had been vigorously critical of both the expensive recruitment and the admission of "culturally inferior" immigrants, they too had to consider Canada's dependence on immigrant labour. Indeed, immigration expenditures increased to an all-time high of an estimated $1,450,000 in 1914,[30] and the number of immigrants from continental Europe continued to rise. The Ukrainians were no exception: between 1912 and 1914, 49,437 entered Canada.[31] By 1914, the total count was 171,538.[32] Ultimately, it was not government policy — either Liberal or Conservative — that brought Ukrainian immigration to a sudden halt in Canada, but the advent of World War I.

The Shifting Frontier

Between 1905 and 1914, wherever labour-intensive industries flourished, Ukrainians could be found. They worked almost exclusively at the lowest levels — as railway navvies, underground miners, miner's helpers, ditch diggers, road builders, and general labourers in mills, foundries, and meat-packing houses. The percentage of Ukrainian immigrants entering the industrial labour market rose steadily. In 1901-02, 25.5 per cent entered occupations other than farming; in 1902-03, the percentage increased to 36.7, and in 1903-04, to 40 per cent.[33] As Table 10-1 illustrates, there was a significant increase of general labourers over farmers and farm labourers. Out of a total of 78,899 Ukrainian males who arrived at Canadian ports between 1905 and 1914, 44,029 stated their occupation as general labourer; 32,834 were listed as farmers and farm labourers. By 1914, 53.9 per cent were general labourers.

There was also a significant shift of destinations from the prairie provinces to eastern Canada. Almost all Ukrainian immigrants entering Canadian ports before 1905 named the North-West as their destination;

Table 10-1[34]

Ukrainian Occupations Stated at Port Arrivals, 1905-1914 (Males)

Year	Males[1]	Farmers or farm labourers	General labourers	General labourers as % of male immigration	Misc. occupation and not classified	Total arrivals incl. females, children[1]	Males as % of total immigration
1905[2]	5,436	3,024	2,149	39.53	263	8,052	67.51
1906[3]	4,762	2,011	2,516	52.83	235	7,277	65.44
1907[4]	1,442	240	1,105	76.63	97	2,184	67.13
1908[5]	12,224	3,821	7,944	64.99	459	17,325	70.56
1909[5]	6,137	2,217	3,667	59.75	253	8,339	73.59
1910[5]	2,810	1,724	878	31.25	208	4,661	60.29
1911[5]	5,065	2,379	2,566	50.66	120	7,122	71.12
1912[5]	11,526	6,718	4,753	41.23	55	15,268	75.49
1913[5]	13,340	6,387	6,794	50.93	159	18,604	71.71
1914[5]	16,157	4,313	11,657	72.14	187	21,619	74.74
Total	78,899	32,834	44,029	53.90	2,036	110,451	

Notes:

[1] includes only those who stated their nationality either as Bukovynian, Galician, or Ruthenian.

[2] arrivals for Canada at Ocean Ports for the Fiscal Year ending 30 June 1905.

[3] arrivals for Canada at Ocean Ports for the Fiscal Year ending 30 June 1906.

[4] arrivals for Canada at Ocean Ports for the fractional Fiscal Year 1906-07 (nine months ending 31 March 1907).

[5] arrivals for Canada at Ocean Ports for the respective Fiscal Years ending March 31.

Table 10-2[35]
Destination Stated at Ports

Year	Total male, female, and children	Maritime provinces	Quebec	Ontario	Manitoba	Saskatchewan	Alberta	B.C.	Yukon	Man., Sask., and Alta. as % of total
1905	8,052	61	986	388	5,513	10	88	16	—	69.68
1906	7,277	235	1,200	608	3,973	873	355	33	—	71.47
1907	2,184	65	395	339	1,099	148	113	25	—	62.27
1908	17,325	378	3,748	2,128	8,526	1,333	1,087	125	—	63.18
1909	8,339	272	1,400	1,167	3,959	855	608	78	—	65.02
1910	4,661	104	944	887	1,556	595	475	100	—	56.34
1911	7,122	239	1,784	1,404	2,217	753	708	127	—	51.64
1912	15,268	265	4,212	3,081	4,845	1,572	1,099	194	—	49.23
1913	18,604	309	5,349	4,102	5,855	1,655	1,246	178	—	47.07
1914	21,619	267	6,919	5,108	5,914	1,545	1,610	256	—	41.95
Total	110,451	2,085	26,937	19,122	43,457	9,329	7,301	1,132	—	—

however, as Table 10-2 indicates, between 1905 and 1914 only 57.7 per cent intended to proceed to the prairies. Out of a total of 110,451 arrivals, 48,144 stated eastern provinces as their destination. Obviously, eastern Canada (especially Quebec and Ontario) became the new mecca for Ukrainians in search of work.

The disproportionate number of men to women and children was another strong indication of the emerging Ukrainian-Canadian proletariat. Tables 10-1 and 10-2 show that 74.4 per cent of the total Ukrainian immigrants arriving at Canadian ports were males — 78,899 compared to 17,462. The full implication of this imbalance can only be appreciated when geographical placement is considered. Census figures of 1911 indicate that the prairie provinces claimed the following percentages of the population of Ukrainian men: Manitoba, 54.8; Alberta, 57.5; and Saskatchewan, 55.9.[36] In contrast, the percentages in British Columbia, Ontario, Quebec, and Nova Scotia were 89.5, 82.5, 76.6, and 95.5, respectively.[37] In the prairie provinces, women were crucial to the success of the farm, doing a great share of the work and, when the men were away on seasonal jobs, doing it all. In British Columbia, Ontario, Quebec, and Nova Scotia, however, the traditional agricultural role of the women was eliminated; the men were labourers, often transient, and women could only be an encumbrance. Consequently, most of the Ukrainians who came to Canada as general labourers were either single or had left their families in the old country until they could earn enough money to send for them.

Among the Ukrainian women arriving in Canada between 1905 and 1914, there was a notable shift from those claiming to be farmers and farm labourers to those stating their occupations as general labourers and domestics. As Table 10-3 illustrates, only 38.8 per cent stated their occupations as farmers and farm labourers, while 20.9 per cent stated that they were general labourers and 32.8 per cent indicated that they were female domestics. A great many, it appears, decided to enter the labour force in their own right.

Railway construction and mining were the most visible occupations which employed Ukrainians. Approximately every second Ukrainian in Canada was at one time or another employed directly or indirectly by a railroad company. It has been estimated that 10,000 Ukrainians were engaged in constructing railroads during 1906 and 1907.[39]

In the mining industry, the Ukrainian work force was no less pronounced. Of the 62,767 miners in Canada in 1911, more than half were immigrants.[40] There are no exact figures specifically for Ukrainians in mining, but it has been estimated that by 1911, 10 to 20 per cent of the labour force in the Crowsnest Pass coal-mining region and the mining regions of northern Ontario was Slavic.[41] Even those regions that tradi-

Table 10-3[38]
Occupations Stated at Ocean Ports 1905-1914 (Females)

Year	Females	Farmers or farm labourers	As % of total female immigration	General labourers	As % of total female immigration	Female servants	As % of total female immigration	Misc. occupation and not classified
1905	1,195	724	60.59	129	10.79	248	20.75	94
1906	1,214	529	43.57	262	21.58	362	29.82	61
1907	380	83	21.84	122	32.10	122	32.10	53
1908	2,563	783	30.55	630	24.58	1,001	39.06	149
1909	1,102	423	38.38	181	16.42	391	35.48	107
1910	933	531	56.91	121	12.97	211	22.61	70
1911	1,157	452	39.06	199	17.20	420	36.30	86
1912	2,248	1,008	44.84	299	13.30	872	38.79	69
1913	3,218	1,056	32.82	753	23.40	1,233	38.31	176
1914	3,452	702	20.33	1,290	37.36	1,229	35.60	231
Total	17,462	6,291	43.21	3,986	20.47	6,089	32.88	1,096

tionally had a higher percentage of British-born miners — the coal-mining districts of Vancouver Island, Sydney, and Glace Bay in Nova Scotia — received a substantial increase of Slavic miners, among them Ukrainians. In Sydney, for example, Ukrainian labourers from Besarabia and Podilia arrived in 1904; they were followed by others from Bukovyna and other parts of western Ukraine in 1907.[42] Between 1906 and 1914, 2,500 Slavic miners were imported to Canada;[43] 591 Ukrainian men coming to Canada in this period listed their occupation as miner.[44]

Ukrainians also gravitated to the expanding urban centres. In the west, Winnipeg consolidated its position as a focal point for Ukrainians, who continued to arrive in the North End while the city grew to become Canada's fourth largest industrial and manufacturing centre by 1914. In the east by World War I, there were about 40,000 Ukrainians in Ontario, Quebec, and the Maritimes, most of whom worked in cities. According to one estimate, "Toronto led with 9,000, Windsor next with 8,000 followed by Sudbury's 6,000, Montreal had 5,000, Hamilton 3,000, Sault Ste. Marie 2,000, Ottawa 1,000, Oshawa 500 and such places as St. Catharines, Thorold, Welland, Niagara Falls, Guelph and others having 200 to 300 each."[45]

These are, of course, only approximate figures, but their value lies in delineating general trends. Statistics for this period are not necessarily precise. For example, census figures indicate that between 1901 and 1911, 195,690 Slavs entered Canada, yet the total population increase of Slavs was only 166,843.[46] Obviously, many went to the United States or back to the old country.

The Stirrings of Revolt

The creation of a permanent industrial proletariat during this period was a new dimension of the Ukrainian experience in Canada. Ukrainians as temporary labourers had shunned unions, strikes, and any other actions which might threaten their "grubstake." After 1905, many suddenly found themselves locked into the labour market. They also found that they were being mercilessly exploited in an impersonal economic system where the maximization of profits at all costs was the objective.

This was particularly true of mining and railway construction. Not only were the wages poor and the working conditions deplorable, but there was a remarkably high injury and death rate. Those working on railway construction, for example, found that if poor food, disease from unsanitary housing, or just plain exhaustion did not seriously affect their health, then the lack of any safety precautions on the construction sites did. According to statistics for all railway workers, the number of people killed on Canadian railway construction sites between 1901 and 1918 was 3,667; in addition, 42,274 people were injured.[47]

Employment in mines was even more hazardous as mining, unlike railway construction, was a year-round operation. Mine managers were often not concerned with the safety of their men; the replacement of dead or injured men was cheaper than instituting safety programs. This callous approach resulted in a horrendous working environment which invited fatigue, disease, and mining disasters. E.T. Corkill, Ontario Inspector of Mines, reported that "32.6 per cent of the accidents which have resulted in fatalities in 1908 in Ontario were caused by neglect, carelessness or incompetence of mine managers. . . ."[48] Indeed, throughout the period, the reports of Ontario, Alberta, and British Columbia mining inspectors were generally critical of high accident rates, especially among immigrant workers.[49] Immigrant miners were particularly vulnerable because they often lacked experience, had difficulty communicating with fellow workers, and were given the most dangerous tasks.

The growing sense of hopelessness in the Ukrainian-Canadian proletariat between 1905 and 1914 found expression in increased participation in trade union activity and the creation of socialist organizations. Led by old world socialists who after 1905 came to Canada in ever-increasing numbers, a working-class consciousness developed among Ukrainians — a consciousness more in tune with the need for a collective proletarian struggle against the injustices of capitalism than the development of a Ukrainian national identity. This period prompted the beginnings of a Ukrainian-Canadian radical tradition — a tradition which ran counter to the nationalistic stirrings in the community. The full import of Ukrainian-Canadian radicalism would not become evident until World War I, when the Ukrainian workers would be regarded as "enemy aliens." But the die had been cast in this preceding decade.

CHAPTER 11

LABOUR AND THE SOCIALIST PERSPECTIVE

In the decade before the Great War, Ukrainian–Canadian workers found themselves at the bottom of the Canadian industrial system. Grossly exploited, alienated from the mainstream of Canadian society, Ukrainian labourers lived in crowded, unsanitary urban ghettos and in isolated railway camps and mining towns. They were shunned by many established unions, who saw them as a threat, and manipulated by employers, who sought to break unions. Most had little choice but to accept their circumstances and map out a strategy for survival. Life in the new country seemed as harsh as in the old.

Yet during this period there were many exceptions. The Ukrainian workers fought back, in some cases on their own, and in other cases as a major contingent within the nation's group of foreign-born workers. In the railway construction camps and in the coal mining regions of western Canada, Ukrainians supported unions, often militant ones, such as the Industrial Workers of the World (I.W.W.) and the United Mine Workers of America (U.M.W.A.). As rank and file members, they participated in some of the most bitter and violent strikes in pre-war Canada.

Beyond the unions, a minority supported the sprouting socialist movements. Some operated within the confines of Anglo-Canadian socialism and others turned to the "Ukrainian"[1] socialist movement which was organized in Canada after 1907. The appeals for international class solidarity against social oppression and economic exploitation found fertile ground in the Dominion. But the utopian ideals of the early Ukrainian socialists, although fragmented in the new world, ensured the limitation of Ukrainian support for international solidarity.

Immigrant Labour and the Union Hierarchy

Canada was a nation of contrasts. Unprecedented economic development was accompanied by industrial mergers which put enormous concentrations of wealth and power in the hands of a few. At the same time, many lived in poverty, struggling to survive in a period where prices were generally rising faster than wages. The industrialists had at their disposal not only tremendous financial resources, but the power of the state. The Canadian government, anxious to encourage the economic growth generated by resource exploitation, railway building, and capital investment, adopted a policy of granting land and monopolies to large companies. It supplemented this policy by protecting the companies through the courts, the military, and police forces when conflicts erupted between employer and employee.[2]

Protection and security within an impersonal industrial system were important goals for Canadian labourers. The most obvious way to achieve these goals was unionization. Two labour organizations predominated: the international unions, associated with the American Federation of Labour (A.F.L.), and the Trades and Labour Congress of Canada (T.L.C.), which aimed to be the labour centre for Canadian unions. Both the A.F.L. and the T.L.C., however, limited their activity to organizing skilled craftsmen — the aristocracy of Canadian labour. Consequently, the vast majority of unskilled general labourers (which, of course, included most of the recently arrived immigrants) was left out of the mainstream of organized labour. Ironically, unskilled labourers were the ones most in need of protection.

The craft-union orientation of the A.F.L. and the T.L.C. (which, after 1902, became a satellite of the A.F.L.) produced a xenophobia toward these general workers, especially the foreign-born. The flood of new immigrants was seen as a threat to the attainment of higher wages and better working conditions. The T.L.C., for example, campaigned continuously against the open-door immigration policy, criticizing Ottawa which was "spending the people's money by granting assisted passage to immigrants who became a source of cheap labour for employers after they arrive."[3] As one journalist of the period wrote of the Ukrainians in Winnipeg:

> The Galicians are the cause of much concern where they are located in Winnipeg. . . . Practically all of them are labourers and they don't get to the front rank rapidly. On account of their ability to live

cheaply, they militate against the wages of natives. The more of them there are to reduce the prices of labour the greater becomes the tendency to Anglo-Saxon suicide.[4]

The immigrant not only accepted lower wages, but he was frequently employed as a "scab" to replace those who were on strike.

The hostility toward the immigrant worker filtered through to the rank and file union members. Among most Anglo-Canadian and British workers there was a prejudice against the "bohunks" and "wops" which reflected the prevalent notions of Anglo-Celtic superiority — a superiority which could only be undermined by the importation of these cheap labourers. The Ukrainians, Italians, and others who arrived in great numbers were seen as competitors with foreign ideas who would undermine organized labour. In fact, it was believed that they could not be organized; not only were they evidently prepared to work in disgusting conditions and subsist on low wages (which in many cases were still an improvement over their old world experience), but their cultural and language differences were an insurmountable barrier to union solidarity. Thus, few genuine attempts were made by the established unions to include in their ranks the ethnic proletariat.

Employers, for their part, thrived on this state of affairs. They resisted all forms of labour organization with evangelistic fervour. They used the foreign-born as a powerful weapon against unions. According to one mine manager who preferred a high percentage of Europeans among his employees:

> In all the lower grades of labour . . . it is necessary to have a mixture of races which includes a number of illiterates who are first class workmen. They are the strength of an employer and the weakness of the union. How to head off a strike of muckers or labourers for higher wages without the aid of Italian labour I do not know.[5]

This reasoning was common; employers believed that European immigrant workers could be easily manipulated.

Such reasoning, however, proved to be erroneous. Between 1905 and 1914 there was unparalleled labour unrest and employer-employee confrontations involving mob violence, property damage, personal injury, and death. The immigrant worker quickly "wised up to the rotten system of robbery and peonage practised on his kind,"[6] demonstrating a capacity for spontaneous rebellion and revolutionary action. Employed in large numbers in the most volatile industries, the Ukrainians played a prominent role in the labour disputes which plagued Canada during the decade before the war.

The Struggle for Union Recognition

Many Ukrainian-Canadians had already experienced the process of industrialization in the old world. When displaced from farms, they sought employment in urban centres; there they swelled the ranks of the labour supply, coming into contact with employers, working conditions, and living standards that were all equally harsh. They also became familiar with trade unions, socialist organizations, and collective self-help through benevolent societies. Those who still clung to their land often supplemented their incomes through seasonal employment, becoming part-time industrial workers in neighbouring countries — in the coal-mining and steel-producing areas of Germany, for example.

Yet by and large they retained their conservative, peasant outlook. Their expectations were low, revolving around work and survival. Indeed, they were preoccupied with survival; it was the operative factor which enticed them to Canada. They were willing to work long hours and endure much discomfort if it allowed them security and a viable future for their offspring. They settled for the concept of "limited good," but if their modest stipulations were not met, they reacted in a variety of mutinous ways.

The most direct method of collective protest used by Ukrainians was the spontaneous strike. This was usually generated by a specific grievance or incident. The labourers would simply lay down their tools and set up crude picket lines. Such action was not uncommon among Ukrainians in the Austro-Hungarian Empire. In 1902, for example, agrarian labourers from nearly 400 village communities in 20 east Galician districts had staged a massive strike. In Canada, one such work stoppage occurred in the Winnipeg C.P.R. yard on 1 August 1905. Approximately 200 Ukrainian workers demanded higher wages of $1.50 to $1.75 per day. In this case, their demands were granted.[7] Another spur of the moment rebellion occurred on 12 May 1912 when Ukrainian labourers digging sewers in north-end Winnipeg discovered that workers in other parts of the city, performing the same job, were receiving higher wages.[8] Again, withdrawing their services was effective. Such examples of collective action were widespread, although usually they did not force the desired outcome.

Most often, spontaneous strikes were made in conjunction with other ethnic groups. A case in point was the violent rebellion of freight handlers in Fort William in 1909. Here the C.P.R.'s time-tested tactic of pitting ethnic groups against each other did not work. More than 700 Greeks, Italians, Ukrainians, and other nationalities struck for "wage increases above the prevailing rates of 17½ cents an hour for day work, and 20 cents for night work, as well as for discontinuation of the bonus system whereby the company withheld an additional one cent an hour until completion of the season's work."[9] The Ukrainians were not in the forefront of this strike, but they supported the initiatives of the Greeks and Italians. Working-class solidarity was achieved. Indeed, shortly after the strike's commencement, an inter-ethnic committee was directing it, despite the fact that "the men still had no union."[10] The Greeks and to a lesser extent the Italians were blamed for intimidating the other nationalities into joining them.[11] But the unity demonstrated throughout the strike did not indicate domination by one ethnic group.

During this particular strike, unfortunately, the C.P.R. brought in 30 specially armed constables, followed by 100 strikebreakers. There was a half-hour gun battle before local officials intervened and the militia arrived, establishing an uneasy truce. A number of men on both sides had been injured. Ultimately a Board of Inquiry was successful in settling the dispute. The workers were granted a wage increase of 3 cents an hour and the bonus system was abolished.[12] Both the C.P.R. and the C.N.R., however, continued to earn the wrath of their employees and the Lakehead was the scene of more work stoppages involving the foreign-born in 1912 and 1913.

The largest and often most bitter disputes in Canada between 1905 and 1914 took place in the railway and coal-mining industries. Both industries had their share of spontaneous revolts, but they were also the target of organized strikes. The Industrial Workers of the World (I.W.W.), founded in Chicago in 1905, was instrumental in making these strikes possible. An American-based Marxist union, the I.W.W. sought to link the bread and butter struggles of labourers with a class-conscious, revolutionary aim.[13] By 1908, I.W.W. organizers had crossed the 49th parallel and moved into the mining regions of the Kootenay. Between 1908 and 1914, they organized the same constituency in western Canada as they had in the United States: the unskilled itinerant labourers, loggers, harvesters, and longshoremen.[14] Their greatest coup, however, was gaining the support of immigrant workers employed by the Canadian Northern and the Grand Trunk Pacific railways.

The I.W.W. attracted the foreign-born for a number of reasons. First, it was especially attuned to them, pointing out their self-worth and circulating propaganda in many different languages. I.W.W. organizers realized that the western Canadian proletariat was composed largely of Ukrainians, Italians, Poles, Greeks, and Swedes, and that the support of these nationalities was the key to success. Second, it advocated direct action — a philosophy that the foreign-born could readily understand. Appealing to the workers' deep sense of grievance, they preached general shutdowns and even sabotage. They emphasized that the state offered no protection; indeed, it was their enemy. This, too, was readily comprehended. The immigrants' distrust of the state in the old world was reinforced in Canada, where the federal and provincial governments frequently quelled protests by employing police forces and the military on behalf of the employer. Finally, the I.W.W. welcomed the immigrants with open arms as equals, while at the same time heaping criticism on the A.F.L. and the T.L.C. which had shunned them.

The first major strike lead by the I.W.W. in the railway camps lasted from April to June of 1912 along the main line of the C.N.R. from Kamloops to Hope. Between 6,000 to 7,000 navvies, most of them foreigners, laid down their tools — some Ukrainian workers destroyed their tools[15] — and started picketing. Along the 3,000-mile strike line, I.W.W. organizers attempted to maintain discipline and keep up the workers' morale by providing food, giving lectures, and generally inculcating revolutionary fervour. But there were insufficient funds coming from the I.W.W. headquarters in Chicago and from other sympathizers. Meanwhile, the Canadian Northern appealed for support from both Ottawa and the provincial government of British Columbia. It promptly received a hearing. While Ottawa relaxed immigration regulations to allow for the importation of strikebreakers and rejected a conciliation board suggested by the I.W.W.,[16] the provincial government dispatched a special police force which harassed the union organizers and protected the incoming strikebreakers. By June, a great many I.W.W. organizers had been either jailed or deported, and the destitute, isolated men had no choice but to return to work.

A month after this strike ended, the undaunted I.W.W. attempted to lead another revolt which developed among 3,000 men employed on the Grand Trunk Pacific from Prince Rupert to Hazelton. This strike also ended in failure, and most of the strikers involved were fired. The following year, the I.W.W. led a number of other navvy rebellions ranging in size from 400 to 1,500 men, but these too proved unsuccessful.[17]

Finally, the I.W.W. attempted to organize the unemployed in the prairie provinces. By 1913, it appeared that Canada's golden age had suffered a setback. A pre-war depression set in, while the completion of railway construction projects threw thousands of unskilled labourers out of work. Many flowed into the urban centres — Winnipeg, Edmonton, and Vancouver — a faceless mass of teeming resentment. Edmonton in February of 1914, for example, had more than 4,000 unemployed men; 600 of these (80 per cent were described as either Ukrainian, Russian, or Polish) held a protest parade organized by the

I.W.W.[18] Protests of this sort to city officials, however, proved futile, and in this particular case 13 "foreigners" were arrested and the I.W.W. leaders were either deported or jailed.

By the beginning of the war, the I.W.W. was a spent force. Opposed by employers and suppressed by the state, the *coup de grâce* came when most of its supporters were dispersed by the end of the railway-building boom and the onset of the depression.[19]

Despite its failure, the I.W.W. left its legacy within the context of immigrant labour history and, more specifically, the history of the Ukrainian-Canadian proletariat. Other unions had ignored north-end Winnipeg, but the I.W.W. local had recruited almost 400 Ukrainians and Poles from the area.[20] While giving the immigrant worker a sense of worth, it also complemented his tradition of direct action. Finally, its activities exposed a myth: foreign-born workers did not shun unions. This was to be demonstrated again in the coal-mining regions.

In the isolated mining towns of British Columbia, Alberta, and northern Ontario, Ukrainians found themselves in highly polarized societies. The companies and their managers were one side, and they were the other side; there seemed to be no common ground. They occupied segregated ghettos on company-owned land, living in company-built shacks, and buying from company-controlled stores. Within the miners' world, Slavs and Italians in particular were at the bottom as the muckers and miners' helpers. In the "slavtowns" and "dagotowns," solidarity formed quickly. These workers had to depend on each other below the ground. Appalling living conditions and frequent periods of prolonged unemployment in times of market uncertainty dictated that they depend on each other above ground as well. It was a matter of survival. The miners' union would provide a measure of security. It would provide a social forum too; within its halls, miners could meet, drink, and discuss their problems. In some cases, it was also the only dispensary for medical services.[21]

The most successful miners' union that counted a high number of Ukrainians in its rank and file was the United Mine Workers of America (U.M.W.A.). It began its activities in the metal and coal mines of Alberta and British Columbia when its predecessor, the radical Western Federation of Miners, dissolved because of setbacks suffered at the hands of employers and the provincial and federal governments.[22] The U.M.W.A., which had success in organizing immigrant workers in the coal-mining districts of Pennsylvania,[23] appealed, like the I.W.W., directly to immigrant workers, distributing union literature in a number of languages (including Ukrainian) and appointing Slavic-speaking organizers.[24]

The U.M.W.A. expanded rapidly, establishing District 18 with jurisdiction over Alberta and British Columbia. During 1906 and 1907, it led determined strikers who won union recognition from various coal operators. For example, the Crowsnest Pass Coal Company experienced a strike of 1,600 workers employed at its Fernie and Michael operations from 22 September to 13 November 1906. The cause was the workers' refusal to work with non-union employees; they eventually won their point. Another strike occurred from 4 March to 2 December in the same year, involving some 500 miners employed by the Alberta Railway and Irrigation Company. The demands included union recognition, an eight-hour day, and wage increases. Some of the strikers' demands were met. Strikes over similar issues also developed in 1907, 1909, and 1911.[25] Ukrainians assumed a major role in all these strikes and were often among the most militant.

Ukrainians obviously knew the value of collective strength and used it to enhance their chances of survival within the Canadian industrial system. It should be emphasized, however, that despite this activity the majority of Ukrainian-Canadians between 1905 and 1914 would remain unorganized, dependent upon their individual strength and ingenuity. While many looked toward unions to ameliorate their condition, others were attracted by socialism and the socialist parties which were then being organized in Canada and within the Ukrainian community.

The Socialist Perspective on Canada

The nature of Ukrainian-Canadian socialism was predisposed by old world allegiances. Ukrainians in the Austro-Hungarian and Russian Empires found a confusing but rich selection of socialist organizations sprouting in their midst. There was the Ruthenian-Ukrainian Radical Party founded in 1890 by Mykhailo Drahomanov, Ivan Franko, and Mykhaylo Pawlyk. Aside from its anti-clericism and moralist brand of socialism concerned with elevating the dignity of the Ukrainian peasant, its major platform included universal suffrage for both men and women, free elementary and secondary education, and autonomy for Galicia. There were also the two groups that broke away from the Radical Party: the nationalist Ukrainian National Democratic Party and the Marxist Ukrainian Social Democratic Party. The Revolutionary Ukrainian Party came into existence in 1900, created mostly by university students who believed in revolutionary proletarian internationalism. In 1904, its extreme left wing formed the Ukrainian Social Democratic Union (Spilka) within the Russian Empire. Finally, Ukrainians participated in the Russian Social Democratic Workers' Party, established in 1898. In 1903, it split into two factions: the Mensheviks, who believed that the historical process of worker emancipation would inevitably come to pass, and the Bolsheviks, who argued that a highly centralized, disciplined party of professional revolutionaries was needed to bring change. These parties, at various points in their development, were not mutually exclusive, and Ukrainian radicals were often influenced by all of them at different times in their ideological growth.

In Canada, this bewildering disarray from the old world found two common issues. First, just as socialists denounced the regimes in the Austo-Hungarian and Russian Empires, so too they were critical of Canadian capitalism. They detested the leaders of the Ukrainian-Canadian community who not only accepted the tenets of Canadian capitalism but urged Ukrainians to adapt themselves to it. Second, they had no use for the "Ruthenian" Catholic Church which, in Galicia, perpetuated the status quo, and in Canada after 1912, attempted to establish hegemony over the Ukrainians.

Ukrainian-Canadian socialists saw Ottawa's immigration policy as little more than a means of creating a cheap labour supply for its railway building and development of natural resources. They believed that those Ukrainians who emigrated to the "promised land" were just as exploited by the Canadian capitalists as they had been by the ruling elite in the Austro-Hungarian and Russian Empires. As one Ukrainian-Canadian socialist newspaper expressed it:

> And don't you think . . . that the Canadian gentleman brought you here with humanitarian intentions in mind so that you could live well . . . ah no! They didn't call us out of sympathy, for underlying their actions are their own motives. By the work done by our calloused hands, they wanted to ensure their rule over us, not only for themselves, but for their children, grandchildren and great grandchildren.[26]

To the Ukrainian socialists, labourers in general and East European immigrants in particular were simply "free white slaves"[27] and "white niggers."[28] Consequently, the socialists attempted to integrate the Ukrainian worker into a broad working-class movement of all the Canadian proletariat while at the same time promoting a sense of "Ukrainian" national identity. The Ukrainians who accepted the Canadian system, however, were mostly school teachers and professional men. They followed a pragmatic policy of Ukrainian self-help through the establishment of cooperatives and credit unions, or they encouraged bilingual education and promoted Prosvita Halls as centres of community activity.[29]

The anti-clericalism of Ukrainian socialists represented another aspect of Ukrainian exploitation. In Galicia, the Greek Catholic Church was seen as a reactionary force supporting the policies of a despotic regime. In Canada, when the "Ruthenian" Catholic Church was granted recognition and attempted to direct the spiritual and secular affairs of Ukrainians, the socialists reacted with violent denunciation. Indeed, the socialists were the first to use the term "Ukrainian" to represent their nationality because Greek Catholics referred to themselves as "Ruthenians."

Ukrainian-Canadian Socialist Parties

The Taras Shevchenko Reading Hall, originally organized by Kyrylo Genik in north-end Winnipeg, was the home of the Ukrainian socialist movement. The movement was very much disorganized until 1907, when Myroslav Stechishin and Pavlo Krat gave it dynamic, if somewhat erratic, leadership.

In 1906, Stechishin was instrumental in organizing the Shevchenko Educational Society at the hall, where young Ukrainian students — many of whom attended the Ruthenian Training School for bilingual teachers in Winnipeg — came to debate social, economic, and political issues relating to both the old country and Canada.[30] Stechishin was an idealistic social democrat. Born in Galicia in 1883, active in socialist circles as a student, he arrived in Canada in 1902. He did not stay long, however, being persuaded by Genik to move to California as a member of the Ukrainian Brotherhood Commune. After that disastrous experiment in romantic idealism, he returned to Winnipeg in 1905 where, as an organizer and journalist, he attracted a following.

Stechishin was overshadowed at the Shevchenko Reading Society by a new arrival, Pavlo Krat. Krat, born in 1882 in the province of Poltava, had a colourful career before arriving in Winnipeg in 1907. He had been briefly a member of the Revolutionary Ukrainian Party and helped to establish the Ukrainian Social Democratic Union (Spilka). He participated in the Russian Revolution of 1905 and was sentenced to death by the Tsarist Regime for his role in the Poltava uprising. Managing to escape to Lviv, he played a significant part in the demonstrations against the Polonization of the University of Lviv. Again under threat of arrest, he fled to Canada and to Winnipeg, choosing his destination, in part, on the strength of a letter from Stechishin, which stated that Canada was in desperate need of political organizers for its Ukrainian community.[31]

Stechishin and Krat were to provide the nucleus of an organized Ukrainian-Canadian socialist movement based on old world politics and new world conditions. The formal organization took the peculiar form of grafting Ukrainian socialism to that of doctrinaire Anglo-

Canadian socialism. The vehicle was the Socialist Party of Canada (S.P.C.) which, at this particular time, was in a period of ascendancy. An organization based in British Columbia, it espoused a revolutionary philosophy based on three premises; that capitalism could not be reformed, that trade unions provided no benefit for workers, and that only class-conscious political action could destroy capitalism.[32]

The S.P.C.'s power base originally came from the coal miners of British Columbia and Alberta, but after the Russian Revolution of 1905 the party worked to broaden its support by including European intellectuals who had come to Canada as exiles.[33] Both Stechishin and Krat were receptive to the S.P.C.'s approach; it provided an opportunity for the revolutionary socialism they preached to be applied within the wider Canadian context. In November of 1907, Stechishin proposed to the executive of the S.P.C. that his group become an autonomous national unit within the party. Winnipeg became the major Ukrainian branch of the S.P.C., but branches were formed in Portage la Prairie and in Nanaimo, British Columbia. In 1908, the S.P.C. headquarters hired two Ukrainian organizers — Thomas Tomaschevsky in Alberta and Herman Sliptchenko in Manitoba — to organize on behalf of the party. The S.P.C. also translated its platform, not only into Ukrainian but also into Finnish and Italian.[34]

Meanwhile, the *Chervony Prapor* (Red Banner) was issued as the official organ of the Ukrainian branch of the S.P.C. The first paper appeared on 15 November 1907 with Krat as editor. Its *raison d'être* was outlined in its first editorial:

> Our paper . . . as the organ of the Socialist Party of Canada designated to serve that section of the Canadian proletariat that speaks the Ukrainian language has given itself the aim of helping this section in its education, enlightenment and organization, toward a clear understanding of the mighty ideas of socialism. Chervony Prapor will lead the working masses in the struggle with injustice, exploitation and slavery, over the ruins of capitalism toward the sunlight and life.[35]

Krat remained the editor for the subsequent 17 editions until August of 1908, when the *Chervony Prapor* ceased publication because of financial difficulties and because a restless Krat moved for a brief period to Edmonton.

Despite the activity, little was accomplished. The S.P.C. executive appeared reluctant to share the leadership of the party with foreign-born socialists, and its uncompromising opposition to female suffrage and trade unionism alienated many Ukrainian-Canadian socialists. There was also a basic misunderstanding between European socialists and those of British or Canadian origin. As one English-speaking party member observed of the ethnics: "the great bulk of feeling and sentiment exhibited . . . had not been born nor was it the outcome of Canadian life and conditions.[36] There was also a rift within the Ukrainian branch of the S.P.C., between Krat and Taras D. Ferley (the latter a founding member of the Shevchenko Educational Society).[37] Ferley became disenchanted with Krat and his radical associates and he and his followers from the Ruthenian Training School decided to leave the Educational Society. This rift was significant because the Ferley moderates would become the nucleus of an independent liberal Ukrainian intelligentsia which, within two years, would have its own newspaper, the *Ukrainskyi Holos* (Ukrainian Voice). They would also become bitter opponents of the socialists.[38]

In an attempt to revitalize the Ukrainian socialist movement after the collapse of the *Chervony Prapor*, the *Robotchyi Narod* appeared in May of 1909, edited by Stechishin. The first issue called for the formation of a "Ukrainian Socialist League" whose purpose would be to "propagate socialist ideas amongst Ukrainian citizens of this country and to organize our working masses for battle against our exploiters for a socialist Canada."[39] Shortly thereafter, a conference of the existing Ukrainian socialist groups was held on 12 November 1909; it accomplished its aim in forming a new organization: the Federation of Ukrainian Social Democrats in Canada (F.U.S.D.C.). Stechishin was elected secretary of the organization, with an executive committee composed of seven members — two from Manitoba, two from Alberta, and three from British Columbia.[40] Federation branches included Winnipeg, Brandon, Calgary, Cardiff, Vostok, Hosmer, Phoenix, and Canmore in the west, and Montreal in the east.[41] Participants at the conference resolved that they were a class-based rather than ethnic-based organization, and expressed their support for Ukrainian Social Democrats in Europe, the Industrial Workers of the World, and farmer cooperatives. They severely criticized the "elitism" of the S.P.C. and vowed to cooperate only with those branches of the party that refused to follow the national executive.

Stechishin had not given up the idea of cooperating with Canadian socialist parties, but the F.U.S.D.C. could not work within the confines of the S.P.C. In July of 1910, it broke all affiliation with the S.P.C. and, under Stechishin's direction, became a founding group of a new socialist party, the Social Democratic Party (S.D.P.). The S.D.P., which was designed to unite eastern Europeans with moderate British socialists, included such notable personalities as Herman Saltzman, R.A. Rigg, and Jacob Penner — all prominent in Winnipeg's socialist movement. More practical in its orientation than the S.P.C., the S.D.P.'s immediate goal was to gain for workers every concession possible within the existing capitalist system, while maintaining as its ultimate goal the destruction of capitalism.[42] In August of 1910, the F.U.S.D.C. became formally affiliated with the S.D.P., and *Robotchyi Narod* became an offical party organ.

Despite its dedication to the Ukrainian-Canadian proletariat, the F.U.S.D.C. was a hybrid with roots still deeply planted in the struggle of Ukrainians in the old world against despotic regimes. The "Sichinsky Affair" illustrated this: Myroslav Sichinsky was a student at the University of Lviv, who, in a moment of nationalistic passion, assassinated Count Potocki, the repressive Polish governor of Galicia. The F.U.S.D.C. decided to form a "save Sichinsky committee." The Committee of Seven, as it was called, included Krat, Stechishin, and Tomaschevsky, among others, and resolved to free Sichinsky from prison by any means possible. It also contributed moral and financial support to the Ukrainian liberation movement within the Austrian and Russian Empires.[43] Sichinsky became a cause célèbre and, for a while, garnered the F.U.S.D.C. increased support among Ukrainians in Canada. Moreover, the party's support of the assassin-hero proved fruitful. In 1911, Sichinsky escaped from prison after the guards had been bribed with money collected by the Committee of Seven and other activists. While Sichinsky remained in hiding, the F.U.S.D.C. brought those responsible for his rescue to Canada to tour union locals.

The F.U.S.D.C. did not prosper long, however. Most of 1911 and 1912 was marred by seemingly interminable personality and ideological clashes within the party. At its convention in 1910, a new executive was elected which was based primarily in Alberta. The newly elected secretary, Roman Kremar-Solodukha, was soon involved in a dispute with Stechishin and others connected with the *Robotchyi Narod*. Kremar-Solodukha and his Alberta colleagues wanted to transfer the newspaper to Edmonton. The personal and ideological conflict escalated when, rebuffed, the Edmonton group began to publish the *Nova Hromada* (New Community) in February of 1911. A small four-page gazette, the *Nova Hromada* sharply criticized the *Robotchyi Narod* while declaring itself the "official organ of Ukrainian Social Democrats in America."[44] A number of meetings were held between both sides and an appeal was made to the Ukrainian Social Democratic Party in Austria to intervene. The solution came, however, when after 67 issues the financially ailing *Nova Hromada* ceased publication in September of 1912, and Kremar-Solodukha's followers gradually dispersed. Meanwhile, the split had done little good for either the federation's morale or membership — both fell.

Hardly had the movement recovered when Krat and Stechishin became embroiled in a dispute. Krat, who had been living in Edmonton during the quarrel between Kremar-Solodukha and Stechishin, supported Kremar-Solodukha's attempts to transfer the paper to Edmonton. Krat and his followers apparently thought that Stechishin was "empire-building" and attempting to impose personal rule over the F.U.S.D.C.

The specific nature of the squabble revolved around the use of the funds raised by the Committee of Seven. Krat believed that the money should be distributed to federation organizers and *Robotchyi Narod*. Stechishin argued that its specific purpose was to secure Sichinsky's release and that since Sichinsky was still a fugitive and his future uncertain, the funds should remain in trust. When Stechishin discovered that Krat and his followers had used a large part of the collection of $2,200 to pay federation organizers, he had had enough. In September of 1912, he resigned from the federation and from the editorship of the *Robotchyi Narod*.

The federation had lost a key member. Stechishin never looked back. After spending 1913 and 1914 in Edmonton, he moved to the United States where he worked as a journalist for a number of Ukrainian newspapers. He returned to Winnipeg in 1921, taking the position as editor of the *Ukrainskyi Holos*. He held the post until his death in 1947.

Krat and the federation struggled along, not always together. While Krat wandered through western Canada vacillating between becoming a private citizen and organizing for the F.U.S.D.C.,[45] the federation underwent two years of instability. The *Robotchyi Narod* had a number of editors in rapid succession. For a short time (November 1912 to January 1914), the federation's executive was moved to Montreal. Finally, after a convention in January of 1914, the F.U.S.D.C. changed its name to the Ukrainian Social Democratic Party (U.S.D.P.) and transferred the executive back to Winnipeg.[46]

During this period of chaos, the federation received an infusion of somewhat younger, more radical men who came to Canada after 1910. They represented a different type of socialism, shunning the utopian and visionary idealism of Krat and the departed Stechishin. Influenced by the Russian Social Democratic Workers' Party, they were able organizers with a tough and pragmatic approach. This group included Ivan Navizisky, Danylo Lobay, and Mathew Popovych. These men and their followers, after 1914, were destined to take the nebulous Ukrainian socialist movement within the tight orbit of the Bolsheviks. The U.S.D.P. would be firmly in their hands by 1916 when Popovych became editor of the *Robotchyi Narod*. But first, there was one more internal struggle, this time between Krat and these younger revolutionaries.

Early in 1914, Krat became editor of the *Robotchyi Narod*. But with the outbreak of the Great War he again disrupted the party. War threatened the stability of both the Austro-Hungarian and the Russian Empires. Anticipating their demise, a "Union for the Liberation of Ukraine" was established in Austria in August of 1914. Its purpose, logically enough, was to unite Ukrainians toward a common goal, that of liberating their homeland. Krat was enthralled; he immediately undertook to organize all the Ukrainian forces in Canada into a single unit to support the liberation of Ukraine. Branches of the Tovarysto Samostiina Ukrainia (Society for an Independent Ukraine) were quickly formed in Winnipeg, Vegreville, Cardiff, and Calgary.[47]

But Krat's appeals for a united front of all those Ukrainians in Canada, regardless of their class and religious affiliation, who desired an independent Ukrainian Republic, alienated leading members within the U.S.D.P. The party conducted a referendum on the question of united-front tactics and repudiated any cooperation with non-proletarian, non-agrarian organizations.[48]

The Society for an Independent Ukraine quickly disintegrated. But thanks to Krat's editorship of the *Robotchyi Narod*, many members of the U.S.D.P. had already cancelled their memberships, believing that the society had superseded the party.[49] Discord was rampant within the U.S.D.P. To complicate matters, the unpredictable Krat announced his intention to enter the Presbyterian ministry and commenced work on the editorial staff of the Ukrainian Presbyterian paper, *Ranok* (Morning), while still editing the *Robotchyi Narod*.[50] Many U.S.D.P. members simply thought Krat had taken leave of his senses.

Krat carried on as editor of the *Robotchyi Narod* until 1916, when the executive of the U.S.D.P. demanded and received his resignation. Shortly thereafter, he was expelled from the party. With his expulsion came the end of the pre-Bolshevik Ukrainian socialist movement in Canada. Henceforth, there would be a pro-Soviet, communist element within the Ukrainian-Canadian community. Krat, until he died in December of 1952, would remain on the periphery of Ukrainian socialism.

The impact of the early socialist movement on Ukrainian-Canadians is difficult to measure. Certainly, it had intrinsic value for a minority of educated and ideologically committed exiles who in Canada continued their confusing and often bizarre political battles and assorted squabbles against each other. In the course of their activities, they left a rich literary heritage. Krat, for example, wrote a veritable library of prose, poems, stories, and satire during his Canadian career. Stechishin, too, besides being a first-rate journalist, was a fine writer and translator.

Socialist organizations were a small but nevertheless important force within the Ukrainian-Canadian community. They provided a theoretical critique of Canadian capitalism, attempted to organize the Ukrainian-Canadian proletariat (not only into an ethnically conscious class group but also as part and parcel of a general Canadian socialist movement), engaged in cultural and educational work, often organized relief for destitute Ukrainian workers, and generally seemed to be the only group that cared about the plight of the Ukrainian-Canadian proletariat.

Winnipeg remained the centre of the socialists' activities. The Shevchenko Hall was the site of regular popular lectures for immigrants throughout the period to 1914. Krat, Stechishin, and others introduced their listeners not only to politics, but to world geography, the history of both Ukraine and Canada, human anatomy, physics, chemistry, and culture.[51] The lectures were complemented by social activities, musical recitals, and drama. Mathew Popovych, for example, along with his political endeavours, directed the Tobilevich Drama Circle, which presented fine performances.

Outside of Winnipeg and other major centres, socialists journeyed frequently to isolated mining towns. Stechishin was instrumental in establishing socialist clubs in Nanaimo, Hosmer, and Canmore. Krat also travelled extensively throughout western Canada. The net result was that scores of towns and villages had workers' associations such as "Borotka Za Voli" (Fight for Freedom) or "Volia" (Liberty), usually as branches of the F.U.S.D.C. and later of the U.S.D.P. These clubs were useful not only politically, but socially. Funds were collected for books and newspapers from the old country, debates and reading sessions were held, and popular causes were supported.

Yet the hope of creating a massive socialist following among Ukrainian-Canadians was never realized. Despite the working conditions found in the Canadian industrial system, membership in the F.U.S.D.C. and U.S.D.P. remained low, ranging from 101 in late 1907 to a high of 424 in mid-1913, and levelling off to 238 in early 1914.[52] The majority of Ukrainians remained unmoved by early socialism for no other reason than that it lacked consistency or a sense of direction. Personality clashes, ideological schisms, and rhetorical arguments were simply irrelevant compared to putting food on the table and a roof over one's head. Unlike spontaneous strikes or militant unions, the socialists offered no direct action.

After 1914, the various strands of the socialist movement succumbed to the sterile world of the Bolsheviks; the pro-Soviet stand of those leading the Ukrainian-Canadian socialist movement ultimately alienated the vast majority of Ukrainian-Canadians.

CHAPTER 12

POLITICS AND THE ISSUE OF EDUCATION

As the Ukrainians began to consolidate their economic and political position in the west, they caused great anxiety in the Anglo-Celtic community. The largest and most visible ethnic group, they were not becoming "Canadianized" but showed every sign of remaining apart. Was the west to be "British," culturally homogeneous, English-speaking, or was it to be Balkanized by a conglomerate of races? The outcome was not assured; a strident amalgamation of cultural groups was resisting the Anglo-Celtic melting pot. After 1905, debates about assimilation took on a deeper and shriller tone as the Anglo-Celtic elite marshalled its forces to "Anglicize" and "evangelize" the immigrants.

Led by the emerging intelligentsia, most of whom were teachers and professionals, the Ukrainians shunned the proselytizing efforts of Anglo-Canadian Protestants. Not only did they retain their Catholic and Orthodox religions, but they actively espoused their own national identity. Nowhere was this more evident than in the concern for their language. It was the sacred key, treasured through the centuries, to the soul of the old country — the best of Ukrainian culture, history, tradition, and ideals. Ukrainians would not give up their birthright. Vigorously adopting the concept of bilingual education, the Ukrainians, through their community spokesmen, demanded the right to have their mother tongue taught in the public schools. Inevitably, their aspirations clashed head-on with those of Canadians who saw the public schools as the instrument of Anglo-Celtic conformity.

The Role of Church and School

The unabated stream of immigrants between 1905 and 1914 gave impetus to the movement for the "Canadianization" of the foreigner. To a large majority of English-Canadians it was, perhaps, the most important problem Canada faced. They found evidence of the "danger" to be abundant. In the rural areas of the prairies, block settlements (especially of the Ukrainians) resisted Anglo-Celtic intrusion and continued a mode of life that appeared alien to British traditions and institutions. The rapid growth of cities, which paralleled mass immigration, created urban problems which made the foreigner highly visible. The urban environment contained within it "all the problems of poverty, overcrowding, ill health, social vice, drunkenness, violence, [and] Sabbath desecration . . . ."[1] The immigrant was seen as the chief cause of falling public morality. The Ukrainians, for example, were considered "a dangerous element" in the cities.[2] Their depraved nature, explained by "centuries of poverty and oppression," had "animalized them."[3] It was believed that their susceptibility to alcohol, crime, violence, and prostitution, coupled with their ignorance, superstition, lack of collective wisdom, and untruthfulness, might undermine the "decent standard" of the "Christian" Anglo-Celtics.[4]

In these circumstances, Anglo-Celtics saw their duty clearly — to assist foreigners by "making them English-speaking Christian citizens who are clean, educated and loyal to the Dominion and to Great Britain."[5] The "Canadianizing" movement was taken up in earnest by the Methodists and the Presbyterians. Although competing with each other for souls, they both viewed their responsibilities in terms of an Anglo-Celtic and Protestant nation, which meant not only uplifting the "inferior races," but doing battle against non-Protestant denominations — the Roman Catholic, Greek Catholic, and Greek Orthodox churches to which the majority of immigrants belonged. One missionary explained the logic:

> If from this North American continent is to come a superior race, a race to be specially used by God in carrying on of His work, what is our duty to those who are now our fellow-citizens? Many of them come to us nominal Christians, that is, they owe allegiance to the Greek or Roman Catholic Church, but their moral standards and ideals are far below those of Christian citizens of the Dominion. These people have come to this young, free country to make homes for themselves and their children. It is our duty to meet them with the open Bible and to instill into their minds the principles and ideals of Anglo-Saxon civilization.[6]

The Methodist Church supported missions established to "proselytize the immigrant and to improve the social conditions of immigrant communities."[7] Best known was the All People's Mission in Winnipeg, but others could be found in Toronto, Edmonton, and Vancouver. The Presbyterians attempted to influence foreigners by supporting, until 1913, the Ruthenian Independent Greek Church and creating a number of "school homes" for Ukrainians near unilingual English public schools. Indeed, by 1914, residences had been established in Vegreville, Ethelbert, Sifton, and Teulon. The idea was to create an immigrant elite which would internalize Anglo–Celtic Protestant values and transmit them to the masses.[8]

The efforts of Methodist and Presbyterian missionaries notwithstanding, it was the elementary schools in western Canada that were regarded as the great assimilators of the immigrants. To quote one historian: "Because the elementary school worked with the children, the most adaptable age group, their prospect for success was good. Elementary education, moreover, appeared to the immigrant to be far more necessary for successful life in Canada than did the Protestant religion; therefore educators had an advantage over evangelical Protestants."[9] Starting the assimilation process with fresh young minds, relatively uncorrupted by years of cultural and linguistic saturation, made sense. Because unity of race and religion was admittedly impossible, it also made sense to seek unity through the teaching of common national values in schools.[10]

Missionaries, educators, politicians, and academics agreed that public schools were the training grounds whereby immigrant children would become good Canadian citizens. J.S. Woodsworth, a prominent Methodist minister, wrote: "How are we to break down the walls which separate these foreigners from us? First of all comes the Public school. Too great emphasis cannot be placed upon the work that has been accomplished and may — yes, must be accomplished by our national schools."[11] Woodsworth's conviction was echoed in the reports of school inspectors. The conclusion of T.M. Maguire of Manitoba was typical:

> The great work of the public school in Canada is the foundation and development of a high type of national life. This is particularly true in Western Canada, with its heterogeneous population . . . these incongruous elements have to be assimilated, have to be welded into one harmonious whole if Canada is to attain the position that we, who belong here by right of birth and blood, claim for her. The chief instrument in this process of assimilation is the public school.[12]

Public schools were designated the guardians of Anglo–Celtic culture, linguistic homogeneity, and national unity.

The Language Compromises

The ideal of non–sectarian and unilingual (English) public schools, however, ran counter to reality. The French fact in Canada forced Anglo–Celtics to recognize not only cultural but specifically linguistic duality. Historical circumstances decreed that bilingual schools be accepted in Quebec, Ontario, New Brunswick, and Manitoba. The Laurier-Greenway compromise of 1897, although seemingly a victory for Anglo–Manitoban ascendancy and non-denominational schools, had left an important loophole vis à vis the language of instruction. Not only was it vague on the extent to which the second language might be employed, but it also left open the question of what language (other than English) was acceptable. The compromise had not specified French as the second language but had used the phrase "any other language" to live up to Macdonald's promise to the Mennonites that they would enjoy liberty in education and religion as a condition for their settlement on the prairies.[13] Immigrant groups quickly became aware of this loophole and demanded Ukrainian, German, and Polish bilingual schools as well as training for bilingual teachers.

From Manitoba, the bilingual concept spread to Saskatchewan and Alberta, which became provinces in 1905 and so had jurisdiction over education. In Saskatchewan, although bilingualism as such was not legally allowed in the schools, school ordinances dating back to 1901 did sanction instruction in French at the primary level and in a foreign language between three and four o'clock in the afternoon, if parents financed such instruction and a competent teacher could be found. Although illegal, it became the practice in many ethnic communities to use a foreign language as a medium of instruction for longer than the allotted one hour per day.[14] Alberta had similar provisions, although with the appointment of Robert Fletcher as Supervisor of Schools Among Foreigners in 1906, the use of a foreign language for instructional purposes was severely curtailed.

Despite the prevalent arguments for English non-denominational public schools, all three prairie provinces established special training schools for foreigners between 1905 and 1914. In Winnipeg, a Ruthenian Training School was opened in 1905 for the preparation of Ukrainian and Polish students who would teach in bilingual schools. The Saskatchewan provincial government, using Manitoba as its model, established a Training School for Teachers of Foreign Speaking Communities in Regina in 1909. And, rather belatedly, Alberta followed in 1913, when the English School for Foreigners opened its doors in Vegreville.

Practical necessity and political expediency were the reasons. Teachers were scarce and English-speaking instructors were loath to settle in isolated ethnic enclaves where they were guaranteed "culture shock," low pay, and inadequate housing. Yet schooling was considered important lest an entire generation of immigrant children grow up illiterate. "The future of the West lies in their children," wrote C.B. Sissons. "Thousands of these, at a time when their bright young minds might be molded, are drudges for helpless or short-sighted parents. . . . these neglected children will have developed within a few years into citizens with the aspirations of slaves."[15]

Many Anglo-Celtic educators did not perceive the bilingual principle as a threat to "Canadianization" because they viewed bilingual schools as transitional. Bilingual teachers as intermediaries would gradually "Anglicize" immigrant children until a totally English public school system emerged. The special training schools for the foreigners were designed to achieve this end. J.T. Cressy, the principal of the Ruthenian Training School, reported in 1908 that the aim of the institution was to make bilingual teachers good Britishers so "that in the years to come the Ruthenian people will do their share in making Canada a great nation, and will say as Britishers 'One King, One Empire, One Race and One Flag'."[16]

Pedagogical theory, moreover, seemed to support this view. As one inspector reported of Ukrainian-English schools in Manitoba: "in schools where the teacher is able to speak the two languages and is using the Ruthenian elementary text-book, or some Ruthenian-English dictionary, the children are making better progress in all subjects of study than they otherwise would." Further, this inspector suggested that "the Department take up the matter of providing bilingual readers and Ruthenian-English dictionaries which will be of great assistance to the children in their efforts to master the English tongue."[17] Under the circumstances, many educators believed this the logical course.

Bilingual schools were also entangled in politics. The political equation was simple: numbers translated into votes. As one observer of the period noted, "the North-West is three times more Austro-Hungarian than Indian."[18] Indeed, Manitoba, Saskatchewan, and Alberta had become polyglot provinces. According to the census of 1911, out of 455,000 people in Manitoba, some 30,000 were of French descent, 40,000 Ukrainian, 35,000 German, 12,000 Polish, 10,000 Jewish, and 6,000 Scandinavian. Saskatchewan, in 1911, boasted a population of

490,000, of which 68,000 were of German origin, 41,000 of Austro-Hungarian (mostly Ukrainian), 34,000 Scandinavian, 23,000 French, and 18,000 Russian. Alberta, in 1911, counted 375,000, of which 36,000 were German, 28,000 Scandinavian, 26,000 Ukrainian, and 20,000 French. The Rodmond Roblin government in Manitoba, the Walter Scott administration in Saskatchewan, and the Arthur Sifton regime in Alberta depended on ethnic electoral support. For that support they were willing to grant some concessions; the establishment of special training schools for foreigners was a political expediency which could be justified in educational terms.

By and large, Ukrainians were the most adamant in demanding bilingual schools. In Manitoba, where they comprised the largest "ethnic" group, and in Saskatchewan and Alberta where they were also a significant force numerically, they were in a position to pressure the provincial governments. East of the Red River, in the interlake region along the south edge of the Riding Mountains and around Dauphin, almost exclusively Ukrainian enclaves could be found. Isolated from English-speaking settlers, having built their own churches and community halls, they participated actively in municipal governments and the creation and running of school districts. They generally were willing to accept the necessity of learning the English language but, understandably, they refused to abandon the right to use and teach their own language within their communities.[19] They agitated for teachers who could speak their language and feel a part of their settlements, and who would not only be instructors of their children but counsellors, guides, and interpreters for the communities.[20] Politicians, preoccupied with soliciting votes from ethnic enclaves, and educators, fearful of a large constituency of "illiterate" and "alien" East Europeans populating the province, had little choice but to respond.

An unforeseen outgrowth of training schools for Ukrainian-English teachers, however, was the formation of a Ukrainian intelligentsia. Out of the Ruthenian Training School in Manitoba emerged a recognizable secular group of bilingual teachers who, although moderate and liberal, identified themselves with the interests of the Ukrainian people. In 1907, they established the Ukrainian Teachers' Association which lobbied for bilingual textbooks, a Ukrainian translation of the School Act, and more bilingual teachers. This was followed in 1910 by the formation of their own newspaper, the *Ukrainskyi Holos* (Ukrainian Voice), which sought not only to educate the Ukrainians but to encourage them to participate fully in the economic and political life of the Dominion. By organizing the Ukrainian community along secular lines, by attempting to cultivate a sense of Ukrainian national identity, they were at cross-purposes with the Anglo-Celtic ideal of cultural and linguistic homogeneity. Battle lines were quickly drawn between the two, with the bilingual school question in the forefront.

Most Anglo-Celtic Manitobans assumed that the Ukrainians would be assimilated eventually. Some were more impatient than others. As early as 1901, two Presbyterian delegations met with the Conservative premier of the province, R.P. Roblin, urging him on the one hand to expand public schools in Ukrainian areas to teach them English and, on the other hand, to repeal "bilingual schooling" because it was an obstacle to assimilation.[21] Roblin might have acquiesced had it not been for the Roman Catholic presence in the province.

Manitoba contained a politically potent French element. Led by the "crusty" Archbishop A. Langevin, "an uncompromising ultra-montane oblate" who had been the sustaining force behind bilingual education since 1894, and who, after the Laurier-Greenway agreement was determined to restore bilingual sectarian schools to their former status, French Catholics vigorously opposed any further attempts to "Anglicize" the province. For Langevin, language and religion were inextricably connected;[22] he was therefore greatly disturbed by the Protestant endeavours to "evangelize" the Ukrainians because at the same time they undermined the bilingual principle. Langevin saw Catholic Slavs as potential allies in his struggle to promote French linguistic and religious rights. His reasoning was cogent: if the Protestants were allowed to proceed with assimilation unchallenged, that would bolster the Protestant majority and further weaken the French position in the province. A pro-Ukrainian stance was logical because it fortified the bilingual concept — even if it meant elevating the status of the Ukrainian tongue to that of the French. Although acknowledging that English should be the second language of these foreigners, he unrelentingly supported their right to bilingual schools. Ultimately, Langevin hoped to check Anglo-Protestant ascendancy by promoting a multilingual, multicultural milieu. Such an environment would ensure a special place for French Catholics by protecting and perhaps expanding upon what they had already established.[23] Thus, while publicly embracing Ukrainian demands for bilingual schools and teachers, Langevin, at the same time, lashed out at the Protestants, accusing them of attempting to convert the Ukrainians to Protestantism rather than to advance their education.

As the debate between the Protestants and Catholics over the Ukrainians widened, Langevin approached the Roblin government for support. A tacit understanding was quickly reached; in exchange for ecclesiastical help, the opportunistic Roblin promised policies that would meet with the approval of the Archbishop and his associates. Indeed, the Catholic hierarchy would support certain Conservative candidates in elections while the Premier would grant great "flexibility" to French Catholics in operating their schools. More significantly, Roblin agreed to the demands not only for Ukrainians but for Polish and German bilingual schools.

Politics bred strange bedfellows; in extending the olive branch to the French Catholics and non-British immigrants, Roblin was able to build a powerful, if corrupt, political machine. By granting these concessions, and by manipulating the foreign vote through the distribution of alcohol at election time, falsifying voting lists in ethnic districts, and patronizing immigrant spokesmen, Roblin's administration was able to hold power in the province until 1915.

The Battle over Schools in Manitoba

The government appointed staunch Conservatives to organize Ukrainian-English schools. John Baderski, Theodore Stefanyk, and Paul Grigeychuk, appointed in 1903, 1907, and 1910, respectively, although having no pedagogical training, proved extremely useful in soliciting the Ukrainian vote. When it became evident that there was a great shortage of bilingual teachers in the rural Ukrainian districts, the government opened the Ruthenian Training School in February of 1905. It served the Ukrainian community until 1916.

The training school was a linchpin for the development of bilingual school teachers. The students, between the ages of 18 and 22, were of diverse backgrounds, from those who received some training in gymnasiums in Europe to those who had some knowledge of the English language from elementary schooling in Canada.[24] They were provided with financial assistance on the condition that they would repay the government. Each student received his room, board, and education at the cost of $25 per month. The curriculum included English, British and Canadian history, mathematics, and a smattering of science, art, and music courses. Pedagogical training consisted of six months' attendance at the Provincial Normal School.[25] Very few were proficient enough to complete the full program and to pass the exams that entitled them to a teaching certificate. Most received third-class, nonprofessional permits which allowed them to teach in isolated Ukrainian communities. The objective of the institution was to provide prospective teachers with the equivalent of a Grade 9 education. J.T. Cressy was assisted by a number of Ukrainian-language instructors: James Makohin and Denis Pyrich while the school was located in Winnipeg, and Wasyl Kudryk, Petro Karmansky, Taras Ferley, and Ivan Basarb after it was moved to Brandon in 1907. Through its halls passed approximately 150 future bilingual teachers.

Of the instructors at the institution, Taras Ferley deserves special mention. From the time of his arrival in Canada in 1903, the Galician native was deeply involved in the Ukrainian community; a socialist, he co-founded the Shevchenko Educational Society along with Myroslav Stechishin. In 1909, however, he began shedding his socialist trappings when he became increasingly alienated by Pavlo Krat and Krat's more radical followers. Ferley became convinced that Ukrainian socialists had become too radical and too prone to emphasize working-class solidarity rather than nationality as the crucial component in Ukrainian-Canadian development. He argued that, instead of preaching revolution, socialists should concentrate on more practical objectives such as the establishment of cooperatives among Ukrainians in Canada and the elevation of their culture in the Canadian context. A man "possessed of a winning magnetic personality,"[27] Ferley was able to consolidate a following of young Ukrainian progressives (dubbed "nationalists" by the Anglo-Celtics) who were increasingly estranged by Ukrainian-Canadian socialism. These men, many of whom had received their educations in Canada, were not steeped in the old world milieu which dominated discussions in socialist circles.

The influence of these graduates of the training school in the Ukrainian rural communities cannot be underestimated. They emerged as true community leaders articulating nationalist values. They were, by and large, fondly remembered by their students for their dedication and crusading spirit, which embraced whole settlements. One pupil, described the accomplishments of his first three bilingual teachers, Ivan Kocan, Theodore Marciniw, and Onufrey Kykawy:

> They left an imprint of their personalities on many of us. They were dedicated men and went beyond the ordinary call of duty to make our introduction to education a challenge and stirring experience . . . they took care that the school library was well stocked with books in both languages and organized evening courses for the adults. An annual concert and play or two by the children of the school was part of their programme. It was a schooling in self expression.

> I am not sure how they would have fared under the merit system. Their English was not the best, their academic training did not exceed grade ten, but they gave us something of the intangible and indefinable; a set of values that was our guiding light.[28]

The importance of these men was two-fold: they provided basic education where, otherwise, illiteracy might have prevailed, and they instilled a sense of national identity in the community. Consequently, they were recognized às leaders — people of authority and deserving of respect.[29]

The sense of mission among many Ukrainian bilingual teachers was evident in the Ukrainian Teachers' Association. At their first convention held early in June of 1907, the 40 bilingual teachers present emphasized their support of the bilingual principle, urged the government to intensify the program at the Ruthenian Training School (arguing that 40 teachers were grossly inadequate to meet the needs of the 30,000 Ukrainians in the province), and demanded the establishment of compulsory school attendance.[30] Other resolutions called for the creation of a five-member committee to press the provincial government for bilingual textbooks and for the translation of the School Act into Ukrainian.[31] Both these resolutions were finally accepted by the Department of Education, with the Manitoba government publishing, in 1913, the first Ukrainian-English readers, entitled The Manitoba Ruthenian-English Readers.[32] The teachers' nationalism was also evident in a resolution passed naming Mikhaylo Hrushevsky, noted Ukrainian historian, and Ivan Franko along with other prominent Ukrainian personalities as honorary members of the association, and in the use of the term "Ukrainian" rather than "Ruthenian" in their official designation. Significantly, too, there was discussion at the convention about the need for a truly independent Ukrainian newspaper which could articulate the teachers' views.

This came about at the third convention of the association in 1909, when the Ukrainian Publishing Company Ltd. was formed. The first issue of *Ukrainskyi Holos* appeared on 14 March 1910. W. Kudryk was the editor, with T.D. Ferley, W. Chumer, W. Karpetz, A. Zylch, H. Slipchenko and J.W. Arsenych — all bilingual teachers — as the directors. Dedicating itself to the "aspirations of the Ukrainian citizenry," the first editorial emphasized the essential task of education: "we should cherish our self-respect and not become slaves to others but show that we have national dignity, and deserve, and are entitled to the same rights and privileges accorded to others. To enable us to defend ourselves we must know how this is done — which comes with education and more education."[33] The *Ukrainskyi Holos*, from the outset closely associated with bilingual teachers, became the organ of a broad national sentiment promoting Ukrainian cultural growth, the Ukrainian identity, and the bilingual principle in the Canadian context.

The organization of the Ukrainian Teachers' Association and the publishing of *Holos* were regarded with deep suspicion by the Anglo-Celtics. Here was a concrete manifestation of Ukrainian power which could undermine conformity to British norms. The assimilation of these East Europeans would be stalled by these teachers promoting Ukrainian literature, art, and social and national life through the schools and the press.

Educational standards in Manitoba in general and the bilingual schools in particular were vulnerable to attack. Teachers were scarce, school districts were slow to organize, and above all, there was no compulsory attendance. Illiteracy was rife; one estimate made in 1910 was that close to 30,000 children were not going to school at all.[34] Those who did attended sporadically and received a rudimentary education at best.[35] As shown in the resolutions of the Ukrainian Teachers' Association, the bilingual instructors were well aware of these shortcomings. Two letters to the *Manitoba Free Press* from Orest Zereko, a Ukrainian school teacher and a graduate of the University of Manitoba, argued, however, the viewpoint of the teachers, that inadequate government action, not bilingual schools, was the source of the problem. The absence of compulsory education, the shortage of qualified teachers, and the limited time (one hour) allotted for teaching Ukrainian were items that could only be corrected by changes in government policy.[36] Zereko, however, went further; he linked poor schooling and Conservative Party politics by using the example of school organizers and other appointees who, emulating politicians, "distributed freely Hoffman drops, beer, whisky, cider and other intoxicating liquors . . . to the worst and lowest element of the population."[37] The Roblin regime, Zereko claimed, was more interested in politics than good schools, which was evident in the ineffectiveness of school inspection — especially in bilingual districts.[38]

As the campaign against bilingual schools as a source of the province's educational problems intensified, the Ukrainians through their teachers' association and *Holos* attempted to defend and clarify their position. They supported the bilingual system of schools absolutely, but they also recognized that they had a duty to Canada:

> It is our aim and duty to teach the Ruthenian element what the British constitution and Canadian ideas are. We realize that our people must be familiar with these, in order to become good Canadian citizens. We also realize that the inculcation of love for what is best in our language and literature, in addition to Canadian ideas, tends to make our boys and girls better Canadian citizens and more efficient members of society at large.[39]

The Ukrainian bilingual teachers did not wish to create a "Canadian Ukraine"; they were not race agitators. They simply wanted to educate their people in a bicultural, bilingual context because "no man can be made to love his adopted land or care for education if he cannot be inspired by the memories of his native land, and does not have to remember and cherish what is best and noblest in the tradition, language and literature of his own race."[40] For Ukrainians, a policy requiring that every child in the province learn the tongue of the majority, exclusively, was socially and politically absurd. They did not take a position of isolation and antagonism to the Canadian state, nor did they seek to place their fatherland before the land of their adoption. They emphasized Canada first and shared Canadian aspirations with the English-speaking citizens. Queen's University Professor O.D. Skelton, in one of his more perceptive moments, inadvertently summed up the Ukrainian attitude:

> We want unity, not a drab, steam-rollered uniformity. The man who forgets the rock out of which he was hewn is no better a Canadian for it; to repress old traditions before we have given new ideals is questionable policy. By all means seek to put Canada first in the minds and hearts of every child of Canada by birth or adoption but do so by constructive action, by emphasizing the nation of the future which all share in common, rather than by repressive action, by forcible suppression of the heritage and memories of the past.[41]

Such arguments, however, had little impact in the Anglo-Celtic community. John Dafoe of the *Manitoba Free Press* began to publish, early in June of 1913, a daily series of 65 articles severely criticizing the bilingual schools. On 10 October 1913, the Orange Lodges swung into action, issuing a manifesto urging members to work actively in making Manitoba a British province.[42] The provincial Liberal Party, sensing the vulnerability of the aging and corrupt Roblin administration, agitated for English as the primary language in all public schools. The Liberal Party handbook published shortly before the provincial election of 1914 stated:

> In the French, Polish and Ruthenian settlements of Manitoba, the English language is but poorly understood and indifferently spoken by the children and by a considerable number of the adult population. The Liberals contend that this condition represents not only a wrong inflicted upon these children individually, but a prejudice to the entire province and to the entire Dominion. For this condition of things means that the French children and the Polish and Ruthenian children are being unprepared not only to make their own way of life, but unprepared also for the responsibilities of Canadian citizenship and the burdens of Canadian nationality.[43]

The bilingual principle was under attack, an attack that was supported by changes in pedagogical theory. By the end of 1913, it was concluded that the medium of the mother tongue was no longer the best method of learning English. The most forceful argument came from a widely read book by Norman F. Black which was published in 1913, *English for the non-English*. Black, after making extensive surveys, concluded that the most efficient way to teach English in the public schools was to use English exclusively in the classroom. Therefore, he added, it was not desirable to have teachers drawn from the immigrant communities teaching in the schools of those communities.[44]

The outbreak of World War I added fuel to the opposition. Indeed, the issue burst into flames. Ukrainians were suddenly feared, if not hated; overnight they had become "enemy aliens." The smouldering resentment of "Ruthenian power" could now be displayed unabashedly. The Balkanization of Manitoba had been a perceived danger; the continued expansion of Ukrainian and Polish schools (122 by 1914, employing 114 bilingual teachers)[45] in the mounting hysteria of wartime was ample proof of that danger. Canada and the British Empire were at war with the country from which these hordes had originated. Their schools and their teachers could no longer be tolerated; total Anglo-Celtic conformity was demanded.

Harsh measures came soon enough with the electoral defeat of the Roblin government in May of 1915 and the transfer of power to T.C. Norris and the Liberals. Under the guise of "educational reform" the Liberals lost little time in instituting a new educational policy. It was announced that the Ukrainian and Polish training schools were to be closed at the end of 1915; henceforth, students were to attend normal schools. While compulsory attendance and a uniform inspection of schools were introduced, the new Minister of Education, Dr. R.S. Thornton, ordered the Superintendent of Schools, C.K. Newcombe, to prepare a special report on bilingual schools. The *Newcombe Report* was released on 12 January 1916 in a "highly selective and edited" form which conveyed an unfavourable impression of bilingual schools.[46] The report stated that of the total number of public school students in Manitoba, 16 per cent were enrolled in bilingual schools. It was revealed that the average daily attendance in bilingual schools was lower than in unilingual schools and that the teaching of the English language was very inconsistent.[47] What was not mentioned were the factors that accounted for this state of affairs. Bilingual schools were below the provincial average in attendance because they were rural. The teaching of English naturally appeared below standard; most of these pupils, after all, were not native speakers. And more than 50 per cent of the Ukrainian and Polish bilingual schools had been in existence for less than two and a half years.[48] Although taken in toto the *Newcombe Report* was not as negative as it had appeared in published form, it was used as justification to take a drastic step. On 8 March 1916, by a vote of 35 to 8, the Manitoba legislature abolished bilingual schools.

Ukrainians had, of course, been working to arrest these developments. The *Ukrainskyi Holos* angrily denounced the attacks on bilingual education: "We have had an earful about their superiority and about our lack of culture. They already suggested to withhold our voting rights, to treat us like Hindus and Chinese, and now in the last while they have directed all their energies against our schools and teachers."[49] While the government carried on with its "educational reform," a Ukrainian Central Committee for the Defence of the Bilingual School System was formed. Led by the teacher and nationalist, Taras Ferley, who had been elected to the provincial legislature as an independent in 1915, the committee held rallies and presented to Norris and a number of cabinet ministers, on 3 February 1916, a 6,000-signature petition urging the retention of bilingual schools. These efforts were in vain. The symbolic end to bilingual schools came with the burning of Ukrainian-English textbooks by government officials on the grounds of the Manitoba legislative buildings.

The School Controversy in Saskatchewan

The province of Saskatchewan was born amid a school controversy. In the Autonomy Bills of 1905, which created Saskatchewan and Alberta, Laurier attempted to guarantee sectarian or confessional schools. He was forced to withdraw these clauses, however, when he faced a revolt of his English-speaking colleagues in cabinet. Although religious minorities in Saskatchewan ultimately did have the right to erect and maintain separate schools through the Saskatchewan Act, their privileges were minimal, subject to the control of the new province's Department of Education, which insisted on a common program of studies, a common inspection of schools, and common qualifications for teachers.[50]

Even these rights were assailed and became an issue in Saskatchewan's first election campaign. F.W.G. Haultain, leader of the Provincial Rights Party and former territorial premier, forcefully opposed denominational schools, arguing that the province should test the validity of the Saskatchewan Act in the courts. Haultain had no use for the nine separate schools (seven of which were Roman Catholic) which existed in the province in 1905. Walter Scott, the Liberal leader, strongly defended the provisions of the Act on the grounds that the province should guarantee minority rights as they were laid down in 1905. In doing so, Scott and the Liberals were able to identify themselves with minority rights — an identification which was translated into electoral support from ethnic enclaves.[51]

To the Francophones, the Ukrainians, and other ethnic minorities, it was obvious that Scott was more willing to defend their interests and grant concessions than Haultain. Although there was no official language other than English in the province's public schools, ethnic groups could rely on a benevolent government and the Department of Education regulations which allowed each school district to employ a teacher to instruct in French, Ukrainian, or other mother tongue for one hour per day where student numbers warranted it.

Scott won the provincial election of 1905 by using the Roblin technique of soliciting not only the Francophone vote, but also the non-British immigrant vote. Liberal candidates were successful in 12 of the 13 ridings north of the C.P.R. main line, where there was a high concentration of foreigners, while Haultain had his base of support in the southern part of the province, settled before 1900 largely by the British and Ontarians.[52] This electoral pattern held true for subsequent provincial elections.

With its heterogeneous population, Saskatchewan faced much the same practical problems as Manitoba in educating the immigrants. The scarcity of qualified teachers in rural ethnic communities was the main obstacle. The provincial government followed Manitoba's example in 1909 with the Training School for Foreign Speaking Communities in Regina. The school's aim was to raise the academic level of the students to Grade 8 so that they could enter high school and later prepare themselves at the provincial normal school for at least third-class teaching certificates. As in Manotiba, it was assumed that these students would act eventually as suitable agents of assimilation in the ethnic settlements.

Unlike in Manitoba, this institution was open to all ethnic groups. This elicited objections from the province's Ukrainian community, which sought to limit attendance to Ukrainians and to change the name of the institution to the Training School for Ruthenians. Although appearing somewhat presumptuous in their request, the Ukrainians could point to the fact that the overwhelming majority of the school's student population was Ukrainian. In 1912, only 5 out of 42 students were non-Ukrainian.[53] The institution was, in fact if not in name, a Ukrainian preserve. The request, however, was ignored by the provincial government.

Although not as numerous or as powerful as their counterparts in Manitoba, the Ukrainian teachers of Saskatchewan were the dominant force in their communities and the chief political spokesmen. At their first conference, held in Rosthern in 1913, the 50 teachers present passed resolutions pressing the government for more Ukrainian instruction in the schools, Ukrainian textbooks, and a professor of Ukrainian for the training school.[54] These demands, made frequently throughout the period, were largely disregarded by the government. The teaching of Ukrainian, for example, was not included in the curriculum of the training school until 1913.

More significantly, and much to the chagrin of Ukrainians, the training school proved a failure. On 25 February 1914, a petition signed by every student in the institution was presented to the Department of Education. The cause of the petition was Joseph Greer, the principal. Greer, a disciplinarian with no sympathy for the immigrant students, was accused of "poor teaching, injustice, severe discipline for minor infringements of regulations, disparaging remarks concerning students and causes which we do not mention here."[55] A three-man committee established by the Department of Education absolved Greer of the charges but the students remained adamant, refusing to continue their studies. A school with no pupils could not long exist and in March of 1914, after having given instruction to about 104 pupils, the institution closed. Greer was forced to resign. These events seriously jeopardized the continued teaching of Ukrainian in the public schools.

After the closure of the institution, "special classes for foreign-speaking students" were conducted at the provincial normal school. Enrolment, however, declined — from 56 in 1915-16 to 29 in 1917.[56] The government curtailed them also. Enrolment notwithstanding, with the advent of the Great War, Saskatchewan, like Manitoba, was seething with antagonism toward the Ukrainians and their bilingual schools. The case of Nicetus Romaniuk exemplified this: in 1914, Romaniuk, a recent arrival from the Austro-Hungarian Empire, was appointed an instructor in these special classes. Although a successful teacher, he was dismissed in 1916 when accused of "subversive activities." He was guilty by association, as were all the Ukrainians who had come from Austria-Hungary. Why should foreigners perpetuate their native tongue in the province's schools while the English were at war with them in Europe? Saskatchewan, like Manitoba, suddenly could not afford to remain a polyglot province.

Against the background of unabated patriotism and demands for all English public schools, the government moved, albeit more slowly than in Manitoba, to stay with public opinion. On 22 June 1915, Scott announced, rather cautiously, that there was a need for certain reforms in the educational system. He invited opinions from those who were interested in "educational work" in the province.[57] The response was immediate, impassioned, and partisan. A Citizens' Committee on Public Education was formed shortly after Scott's announcement. By September of 1915, it had held a convention in Regina out of which was established the Saskatchewan Public Education League. Led by the fiery Reverend E.H. Oliver, a prominent clergyman and educator, a "Crusade for Better Schools" was launched. Influenced by developments in Manitoba, a great cry against bilingualism arose. The message to the government was clear: foreign-language instruction had to cease "for the good of the future Canadian citizenship of this Province."[58]

The debate continued at a fever pitch into 1917, as resolutions for unilingualism were passed by all major English-speaking organizations in the province — from the Saskatchewan School Trustees' Association to the Loyal Orange Lodges. In June of 1917, the government finally reacted by commissioning an American educational expert, Dr. H.W. Foght, to survey educational conditions in the province, especially in the rural areas.

Foght's report was not flattering to the bilingual schools. In his wisdom, he equated poor school districts with non-English districts. He especially singled out the Ukrainian schools: they were "unsanitary," "very crowded," and without a "class in the government and history of the British Empire and Saskatchewan." Further, the teachers had a "very limited" capacity in English, and their students repeated their grammatical errors. According to Foght, children in these schools were not "getting the training in citizenship that is so essential in a democratic nation." His recommendation, therefore, was blunt: with the exception of French, all languages other than English should be completely excluded from the public schools during school hours.[59]

Foght's conclusion was released in March of 1918 and was supplemented by hundreds of letters to the premier's office from organizations such as the Loyal Orange Association and the Sons of England of Saskatchewan. They demanded English exclusively in the public schools.[60] The pressure was overwhelming. On 27 December 1918, the government of W.M. Martin (Scott retired in late 1916) dealt a death blow to bilingual education by amending the School Act, abrogating the provisions that had allowed instruction in languages other than English. The new regulation stated that with the exception of French, which received minor consideration, "English shall be the sole language of instruction in all schools and no language other than English shall be taught during school hours."[61] In retrospect, a sledge hammer had been used to kill a fly, since there were only 80 French-English, 73 German-English, and 39 Ukrainian-English schools out of more than 4,000 public schools in the province.[62]

There was little that Ukrainians could do against the attack on their teachers and schools. With a suspicious, hostile public and ever-increasing restrictions on their civil liberties becoming a preoccupation, Ukrainian leaders attested their loyalty to Canada and the British Empire and kept a low profile. Their pleas for a more tolerant attitude through delegations, conventions, and the press were ignored. As in Manitoba, the die had been cast.

The School Conflict in Alberta

Although having the same regulations for non-English language study as Saskatchewan, in Alberta the concept of bilingualism never fully materialized. From the beginning, the provincial administration refused to allow any segregation in the educational system and demanded that all teachers in the province conform to minimum qualifications. Two other factors assured the government tight control over educational policy. The English School for Foreigners in Vegreville, not established until 1913, was granted no stipulation that graduates could teach in Ukrainian districts, and Robert Fletcher enforced the government line as Supervisor of Schools Among the Foreigners with the power to act as an official trustee.

Nevertheless, demands for Ukrainian–English schools arose; the source was Peter Svarich of Vegreville. A native of Galicia, a university graduate, and formerly a lieutenant in the Austrian army, Svarich arrived in Canada in 1900, the head of a contingent of 300 Ukrainians. Pursuing activities which ranged from gold mining in the Yukon to operating a store and post office near Vegreville, in 1905 the energetic Svarich was employed by the provincial government to organize and build schools in Ukrainian districts.[63] He did his job well. By 1909, he was the secretary-treasurer of nine schools.[64] Although a staunch supporter of the Liberal administration in Alberta, Svarich became increasingly concerned over the government's lack of educational policy in the Ukrainian districts and over Robert Fletcher's activities as Supervisor of Schools Among the Foreigners.[65] In March of 1909, he called a convention of Ukrainian Liberals in Vegreville. He had drafted a petition which pointed out the critical shortage of bilingual teachers and recommended that Ukrainian teachers be allowed to come from Manitoba and Saskatchewan to teach temporarily in Ukrainian districts while a training school was established to prepare Ukrainian–English teachers.[66] The petition was approved and sent to A.C. Rutherford, the provincial premier.

The premier's response was polite but vague; no immediate action was forthcoming. But after a Ukrainian delegation from Edmonton met with the premier in December of 1909 with much the same requests, the government began to take notice. Rutherford agreed to establish a training school (if numbers warranted it) and would "consider" appointing Ukrainian school organizers.[67] Two years later, the promises remained unfulfilled.

Svarich, in February of 1912, convened another convention of delegates from the surrounding school districts. A list of demands from 95 trustees and 66 other delegates was submitted to the government. The list reiterated Svarich's proposals and added demands that the School Act be published in Ukrainian and that the Department of Education approve Ukrainian textbooks that had been prepared by Svarich.[68] Another committee, led by Andrew Shandro, president of the newly established Association of Ukrainian School Trustees, met with the Minister of Education, D.R. Mitchell. Although nothing was resolved in a subsequent exchange of letters between Mitchell and Svarich, who had been made the association's secretary, a training school was promised.[69] Before the matter could be pursued, Mitchell was replaced by J.R. Boyle in May of 1912, when the new premier, A.L. Sifton, reorganized his cabinet. But Svarich was encouraged. The new Minister of Education represented the Sturgeon constituency, which contained a large Ukrainian vote. Perhaps now they would receive a sympathetic hearing. Boyle, in June of 1912, was reminded of the convention resolutions and asked to give an immediate official response.[70] On 23 June, Boyle repeated the old promise to open a training school and intimated that the School Act would be translated into Ukrainian, but that was as far as he went.

Svarich and other Ukrainian Liberals then sought to apply more political pressure. With a provincial election coming up in April of 1913, they began organizing in five constituencies — Victoria, Pakan, Vegreville, Whitford, and Vermillion — where the Ukrainians were most numerous. Their aim was to nominate and elect Ukrainian Liberals so that they could influence policy in the provincial legislature. On 15 January 1913, another Vegreville convention was called to assess the political situation. The immediate problem was the government's proposed redistribution of electoral boundaries, which would ensure that Ukrainian majorities did not exist in the revised constituencies. A committee composed of Svarich, Andrew Shandro, Paul Rudyk, Roman Kremar-Solodukha, Michael Gowda, and Gregory Kraykiwsky, all of whom at least nominally supported the Liberal Party, arranged a meeting with Premier Sifton and Boyle to object to the proposed redistribution. A meeting was held on 21 January 1913, at which the committee members restated their old demands and strongly urged that constituencies that had Ukrainian majorities be formed from which Ukrainian candidates could be elected.[71]

The government chose to ignore these demands. To add insult to injury, no Ukrainian Liberal candidates were nominated, with the exception of Shandro, in the constituencies where a heavy Ukrainian vote could be expected. Furious at the snubbing they had received from the Liberal hierarchy,[72] Svarich, Rudyk, Gowda, Mykailyshyn, and Kraykiwsky decided to run as independent candidates. Mykailyshyn and Kraykiwsky even had the audacity to contest Sturgeon and Vermillion, respectively, against Boyle and Sifton.

All of the independents were defeated. Indeed, only one Ukrainian candidate was elected: Andrew Shandro, who was the official Liberal candidate in the Whitford constituency. Shandro, although he was the first Ukrainian M.L.A. in Canada, proved less than accommodating to his countrymen. Born in Bukovyna in 1886, he came to Canada in 1898. A successful businessman, he became a homestead inspector for the Dominion government and, prior to his election, was the postmaster in the village of Shandro. Although actively involved in school affairs and a member of a number of delegations which met with the provincial administration pressing for Ukrainian school rights, during the election campaign Shandro condemned the use of Ukrainian in the public schools on the grounds that there was no official Ukrainian language or nationality.[73] Nationalist Ukrainians strongly suspected that Shandro was a Russophile. Indeed, this suspicion was confirmed when the Alberta School Act was finally published in the macaronic Ukrainian-Russian dialect favoured by the Russophiles.[74] Boyle publicly stated that the Ukrainian language was a dialect of Russian and that Ukrainians should be referred to as "little Russians" because they were a "branch of the great Muscovite nation."[75] Shandro fully endorsed Boyle's statement.

It appeared that Shandro was being used by the Liberal Party to punish the Ukrainian malcontents. His victory, however, proved illusory. His outraged opponent, Paul Rudyk, initiated court proceedings to have the election declared null and void because "notorious systematic, corrupt and unlawful practices were carried on before, at, during and after the election by Shandro and his agents."[76] It appeared that Shandro had cheated. He was eventually unseated when it was verified that payments were made to certain electors to induce them to vote for Shandro. After a series of court proceedings, a new by-election was ordered for 15 March 1915.

In this election, Shandro's opponent was Roman Kremar-Solodukha, a socialist turned nationalist. The editor of *Novyny* (News), which was founded in Edmonton in January of 1913, Kremar-Solodukha violently opposed the denial of the Ukrainian language in the public schools. He believed the language right to be constitutional.[77] Kremar-Solodukha had been instrumental in establishing, in December of 1913, a 14-man committee on native-language schools in Alberta. Among other activities, the committee collected funds for Ukrainian private schools and to defeat the hypocritical Liberals at the next election.[78] Unfortunately for Kremar-Solodukha, by 1915 bilingual schools had become a spent force as an issue and Shandro, a long-time resident of the constituency (unlike Kremar-Solodukha who was a parachute candidate from Edmonton), emerged victorious.

Events after the provincial election of 1913 conspired against Ukrainians as a political force within the province. The first blow came when Boyle, within a month of the election, cancelled all the teaching permits of Ukrainian teachers. Since 1910, Ukrainians trained at Brandon and Regina had been trickling into Alberta and had been given permits to teach in Ukrainian districts. Suddenly, their livelihoods had been taken away. In Boyle's eyes, these teachers (13 in total) were agitators with ulterior motives to serve; most of them had publicly supported the independent Ukrainian candidates. To the cynical it appeared that Boyle was meting out punishment to the rebellious Ukrainian Liberals.

The government's ostensible argument was that these "intruders" were not qualified to teach in Alberta. The man responsible for the purge was Robert Fletcher. He took his job seriously, and in the process precipitated the "Great Ruthenian Revolt of 1913." Fletcher's target was the Ukrainian enclaves north-east of Edmonton. He visited the school-board trustees of Oleskiw, Podala, Molodia, Zawale, Spring Creek, Parashevia, and Stanislawow and persuaded them in each case to dismiss the "unqualified" Ukrainian teacher and hire a "qualified" Anglo-Celtic. All complied, although with considerable reluctance.

However, at the Vladymir School near Mundare, he ran into difficulty when the school board refused to dismiss its teacher. Fletcher then, with the approval of the Department of Education, dismissed the board and assumed the position of official school trustee. A "qualified" teacher was placed in charge of the school. The same procedure was used for the Kolomea School near Mundare and for the Lwiw School near Lamont.

At the Bukovyna School north of Vegreville, Fletcher encountered yet more stubborn opposition. The trustees of this school refused to fire W. Chumer, the teacher in charge of the school. Fletcher promptly dismissed the trustees and again, with himself as official trustee, appointed a suitable replacement. The matter did not end there, however. On 15 July 1913, 20 ratepayers incensed by Fletcher's high-handed action assembled on the school grounds. An ex-trustee disrupted the class and dismissed the children. A trial ensued after which this ex-trustee was fined and the Anglo-Celtic instructor re-installed. The former trustees then built a private school next to the public school and rehired W.

Chumer as their teacher. Chumer taught about 30 pupils while Mr. Armstrong, the "qualified" instructor, had none. This state of affairs continued until the end of 1913 when the ratepayers were finally forced by heavy fines to conform to the school ordinance.

Meanwhile, on 1 December 1913, Fletcher had discovered that the ex-treasurer was collecting taxes from the ratepayers in order to pay the private teacher for his services. He ordered the "leading belligerents" of the district to pay taxes directly to him or face the confiscation of some of their property. When his warnings were ignored, on 15 December he seized a horse from each of the five culprits he had notified. In one case he ended up scuffling with an old Ukrainian woman who would not give up the family's animal. After seeking legal aid to no avail, the residents finally paid their taxes. The ex-treasurer also paid Fletcher the taxes he collected. By the end of 1913, the "Great Ruthenian Revolt" had been put down.[79]

This most ludicrous series of events was significant. To the Ukrainian community it represented a diabolical plot to subvert Ukrainian aspirations.[80] To the opponents of bilingualism in the prairies, such as J.W. Dafoe and the powerful *Manitoba Free Press*, it was a "decisive stand" on "educational efficiency."[81]

The final blow to bilingualism in the province came with the failure of the School for Foreigners in Vegreville. The institution, under the direction of W.A. Stickles, a former school principal in Calgary, was designed to teach English to those who desired to enter business or the teaching profession. The school opened on 3 February 1913 with a male student population of 9 which grew to 37 in 1914. Problems arose immediately. First, there was a misconception about what the school was designed to do. A great many students believed that they would be granted teachers' certificates to teach after attending the school for one or two years. This was not the case, since there was only one standard for teachers in Alberta and all students wishing to become instructors had to pass departmental examinations and complete their course of training at the provincial normal schools.[82] Second, there were problems with the operation of the institution. The rules and regulations were strict. Students were forbidden to play cards, swear, frequent hotels or pool rooms, and smoke in the school or dormitory. They were to be in bed by 10 p.m. and could not absent themselves from class, meals, or sleeping quarters without the permission of the principal. Finally, only English could be used in class, in the dining room, and indeed in all forms of communication.[83] Many of the students must have felt as though they were in an Anglican monastery. The boiling point was reached when Mrs. Stickles attempted to teach Protestant hymns on Sundays. The students went on strike on 7 December 1913.

When they refused an appeal from Stickles to return to classes, the entire affair was deferred to the Department of Education for resolution.

Stickles was eventually exonerated (in the spring of 1915) and some of the more vocal students were expelled. But after this incident, the institution's days were numbered. Stickles resigned and the school went through two more principals in rapid succession before it was unceremoniously closed at the end of June, 1918. It had failed to graduate a single Ukrainian teacher.

That bilingual schools emerged appeared to most Anglo-Celtics as an aberration caused by militant Catholicism, unworthy politicians, and unscrupulous immigrant nationalists. Catholicism opposed the "national ideal" which demanded that "all children shall meet together in the public school so that the whole mass of the people may be welded together into a homogeneous nationality by the power of a uniform educational system."[84] Corrupt politicians had encouraged the immigrants "to regard their vote as an article of commerce, to be bartered to the highest bidder," in the process granting too many concessions.[85] And the immigrant nationalists found the "right legal procedures that had their English-speaking neighbours at their mercy."[86]

The unilingual movement of the English-speaking population of the prairies was nothing less than a crusade for the future of English Canada. Under the rubric of providing better teaching of English, improving the attendance of students, and strengthening the qualifications of teachers, minority educational rights were suppressed. The coming of the Great War, with its rhetoric about saving democracy (equated with saving the Empire) gave the final push to the unilingual movement. It ensured that Anglo-Celtic conformity would triumph.

CHAPTER 13

CONSOLIDATING THE RELIGIOUS QUESTION

From the day Ukrainian immigrants set foot in Canada, they found themselves in confusing religious circumstances with a multitude of denominations seeking to fill the spiritual vacuum. However, after 1905, the competition for the Ukrainian soul had narrowed somewhat; in the field were the Greek Catholic Church under the jurisdictional control of the Roman Catholic hierarchy, the Independent Greek Church which received financial support from the Presbyterians, and the Russian Orthodox Church directed by the Holy Synod in St. Petersburg.

Eventually, the Independent Greek Church and the Russian Orthodox Church were egested as alien by the bulk of the Ukrainians. The Greek Catholic Church in Canada, after almost two decades of impotence, attempted to break out of the imposed Roman Catholic framework and assert its traditional hegemony over the Ukrainians. It secured a bishop for its Canadian flock.

The emergence of Greek Catholic clericalism under a determined bishop, however, led to a schism. The nationalist intelligentsia, bent on creating progressive secular and ecclesiastical institutions, repudiated the Catholic clergy's claims to spiritual authority and secular leadership and established an alternative: The Ukrainian Greek Orthodox Church.

Roman Catholic Policy and the Ukrainians

Greek Catholic Ukrainians fell under the religious jurisdiction and care of the Catholic administration already in place in Canada — the Oblate

Order of the Latin rite. The result was confusion and misunderstanding. First, Ukrainian Catholics found themselves without genuine religious leadership; priests who knew the Eastern rite were scarce, while Latin missionaries were, by and large, ignorant of the Old Slavonic liturgy and traditions. Second, much to the vexation of the Ukrainians, who were accustomed to married clergy, the Roman Catholic clergy was celibate, contemptuous of married Greek Catholic priests and insistent that only celibate priests enter the country. And third, the Ukrainians, not understanding Catholic jurisdictional regulations or that the church was separate from the state, saw the Roman Catholic ministering as an attempt to subjugate them. This belief was reinforced when the Roman Catholic Church sought to register all Greek Catholic Church buildings and lands under its ecclesiastical authority.

Although sympathetic to the Ukrainians, the Roman Catholic hierarchy had as its prime concern establishing a "Catholic Empire" in the west; it therefore firmly resisted any modification of its authority. Nevertheless, it soon became evident that if steps were not taken to accommodate the Ukrainians, the struggle for the retention of their souls would be lost to the Russian Orthodox Church and to the Presbyterians via the Independent Greek Church.

Many Ukrainian Catholics discovered that they had much more in common with Russian Orthodox missionaries than they had with the Latin priests. First, the Russian church employed the Old Slavonic and the same form of Mass as the Greek Catholic Church and the Orthodox Church in Bukovyna. Second, Russian Orthodox priests did not demand the incorporation of parish property nor did they charge large fees for their services. They did not need to do so; the Holy Synod in St. Petersburg subsidized the church in North America to the extent of $77,850 annually.[1] And third, the Russian priests were able to convince "the less instructed" Ukrainian Catholics that they were really "little Russians" indistinguishable from the full-fledged Russians.

Under the astute direction of Archimandrite Arsenii Chekhovtsev, the Russian Orthodox Church in Canada forged ahead. Between 1905 and 1911, Chekhovtsev converted many Greek Catholics to Russian Orthodoxy from his base in Winnipeg. In 1908 he began publishing the *Kanadyiskaia Nyva* (Canadian Field), which promoted Pan-Russianism among the Ukrainians. He also initiated a residence school in Edmonton. Chekhovtsev's activities were cut short, however, when he departed for Russia, frustrated by the Holy Synod's failure to name him Canadian bishop. Nevertheless, the church continued to flourish, boasting of 110 parishes by 1916.[2]

Alongside the Russian Orthodox Church, the Independent Greek Church vied for Ukrainian souls. It was an outgrowth of the defunct

"Seraphimite movement."[3] Kyrylo Genik, John Bodrug, and Ivan Negrych, the latter two school teachers and former pupils of Manitoba College, made a secret agreement in 1904 with the Presbyterian Church. In exchange for financial assistance, they promised to follow evangelical Protestant doctrines. Although the church retained the Eastern rite, it was to be Presbyterian in spirit and democratic in form. Independent of the Vatican, the Russian Holy Synod, and all eastern patriarchies, it was governed by a sobor made up of clergymen and by delegates from each congregation which met at intervals (of one to three years) to elect a consistory. The consistory — president, secretary, treasurer, and superintendent — served as the executive body of the church and had as its prime responsibility the ordaining of clergymen. On a local level, parishes were governed by their ministers and three elected lay trustees.

Presbyterian leaders, realizing that Ukrainians would not accept the Scottish church outright, encouraged this peculiar method of proselytism. It seemed the only viable way of "Canadianizing" and "Christianizing" the Ukrainians.[4]

For a time this arrangement proved successful. In 1905, the Ukrainian-Presbyterian newspaper, *Ranok* (Morning), began publishing. Meanwhile, a residence school for young Ukrainians was established at Manitoba College; between 1905 and 1912 it attracted more than 200 students who studied the Bible from a Protestant perspective.[5] Other residence schools made their appearance in Teulon and Sifton (Manitoba) and Vegreville (Alberta). The Report of the Board of Home Missions of the Presbyterian Church claimed that, in 1907, 2,484 families throughout the prairies were members of the church while another 948 families were sympathizers. Of the 24 ministers working in the Ukrainian districts, 11 were full-time, receiving a total salary of $480,000 annually from the Home Mission Board.[6] By 1911, the Independent Greek Church had 72 congregations, 40 churches, and employed 19 full-time ministers.[7]

With the Russian Orthodox Church and the Independent Greek Church apparently making great progress in wooing Ukrainian Catholics, the Roman Catholic leaders became alarmed. As one devoted Catholic author noted:

Thousands and thousands of these Greek Catholics were scattered through the prairies; roaming flocks without shepherds, a prey to ravening wolves. Heresy, schism, atheism, socialism and anarchy openly joined hands to rob these poor people of the only treasure they had brought with them from the old land — their Catholic faith. Presbyterian ministers . . . celebrate among them "bogus masses";

schismatic emissaries . . . bribe them with "Muscovite money". . . .[8]

For many pious Catholics the struggle for mastery of the Ukrainian soul took on large proportions; Catholicism could not afford the weaning of new Canadians from the faith of their fathers. If the Ukrainians were to be assimilated, it had to be carried out by Catholic agents who would "build around them the protective wall of Catholic life."[9]

Without relinquishing their jurisdictional authority, French-speaking bishops sought ways to alleviate the prejudices of Greek Catholics toward the Roman Catholic Church. Between 1896 and 1904, Archbishop Langevin, Bishop Albert Pascal of St. Albert (Saskatchewan), and Bishop Emile Legal of St. Albert (Alberta) made requests in Rome, Vienna, and Lviv for celibate Ukrainian priests. Their efforts, however, bore little fruit, simply because only three per cent of the Ukrainian clergymen in Galicia were celibate to begin with. A number of Roman Catholic missionaries then adopted the Eastern rite in hopes of finding acceptability among the Ukrainians. Redemptorist Fathers from Belgium — A. Delaere, H. Buls, M. Decamp, and K. Tesher — and priests such as A. Sabourin, D. Claveloux, O. Gagnon, A. Desmarais and Fr. Jean, with the newly learned Eastern rite, performed missionary work among the Ukrainians.[10] They all encountered difficulties; because they submitted to the Latin bishops they were viewed as Judases attempting to "Latinize" the flock which, in old country terms, meant Polish domination.

Slowly it was realized that only the establishment of a Greek Catholic Church eparchy, with a Ukrainian bishop, would suffice to overcome the problem of supervising the Ukrainian Catholics. No one was more aware of this than Father Delaere, "the first monastic missionary priest to undertake systematic and continuous work among the Ukrainians in Western Canada."[11] In 1908, he wrote a long memorandum on Catholic Ukrainians, stressing the inadequacy of Ukrainian Catholic services and the danger of conversion by the Presbyterians.[12] Delaere came to the conclusion that the appointment of a Ukrainian bishop in Canada was essential to the welfare of the Ukrainian Catholics.

The "Ruthenian Question" was given wide publicity at the first Catholic Missionary Congress in America in Chicago, 15 to 18 November 1908. A representative of the Catholic Church Extension Society of Canada, quoting extensively from Delaere's *Memorandum*, declared that there were 100,000 Ukrainian Catholics in western Canada without parishes or priests.[13] Thereafter, a number of articles on the subject appeared in the *Catholic Register,* suggesting that action be taken by the National Catholic Council which was scheduled to convene in Quebec City in 1909.

The highest Catholic Church official in Canada, the Apostolic Delegate His Excellency S. Sbarretti, also became immersed in Ukrainian religious affairs. He wrote to Delaere in June of 1909 requesting him to prepare a report for the council. Delaere obliged and, as a result, Sbarretti presented a forceful brief on the condition of the Ukrainian Catholic Church. Signed by Delaere, Reverend A. Fylypiw, representing the Basilian Fathers, and Sabourin on behalf of the secular priests, the document, entitled *The Memorial in Regard to Ruthenians of North-Western Canada,* was the first explicit statement supported by the Canadian priesthood which advocated the appointment of a Ukrainian bishop for Canada.[14] Thus, through the initiative of Delaere, the interest of Sbarretti, and the alarm of the French-speaking bishops, the Ukrainian Catholic Question was brought not only to the attention of the whole Canadian Catholic hierarchy but of the Vatican as well.

Ecclesiastical decision-makers were cautious and proceeded without haste, especially as the appointment entailed a substantive change in church policy. Indeed, Rome may have temporized or set the question of a Ukrainian bishopric in Canada aside indefinitely had it not been for the timely visit to Canada of Metropolitan Andrew Sheptytsky.

The Catholic Accommodations

Andrew Sheptytsky, Metropolitan for Ukrainians in Galicia, Archbishop of Lviv, and bishop of Kaminetz Podilsky, was well-known to the Catholic hierarchy in Canada. As early as 1900, Reverend Father Albert Lacombe had visited Sheptytsky and extended an invitation from the western Canadian hierarchy to tour Ukrainian settlements. The Metropolitan was receptive, but he was denied a trip at that time because the Roman Congregation of Propaganda Fide objected. He required the permission of Count Mieczyslav Cardinal Liedechowski, who, as representative of the Polish aristocracy, scoffed at such a journey.[15] Nevertheless, Sheptytsky familiarized himself with the "Ruthenian problem," writing two pastoral letters to his uprooted flock and sending his personal secretary, Reverend Vasyl Zholdak, to act as a liaison between the Latin rite bishops and the few Eastern rite priests in the country.

Sheptytsky finally did manage to come to Canada in 1910 to attend the International Eucharistic Congress in Montreal. After a ceremonious welcome by Archbishop Langevin, Bishop Legal, and Bishop Pascal, he undertook a two-month tour of Ukrainian settlements to assess their needs. As a result of this sojourn, in March of 1911 Sheptytsky prepared an *Address on the Ruthenian Question to Their Lordships the Archbishops and Bishops of Canada*. In cogent form he presented arguments for the creation of a separate Greek Catholic eparchy and for the appointment of a Ukrainian Greek Catholic bishop.

For Sheptytsky the critical question was whether the coming generation of Ruthenians would remain Catholic or become Protestant or schismatic. The Ukrainian Protestants who, in Sheptytsky's mind, were aided by the Radical Party of Galicia, were the most dangerous. He attributed their success to a zealous organization, the fact that they had infested the teachers' training schools, and their control of public opinion through a number of periodicals. Whereas the Protestants had at least five Ukrainian-language newspapers promoting their views, Ukrainian Catholics had none. Sheptytsky noted:

> Protestants have managed to get hold of the public and national opinion of the Ruthenian-Canadians. They it is who give the tone, who decide what constitutes the public and national good; they it is who present themselves before the Government as representatives of the Ruthenian people and this is a victory gained . . . which has been most fruitful to them.[16]

The problem, Sheptytsky believed, could not be solved by simply increasing the number of priests. It was "absolutely necessary to obtain from the Holy See the nomination of a Bishop of Ruthenian Rite and nationality, who has entire jurisdiction over all the Ruthenians, or, at least . . . a separate diocese with a limited territory, however small in size and delegation of the bishop of the place in other dioceses."[17] The Ukrainians desired their own bishop; otherwise, outstanding problems, such as the registration of church property in the name of ecclesiastical authority, would not be solved. As Ukrainian Catholics bluntly told him: "To give up our church to ecclesiastical authority can only be done in return for the help of the Latin bishops in obtaining a Ruthenian bishop: if we give it up without condition we run the risk of never getting a bishop of our own."[18] Thus, Sheptytsky emphasized that although only 21 out of 93 churches were registered, "the others . . . could easily be registered in the name of a Ruthenian bishop and are only independent because there is not one."[19]

Sheptytsky was willing to accept compromises in exchange for an Eastern rite bishopric. These included only celibate priests and the continued missionary work of Latin rite priests among the Ukrainians, provided they used the Eastern rite and learned the Slavic language.

In his recommendation of a Ukrainian bishop for Canada, Sheptytsky could point to one other important fact: the Ukrainians in the United States had their own bishop. After 20 years of conflict between the Roman Catholic bishops, mostly Irish, and Ukrainian Catholics, in 1907 Soter Ortynsky, a Basilian monk, was appointed bishop for Greek Catholics in the United States. Although Ortynsky did not have full autonomy but was an auxiliary of Roman Catholic bishops in whose territories Greek Catholics resided (complete independence for Ortynsky was not given by the Vatican until 1913), Sheptytsky could argue that a precedent had been set which altered a traditional principle of the Roman Catholic Church, that all Catholics living in a given territory were under the jurisdiction of single ordinary.[20] In his *Address*, Sheptytsky defended Ortynsky's appointment, despite Ortynsky's difficulties with the Latin hierarchy, and concluded that in Canada as in the United States, "the nomination of a bishop is the only way to save this people and preserve them from the danger of Protestantism."[21]

As a result of Sheptytsky's pleadings, Archbishop Langevin, who rejected such a proposal when it was first suggested by Father Delaere, Bishop Legal, and Bishop Pascal, informed Sbarretti in a special declaration on 28 July 1911 that all Roman Catholic bishops of northwestern Canada were favourably disposed toward the idea of creating a separate ecclesiastical province of Ukrainians in Canada. With that declaration, the outcome was sealed. In 1912, the Apostolic Capitol formed a separate ecclesiastical province for the Greek Catholic Church and Sheptytsky appointed Reverend Nykyta Budka, the prefect of the theological Seminary of Lviv, as bishop.

Bishop Budka and the Ukrainian Community

It must have been with some trepidation that the head of the newly created ordinarite began his duties. Upon arrival in December of 1912, Budka had at his disposal but 20 clergymen — 5 Basilians, 6 priests of Ukrainian origin, 4 Redemptorists, and 5 French Canadians.[22] According to the census of 1911, they were charged with serving a population of approximately 75,000. A formidable task indeed!

Undaunted, Budka set about consolidating his authority. He requested the Canadian government to pass an Act whereby Greek Catholic churches could be incorporated under his jurisdiction. He was ensured the legal possession of church properties when the House of Commons recognized the "Ruthenian" Greek Catholic Church in 1913. In the same year, the first convention of Ukrainian Catholic priests was held in Yorkton, Saskatchewan, where, under Budka's diligent guidance, the rules and regulations of the church were laid down. Budka was ambitious; his goal was no less than to elevate the Greek Catholic

Church to its "traditional" role of leadership within the Ukrainian community. He fervently desired Greek Catholic hegemony over the Ukrainians in Canada. Determined to unite his flock "as a single people," Budka envisioned himself as the Moses of his people "sent to them in response to their prayers to show them the way out of the desert of neglect, gather them in their misery, lead them, defend and protect them . . . so that they might live as men should and achieve the end for which men are placed on this earth — the attainment of happiness in heaven."[23]

In attempting to realize his objectives, Budka had little difficulty in dealing with the Independent Greek Church and the Orthodox Russian Church, despite all the anxiety expressed in Catholic circles. Nor were the socialists a threat. The challenges to his authority from these groups were subdued. The nationalist intelligentsia, led by the bilingual school teachers and their newspaper, *Ukrainskyi Holos*, was a different matter totally.

Support for the Independent Greek Church was waning even before Budka's arrival in Canada. By 1912, the Presbyterian Church was heavily in debt; statistics for 1911-12 revealed that the expenditures of the church exceeded its income by more than half a million dollars.[24] With financial matters weighing heavily on their minds, Presbyterian leaders began to question their policy of giving aid to the missions of other nationalities. Why were they "paying good Presbyterian dollars to help the service of another church, a very ritualistic church at that?"[25] Most did not advocate abandoning the Independent Greek Church but rather forcing it to conform more closely to Presbyterian practices in exchange for continued financial support. To this end, the Synod of the Presbyterian church demanded that the Independent Greek Church abolish its consistory and compel its clergymen to submit directly to the Synod.

The actions of the Synod resulted in a protest against Protestantism. Rather than submit to the Synod, a number of priests resigned. A series of lawsuits over the possessions of the churches followed. When the courts decided against the Independent parish trustees in favour of the Presbyterian Church, independents defected en masse. Prominent among these was Ivan Bodrug, the co-founder of the Independent Greek Church. He refused to join the Presbyterian Church, stating that:

> Every nation has its own specific psychology and culture and every national church has to reflect and represent the psychology and culture of its nation. And if any steps, at any given church, are to be taken then the same reformation must be taken gradually, in line with the spiritual growth and respect for the traditions of that nation. . . .

The forcing of some alien idea upon any nation or compelling some people to accept another's denomination never succeeds.[26]

Indeed, the marriage between Ukrainian Orthodoxy and Scottish Protestantism came to an end when, in 1912, the Presbyterian Church curtailed its subsidy and closed the residence school. The 21 clergymen who had not defected formally joined the Presbyterian Church.[27] The majority of disenchanted followers, with Budka's encouragement, flocked to the Greek Catholic fold.

Others, however, went to the Russian Orthodox Church. Yet Budka's appointment robbed that church of its vitality. He offered an alternative which appeared wholly Ukrainian. In the end, however, two developments overseas completely undermined the Orthodox Church. The Russian Revolution of 1917 deprived the church of its source of revenue, and the short-lived independence of Ukraine, which stimulated Ukrainian nationalism, drained the church of its authority.

Meanwhile, the socialists promulgated anti-clericalism. *Robotchyi Narod* accused all churches of subverting the teachings of Christ and the priests of forgetting the "apostolic, humanitarian duties introduced by Christ."[28] With the arrival of Budka, the publishers of *Robotchyi Narod* stepped up their anti-clerical campaign by issuing, in May of 1913, a monthly periodical entitled *Kadylo* (Censor). Edited by Pavlo Krat, the journal, in a humourous but vicious tone, waged war on all priests, especially the Catholic clergy. Its favourite themes were the clerical exploitation of Ukrainian immigrants and the alleged licentious habits of celibate priests. Muckraking articles supplemented by colourful cartoons and satirical verse no doubt brought both amusement and irritation, but hardly persuaded parishioners to denounce their priests or abandon their churches.

Far more formidable was the nationalist intelligentsia, which rejected Budka's claim to Ukrainian leadership under the Greek Catholic Church and insisted that "secular enlightenment" was key to the healthy development of the Ukrainian-Canadian community. From the day it began publication, *Ukrainskyi Holos* became the undisputed mouthpiece of this group. Led by former school teachers — Wasyl Kudryk, the paper's first editor, Taras Ferley, its first manager, and J.W. Arsenych, president of the Ukrainian Publishing Company — *Holos* approached religion from a "rational scientific perspective." "It is necessary," an editorial stated, "that the people do not allow themselves to be led blindly by any kind of religion or church. . . . The concern is not about religion on paper but about religion in life. Let us remember that learning and justice is the greatest religion."[29]

The nationalists' distrust of church politics was underlined when in

Winnipeg Sheptytsky celebrated Mass in the Basilian church and in the Polish Roman Catholic Holy parish but refused to enter a Greek Catholic Church which did not recognize the authority of Archbishop Langevin. *Holos* also pointed to some of Sheptytsky's old world sins, such as his condemnation of Myroslav Sichinsky, the assassin of the Polish Governor of Galicia, and of Adam Kotsko, a student who was killed by Polish police in 1908 during a violent demonstration for the establishment of a Ukrainian university in Lviv. *Holos* concluded that Sheptytsky's visit to Canada was not only a "sham" but would soon be forgotten.[30]

In its first pronouncement on the first Ukrainian bishop, *Holos* noted that "English papers called the Ruthenian bishop also a Roman Catholic Ruthenian bishop and not Greek Catholic. . . ."[31] While demanding clarification, it continued its bitter attack on the French Greek Catholic priests, labelling them "spies" of the Roman Catholic Church.[32] *Holos* proposed that all Redemptorists be recalled by Rome and the order abolished, that the priests be of Ukrainian nationality exclusively, and that the Eastern rite be strictly adhered to with no modification toward the Latin rite. Budka, financially dependent on the Roman Catholic hierarchy, was in no position to grant such demands.

The nationalist intelligentsia concluded that if Budka had no real power, Greek Catholic churches should not be incorporated under his authority. Wasyl Kudryk, after a tour of Ukrainian communities, pointed out that the "Act to Incorporate the Ruthenian Greek Catholic Episcopal Corporation of Canada" did not stipulate that a Ukrainian must be bishop but left it open to interpretation so that, conceivably, the future "bishop for Ruthenians" could be of any nationality. Thus, there was no guarantee that property incorporated in Budka's name would remain firmly in Ukrainian hands.[33] Budka's position was further undermined in the eyes of the nationalists when, by a decree of the congregation of propaganda *Ea Semper*, 11 August 1913, married priests were forbidden to enter Canada.

At the instigation of *Holos*, a number of protest meetings were organized to denounce the *Ea Semper* and demand the eviction of French and foreign priests. At least 10 Greek Catholic parishes heeded the appeal of *Holos*, refusing to have their church property incorporated under the charter of the bishop until the demands of *Holos* were met.[34] If Budka failed, *Holos* suggested that perhaps it would be better "to return to the faith of our forefathers, to the true Ruthenian faith, to Orthodoxy and to send for Orthodox clergy."[35] Other articles followed, advising the establishment of an independent national church. By 1914, *Holos* was taking a strong pro-Orthodox position, insisting that "in Catholicism as in Russian Orthodoxy, Ukrainian patriotism is not compatible. The one and the other desire to make a Ukrainian a servile slave and not a patriot, not even a man, but only a blind tool of their own interest."[36]

The beleaguered bishop was not an individual to tolerate such attacks for long. He began a counter-offensive against the nationalist intelligentsia and their irreverent newspaper. His mouthpiece was the *Kanadysky Rusyn* (Canadian-Ruthenian). Established in May of 1911 with financial aid from the Roman Catholic hierarchy, the newspaper's chief aim was "to propagate and defend the foundations of the Greek Catholic faith."[37] Reflecting on Budka's views, *Kanadysky Rusyn* condemned those of the intelligentsia who exhibited "a hostile attitude toward our beautiful ancient Greek Catholic Rite and religion."[38] Throughout 1913 and 1914, the newspaper directed an unrelenting stream of abuse on all who would criticize the bishop and Catholicism.

Immediately after the outbreak of World War I, however, Budka got into trouble. Austria-Hungary, in an effort to promote unity within its ethnically diverse empire, promised to create a separate Ukrainian state if the empire was on the winning side. Budka was sympathetic to Austria rather than to Russia, especially as the Tsarist regime was attempting to annex eastern Galicia. Describing Austria as "the threatened fatherland," he urged all male Ukrainians to "immediately report to the consulate and leave for the old country."[39] Such a call may have resulted in severe political and social repercussions against the Ukrainian immigrants, as Russia was Britain's ally. Fortunately, it found little support in Canada. Budka quickly realized his blunder and repudiated it within a week. However, it gave more ammunition to the nationalist intelligentsia, which promptly denounced it as another example of Budka's subservience to Austro-Polish interests.

The Rise of an Independent National Church

World War I soon subdued the debate between Budka and the nationalist intelligentsia. In 1916, however, there was a sudden escalation of the war of words between *Kanadysky Rusyn* and *Ukrainskyi Holos*. It occurred over the type of schooling Ukrainian students should receive. With the Norris government in Manitoba committing itself to the abolition of the bilingual school system, the Ukrainians in Manitoba turned their attention to establishing private institutes or "bursas" in an effort to maintain and promote the Ukrainian language and culture. On 3 July 1915, a general public meeting was held in the Procathedral of St. Vladimir and Olga, Winnipeg, with the aim of founding a Ukrainian bursa. All did not proceed well, however; opinions quickly divided when a nationalist-inspired group proposed that the bursa be non-sectarian in character and earnest Greek Catholics insisted on strict adherence to the Catholic denomination. The Catholics were out-voted and the Adam Kotsko Bursa opened its doors in 1915 on an inter-denominational basis. Unfortunately for its sponsors, it existed for only two years because the alienated Catholics gave it no financial support. Meanwhile, not to be outdone, the Catholics set up their own bursa: the Metropolitan Andrew Sheptytsky Bursa in St. Boniface.

The parting of ways over the Adam Kotsko Bursa was but a prelude of the breach to come. In March of 1916, the Ukrainian Student Club of Saskatoon met to establish a steering committee for a proposed bursa in that city. Named after Petro Mohyla, a seventeenth-century Orthodox leader, the bursa was to be secular, encouraging Ukrainian students of all denominations to attend and soliciting support from all sectors of the Ukrainian community. And indeed, when it did open in 1916, such was the case: of the 35 students in the residence, 23 were Greek Catholic, 6 were Protestant, 4 were Orthodox, and 2 were Roman Catholic.[40]

Initially, Budka supported the creation of the bursa; he participated in the First National Convention, 4 and 5 August 1916, and delivered a two-hour address before 500 people indicating his approval. Nor did he object to the elected executive which included Osyp Megas as president, Vasyl Swystun as vice-president, Myroslav Stechishin as treasurer, and A.T. Kibzey as secretary.

By the spring of 1917, Budka had second thoughts. Indeed, he bluntly demanded that the executive incorporate the bursa under the episcopal charter and limit admission to Catholic students. Budka's "Catholic only" stance infuriated the nationalists. A delegation consisting of Stechishin, Swystun, and Ferley met with Budka on 16 June 1917 in the hope of dissuading the bishop from such a position. When Budka refused to budge, an angry Swystun let his feelings be known in *Holos*:

> What will you say about this, member share-holders of the P. Mohyla bursa? Will you permit the bishop to grasp the property of the bursa, of which you and all the people with you are joint-owners, not only for himself but also for all his successors and not only for the time of his life but forever and forever? . . . Will you permit the expansion of the clerical group which wants to control your property and all your cultural gains?[41]

In a show of defiance, Swystun and the bursa executive proceeded to acquire a charter under the Companies' Act, 20 January 1917, which renamed the bursa the Petro Mohyla Ukrainian Institute, thus short-circuiting Budka's bid at episcopal incorporation. In explaining this move, Stechishin pointed to the fact that the charter of the episcopal corporation did not guarantee that the Greek Catholic Church would always have a bishop of Ukrainian nationality.[42] Such a rebuttal to Budka was endorsed at the Second National Convention of the institute shareholders held in Saskatoon in December of 1917. More than 700 delegates pledged their moral and financial support to the institute and accused Budka of unfairly attacking "all national work among Ukrainian people in Canada" because it was "independent of the Episcopal Church Corporation."[43]

Budka and *Kanadysky Rusyn* launched an all-out campaign against the institute and its nationalist leaders. For example, it was reported that Belgian Catholic priests in Yorkton refused to give confessions to those who supported the institute, while other priests declared that those who died without confession would not be buried in consecrated ground. Budka himself, in a sermon delivered on Easter Sunday, stated that anyone supporting or sending children to the institute was not Catholic and therefore he would forbid such people marriage, christening of children, and burial in the cemeteries.[44]

These rather high-handed tactics led Swystun to convene protest meetings throughout western Canada. At Meacham, Saskatchewan, for example, resolutions were passed condemning Budka's attack on the institute, emphasizing that the institute was not irreligious as it allowed religious instruction. Secular leaders threatened to embrace Orthodoxy if Budka persisted in maligning them. Those present at the Meacham meeting also demanded changes to the bishop's charter which would guarantee a bishop of Ukrainian nationality, allow church property to remain in the hands of the congregations, and prohibit French and Belgian priests from working among the Catholic Ukrainians.[45]

By 1918, Budka and the nationalist intelligentsia had reached an impasse. Budka would not yield and the nationalists would not compromise. Alienated totally from the Greek Catholic Church, many nationalists saw but one course of action: the creation of their own church which would be progressive and incorporate their ideals while meeting the spiritual needs of Ukrainians.

The movement toward a Ukrainian national church begun in *Holos* gathered momentum in *Kanadiiskyi Farmer*. O.H. Kykawy, a former teacher and the editor of *Kanadiiskyi Farmer*, repeated the criticism that Budka was only a titular bishop of a non-existing diocese.[46] A series of articles followed over a seven-month period. Signed by "Narodyny Svyashchenyk" (National Priest),[47] they proposed a method of organizing the Ukrainian national church. The general characteristics of the proposed new church reflected the ideals of the nationalist intelligentsia: it was to be democratic and national with a bishop and clergy elected by the people and approved by a synod composed equally of clergy and layman. Because the Greek Catholic Church had been an Orthodox Church until 1596, when it recognized the supremacy of the Pope, it was suggested that the new church subscribe to the precepts and practices of the Eastern Orthodox Church.

During this period, letters approving of the national church concept and organization deluged the newspaper. When in March of 1918 Swystun and Stechishin called for a national church convention to examine the bishop's charter, the "National Priest" published a draft of the constitution of the new church. He proposed that parishes elect delegates to a convention to discuss and adopt the 59 articles put forth in the proposed constitution.[48]

On 16 June 1918, Swystun called a confidential meeting of "leading Ukrainians" to discuss "church and national affairs." More than 300 invitations were printed, the list being endorsed by a national committee of 30 prominent Ukrainians. Among the 30 were Wasyl Kudryk, O.H. Kykawy, J.W. Arsenych, T. Ferley, Myroslav Stechishin, A.T. Kibzey, and Peter Svarich, a veritable Who's Who of the nationalist intelligentsia. Conspicuous in his absence from the committee was Swystun who, as principal of the Petro Mohyla Ukrainian Institute, wanted to avoid involving the institute.

There were 154 Ukrainians at the meeting held 18 July and 19 July in Saskatoon. At the end of the conference, resolutions reflecting the accumulated grievances against Budka and the principles of the new church were adopted (see Appendix II for resolutions). A Ukrainian Greek Orthodox Brotherhood was organized to "conduct all the church activities until the time when there will be a legally elected and consecrated bishop, in conformity with the Eastern Orthodox Church."[49] Despite Budka's and *Kanadysky Rusyn*'s condemnation of the "Godless Church," the Ukrainian Greek Orthodox Church came into being.

From the beginning, the Greek Catholic Church was at a disadvantage. Subordinated to the Roman Catholic hierarchy during the critical years of Ukrainian immigration and settlement in Canada, it never recovered to assume its traditional leadership role. After 1910, when the church attempted to establish hegemony over the Ukrainians, it did so from an old world perspective; Budka insisted on a centralized, authoritarian, hierarchical structure which did not reflect the ideals of the intelligentsia or the reality of Canadian life. The result was a schism — the first the Greek Catholic Church had suffered in its 320-year history.

The nationalist intelligentsia, by taking control over the religious destiny of Ukrainian-Canadians, in a real sense re-defined the kind of church many Ukrainians had desired. Still a protector of historical tradition, at the same time the Ukrainian Greek Orthodox Church was in tune with a more democratic and egalitarian environment.

Yet there was nothing inevitable about the process which resulted in the emergence of two dominant Ukrainian churches. Both desired to unite the Ukrainian Canadians, but under different rubrics. Both chose polemics and confrontation rather than understanding and compromise. Conceivably, had Budka been more of a statesman, more tolerant of dissenters, and more appreciative of the role played by the nationalist intelligentsia within the immigrant community, the schism may have been avoided. Conversely, the members of the nationalist intelligentsia, in prompting the schism, believed with equal righteousness that they were restoring the traditional faith while pointing the way to self-reliance and self-esteem. Had they been less hostile and more cognizant of the constraints under which Budka laboured, perhaps the bishop would have been willing to accommodate them.

In the end, the churches retained affinities — both were cut from the Byzantine cloth. The divergence was in the organization. The Greek Catholic Church remained centralized and rigid in its structure; the Greek Orthodox Church provided greater scope for participation by the laity. After 1918, a new chapter in the history of the two churches began, as each sought to consolidate its position at the expense of the other.

CONCLUSION

The beginning of World War I marked the end of the first wave of Ukrainian emigration to Canada. From 1915 to 1919, a total of 10 Ukrainians entered Canada.[1]

The Great War would open another turbulent chapter in the life of Ukrainians in Canada. In its wake, Galicians and Bukovynians would become the objects of suspicion, harassment, and intimidation. As enemy aliens, they would be subject to restrictive regulations and, in many cases, internment and deportation. Events in the old country would also greatly affect the gestalt of the immigrant community. The Ukrainian Revolution of 1917-21, during which Ukrainians declared their independence from Bolshevik Russia, would give the final push toward a national identity: Galicians and Bukovynians would become, collectively, Ukrainians.

Yet that was the future. What of the years 1891 to 1914? The period was doubtless a watershed. For Canadians, prosperity had been achieved, but at the price of an "alien" North-West. For Ukrainians, new seeds had been successfully planted, but with the harvest came the old weeds. For both the host society and the "stalwart" peasants, this period was fraught with new visions, shattered dreams, and sober readjustments.

Summary

In the context of Imperialistic thinking, the North-West represented a hinterland which, when fully developed, would ensure the destiny of

Canada by a continuation of the best that British traditions had to offer. New settlers upholding British-Canadian values would enable the Dominion to shed its peripheral existence within the Empire and assume equal partnership with Great Britain. That was the plan, yet the plan was drastically altered. Strangers ignorant of "British institutions and principles of life" populated the North-West.

The Imperialist concept was subverted by railway and business interests, which forced greater consideration of economic needs rather than social desires. Immigrants thought to be culturally "undesirable" became, in the scheme of things, acceptable for their economic value. The fruition of this policy came during Clifford Sifton's term as Minister of the Interior.

Under Sifton, economic utility outweighed Imperialist sentiment. Through his adherence to "economic benefit," Sifton struck a fatal blow to the notion of a British-Canadian west. The vision of the North-West as the last British outpost was shattered. It would be impossible to make Britishers out of Ukrainians.

After 1905, as the pace of Canada's economic development quickened, there was an increasing demand for cheap, unskilled labourers. The East European tap could not be turned off. Ukrainians were welcome, not only as agricultural settlers but as general labourers in the mines and on the railways. They fulfilled an essential function as "hewers of wood and drawers of water."

Yet the debate over cultural, social, and political acceptability continued. What was to be done about these newcomers? The answer was assimilation; the agents were the churches and the public schools.

Protestants sought to "Canadianize" and "evangelize" the Ukrainians. Their goal was to break the peasant of his old country habits and give him the instruments — linguistic, religious, political, and cultural — to become an Anglo-Canadian. But as the Presbyterian experiment with the Independent Greek Church illustrated, they failed. Protestantism was too alien to grow firm roots within the Ukrainian immigrant community.

The same could be said of the Catholics. Despite the jurisdictional control that the Roman Catholic hierarchy enjoyed over the Greek Catholic newcomers, Ukrainians, by and large, rejected the Latin variant and substituted their traditional Eastern brand. With the official recognition of the Greek Catholic Church and the advent of a Ukrainian bishop, Roman Catholic domination came to an end.

But the Roman Catholic Church, supported by a powerful French-speaking hierarchy in the North-West, had posed a serious threat to the "Canadianization" efforts of the Protestants. Seeking to preserve and nurture the French presence in the North-West, the Roman Catholics promoted bilingual education and separate schools. They emphasized ethnic diversity which, of course, was contrary to the homogeneity espoused by the Protestants. The Ukrainians were caught in the middle of a struggle between two different views of Canada. In the end, both the Roman Catholics and Protestants failed to conscript the immigrants.

Public schools as agents of assimilation were more successful. But after a flirtation with Ruthenian-English schools, a unilingual movement made its bid for supremacy in an English Canada. It appeared that Anglo-Celtic conformity would triumph.

Yet it was impossible to impose Anglo-Celtic conformity on a polyglot populace. It became increasingly obvious to Anglo-Canadians that the North-West would not evolve as a "carbon copy of the east." Pandora's box had been opened; what emerged, however, was not yet clearly defined.

But what of the Ukrainians? Peasants of Galicia and Bukovyna came in search of a new life. Yet in a sense the old world came with them and would act as a buttress against the pressures that threatened their established avenues of existence.

It was difficult to break old world ties and habits. Many never did; from those who did, often a heavy price was extracted. Alienation, self-denial, and hostile surroundings ensured that immigrants lived in crisis, immersed in a world of strangers. Yet there was the one compensation that made it worthwhile, if not for them, then for their children. In Canada, the peasants had a place to stand.

Indeed, a dominant theme in Ukrainian-Canadian history is the land. For a great deal of this period, the Ukrainian immigrants were engaged in the drama of pioneer life with its accompanying horrors — isolation, disease, and death. To "plant an island of domestic life in the wilderness" was a brutal process which often left a bitter legacy.

The process of adaptation was fraught with conflict. It could not be otherwise; old world attitudes interacting with new world realities led to "factionalism" within the Ukrainian immigrant community. Mutually antagonistic groups emerged: Protestants, socialists, nationalists, and clerics.[2]

The Protestant doctrine, to some, was the key to immigrant "enlightment" and "self-improvement." The Independent Greek Church was a manifestation of this belief. While adhering to the Orthodox rite, it preached its dogma in the spirit of Protestantism. Predictably, the church failed.

Others espoused socialism. In the decade before the Great War, the newly created Ukrainian-Canadian proletariat found itself at the bottom of the Canadian industrial system. Given exploitative working conditions, socialism could be expected to have widespread appeal. Yet only a minority supported the Ukrainian-Canadian socialist movement. The utopian ideals of the early Ukrainian socialists, with their roots in old world politics, militated against a large following.

Such was not the case, however, with the Ukrainian nationalist intelligentsia. Identifying themselves with the interests of the Ukrainian people rather than the interests of a particular class, political party, or religious denomination, this group set about organizing the Ukrainian community along secular lines. They emerged as the most articulate and representative group in the Ukrainian-Canadian community.

It was the nationalists who challenged the belated attempt of the Greek Catholic clergy to assert their traditional hegemony over the Ukrainians in the new world. Bent on creating progressive secular and ecclesiastical institutions, they repudiated the church's claims to spiritual and secular leadership and, in the process, established an alternative — the Ukrainian Greek Orthodox Church.

In this formative period of their new world experience, Ukrainians could never be sure of themselves or their actions. Rootless, adrift, living in an unfamiliar milieu, they nevertheless sought, individually and collectively, to establish the viable remnants of their past. Slowly, they discovered the use of power. In spurts, they fought stubbornly to retain and perpetuate their *Weltanschauung*.

By 1914, their place in the North-West was secured, but at a cost. The new world had changed them. They could no longer rely on their heritage to sustain them; they had to adjust. But in the process, they altered their environment.

With the Great War closing in, they wondered, like the Canadians, what the future had in store for them.

Epilogue

The period of Ukrainian immigration into Canada before World War I was succeeded by two others: between 1921 and 1939, approximately 70,000 Ukrainians entered the Dominion, and after World War II (1947 to 1953) a further 30,834 chose Canada as their home. A full history of these inter-war and post-war immigrants is yet to be written, but each group has made a significant contribution by not only preserving but revitalizing the Ukrainian-Canadian community.

Like the first, the second wave of immigrants consisted mainly of peasant farmers. But there were also political refugees and Ukrainian army veterans who fled Soviet Russia after the demise of the short-lived Ukrainian Republic (1917 to 1921). A large number of these tended to enter the industrial sector, gravitating toward urban centres, particularly in Ontario, which in 1941 had a Ukrainian population of 48,158.

The third wave of Ukrainian emigration to Canada was part of the "displaced persons" movement at the end of the Second World War. Many who found themselves in the allied zone of ravaged Europe chose emigration rather than repatriation to their homelands. By and large, this group was highly educated (including intellectuals, professionals, and skilled craftsmen), overwhelmingly urban (the majority settling in Ontario with the Toronto area absorbing 80 per cent), and acutely political (fervently anti-Soviet and dedicated to the ideal of a free Ukraine).

Today there are approximately 600,000 Canadians of Ukrainian origin. Ontario is the home of the largest number, where they are a little more than 2 per cent of the province's population. The Ukrainian fact is most evident, however, in the west, where in Manitoba, Saskatchewan, and Alberta Ukrainians make up 11.5, 9.2, and 8.3 per cent of the population, respectively. Despite their heterogeneous nature and the accompanying mutual suspicion and friction which exists in every immigrant community, collectively Ukrainians have resisted assimilation and have been an important "third force" in promoting and enhancing Canada's multicultural development.

Whether this resistance to assimilation will continue is an open question. Recent studies have reflected the fact that 80 per cent of the Ukrainians in Canada are Canadian-born, and no further notable Ukrainian immigration is expected.[3] The number of Ukrainians in relation to the total Canadian population is declining. The two traditional churches (Ukrainian Catholic and Greek Orthodox) are experiencing difficulty in retaining their membership. Most ominously, descendants of each wave are losing their knowledge of the mother tongue.

But there is also the renewed awareness of ethnic minorities in Canada. In the case of the Ukrainians, this awareness has manifested itself in English-Ukrainian bilingual schools and in the exertion of political pressure to have the linguistic and cultural rights of ethnic minorities recognized and guaranteed in the new Constitution. But perhaps the best safeguard against assimilation lies with the Ukrainians themselves. As this study has shown, they have exhibited a remarkable tenacity in surviving as a group despite the challenges of their history.

APPENDIX I

NATIONALITY AND RELIGION

The following notes and chart provide a short summary of the ethnic background of "Ukrainians," their geographical dispersion, and their religious affiliation.

The Ukrainians: Geo-political Status and Religion circa 1900

	AUSTRO-HUNGARIAN EMPIRE			RUSSIAN EMPIRE
	Galicia	Bukovyna	Carpatho-Ukraine (Subcarpathia)	Ukraine
Political Status	crownland of Austria-Hungary	crownland of Austria-Hungary	in the Kingdom of Hungary (Austria-Hungary)	incorporated into the Russian Empire
Area of occupation (square kilometres)	55,700	5,300	16,700	845,500
Ukrainian Population	3.3 million (43% of the total population)	300,000 (40% of the total population)	400,000	17 million
Dominant Church	Ukrainian Catholic (Uniate)	Ukrainian Greek Orthodox	Ukrainian Catholic (Uniate)	Ukrainian Greek Orthodox

Ethnicity/Nationality

Although **Ukrainian** is the accepted nomenclature to denote ethnicity/nationality, historically Ukrainians have had various names. In the Austro-Hungarian Empire some Ukrainians described themselves as Galician or Bukovynian (Galicia was an old Ukrainian principality dating back to medieval times). Others preferred the designation Ruthenian (in Ukrainian *Rusyny*), which had a religious connotation. Ruthenians were Ukrainian Catholics as opposed to their Orthodox brethren (see note on religion below). In Galicia, Austrian authorities tended to refer to Ukrainians as Ruthenians because the vast majority were Catholic. Part of the confusion over nationality (defined as a group of people of the same race sharing a common language and distinctive cultural traits) was that seldom in their history have Ukrainians been united in a single, geo-political state. Most often they have been subjugated and divided by foreign powers. Thus geographic locale or religious affiliation was tantamount to nationality. Indeed, the Ukrainian peasants from Galicia and Bukovyna, possessing a low level of "national consciousness" and for the most part acquiring only a rudimentary (if that) knowledge of their historical development, often stated their nationality on arrival in Canada as Austrian, Russian, or Polish and were consequently classified as such by Canadian officials. It was not until the census of 1921 that the term Ukrainian was employed to record their nationality. Although in this study the terms Galician, Bukovynian, and Ruthenian have been retained (since they are predominant in the contemporary documentation), they are synonymous with the proper designation, Ukrainian.

Political Status

Galicia, which had been under Polish rule since the latter half of the 1300s, was transferred to Austria in 1772 as a result of the partition of Poland (the first of three) by Austria, Prussia, and Russia. Galicia was to remain under Austrian rule until the break-up of the Austro-Hungarian Empire (1918). Today, of course, Galicia is part of Soviet Ukraine.

Bukovyna was annexed by Austria from Turkish control in 1775. It was appended to Galicia for administrative purposes until 1849; thereafter, it became a separate province and remained so until Austria-Hungary's demise.

Carpatho-Ukraine is included in the table above only to note the other area of the Austro-Hungarian Empire with a significant Ukrainian component. Since very few Ukrainians emigrated to Canada from this region, it is beyond the scope of our discussion.

While Austria-Hungary obtained Galicia in the first partition of Poland, Russia received all the remaining Ukrainian lands that had been under Polish rule (that is, most of present-day Soviet Ukraine). **"Eastern" Ukraine** was brutally incorporated into the Muscovite state and a vigorous attempt was made to obliterate the Ukrainian language and national aspirations. As in Carpatho-Ukraine, very few Ukrainians emigrated to Canada from this territory in the time period covered by this study.

Religion

Christianity came to Ukraine via Constantinople rather than Rome. In 988 A.D., Prince Vladimir the Great adopted the Eastern rite of the Byzantine Church, making **Greek Orthodoxy** the official religion of the Kievan Rus state with Ukrainians owing allegiance to the Patriarch at Constantinople. Except for the use of Old Church Slavonic in the liturgy and ceremonies, the practices, beliefs, institutions, and architecture of the Byzantine Church was transported wholesale to Kiev. Over the course of the next two centuries it was to consolidate its hold not only on the Ukrainians but on eastern Slavs in general.

The Ukrainian **(Greek) Catholic Church** was established in 1569 when a conclave of Ukrainian Orthodox bishops changed their allegiance from the Patriarch of Constantinople to the Pope in Rome. The reason for this is shrouded in historical controversy. Certainly after Poland's conquest of Galicia (in the late 1300s) a vigorous policy of "Catholicizing" and "Polonizing" followed, which, in part, facilitated this Act of Union with Rome. Also, there was general dissatisfaction with the Byzantine Patriarchate, especially after the defeat of Constantinople at the hands of the Turks in 1453, which obliged the Patriarch to recognize the Turkish Sultan. Nevertheless, while acknowledging the supremacy of the Papacy in matters pertaining to dogma, the Ukrainian Catholic Church remained faithful to the Eastern rite, retaining the Old Church Slavonic in its liturgy and abiding by the customs and traditions of the Byzantine Church. Although its proper modern title is the Ukrainian Catholic Church (employed after 1918), earlier in its history it was known as the Uniate Church, the Ruthenian Church, and, under the Austro-Hungarian Empire (1772 to 1918), as the Ruthenian Greek Catholic Church.

APPENDIX II

RESOLUTIONS OF NATIONAL CHURCH MEETING

WHEREAS the head of the Ukrainian Greek Catholic organization in Canada unconditionally demands the title to the church property be given to the Ukrainian Greek Catholic bishopric corporation which, according to its provisions, constitutes the bishop of the Ukrainian Greek Catholic parishes or missions whose only administrator is the bishop, and

WHEREAS according to the regulations of the corporation, Ukrainian Greek Catholic parishes and the congregations are deprived of all rights to manage their own church finances, and

WHEREAS the aforementioned bishop refused to admit married Ukrainian priests into Canada (which is contrary to our rights and privileges) and in fact introduced celibacy, and

WHEREAS the aforementioned bishop gave jurisdiction to the Roman Catholic missionaries, the Redemptorist fathers, amongst our Ukrainian Greek Catholic people, and

WHEREAS the aforementioned bishop accords himself exclusive right and control over all the education, institutions, and aspirations, and

WHEREAS the aforementioned bishop administers religious affairs contrary to the democratic principles of this country, which are upheld by the Ukrainian people in Canada, and

WHEREAS the aforementioned bishop's actions are such that are compromising to the Ukrainian society, and

WHEREAS all petitions and painstaking care urged by the Ukrainian element upon the bishop that he fulfil his obligations with more tolerance and better procedure, revealed to be unsuccessful, and

WHEREAS the aforementioned bishop often in an unChristian manner refuses religious service to those parishes that wish to handle their own church property without the protection of the bishopric corporation, and

WHEREAS the aforementioned bishop threatens excommunication of the members of those various educational organizations in Canada that are not under his jurisdiction and further instructed his priests not to confess these members nor to give absolution, and

WHEREAS the present Ukrainian Greek Catholic church is a result of religious union forced upon the Ukrainian nation by Poland in 1596 and which was supported by Austria,

THEREFORE, we, the representatives of various Ukrainian communities and congregations of Western Canada, resolve as follows:

To organize the Ukrainian Greek Orthodox Church of Canada on the following principles:
(1) This church is in communion with other Eastern Orthodox Churches, and accepts the same dogmas and the same rites.
(2) The priests may be married.
(3) The property of each congregation shall belong to its members who will be entirely responsible for it.
(4) Bishops shall be chosen by the general Sobor or priests and delegates of all congregations, from among qualified candidates.
(5) The appointment and dismissal of priests shall be with the consent of the congregation concerned.
(6) To fulfil the aims and objectives of this conference, it is resolved to organize the Ukrainian Greek Orthodox Brotherhood of Canada, which shall:
  a) incorporate the newly-formed church in Canada
  b) establish a Ukrainian Greek Orthodox Seminary
  c) organize Ukrainian Greek Orthodox congregations
  d) provide priests for each and every congregation
  e) prepare and call a general Sobor of members and followers of the new Ukrainian Greek Orthodox Church of Canada to complete its organization.

Source: Odarky S. Trosky, *The Ukrainian Greek Orthodox Church in Canada* (Winnipeg, 1968), pp. 14–15.

NOTES

Chapter 1: The Dual Frontier

1 A. Shortt, "Some Observations on the Great Northwest." *Queen's Quarterly* 2, no. 3 (January, 1895): 191.
2 J.C. Gwillim, "A Glimpse of the Canadian West," *Queen's Quarterly* 18, no. 1 (1910): 45.
3 Shortt, "Some Observations on the Great Northwest," p. 185.
4 Cited in R.C. Brown, "For the Purposes of the Dominion: Background Paper on the History of Federal Public Lands Policy to 1930," *Canadian Public Land Use in Perspective,* eds. J.G. Nelson, R.C. Scace, R. Kouri (Ottawa, 1973), p. 6.
5 Principal Grant, cited in Norman Patterson, "The Canadian People: A Criticism of Some of their Social Peculiarities," *Canadian Magazine* 13, no. 2 (June, 1899): 135.
6 Douglas Robb Owram, "The Great North West: The Canadian Expansionist Movement and the Image of the West in the Nineteenth Century" (Ph.D. thesis, University of Toronto, 1976), pp. 342, 462.
7 Carl Berger, *The Sense of Power: Studies in the Ideas of Canadian Imperialism 1867-1914* (Toronto, 1973), p. 3.
8 Cited in G. Bryce, "The Canadianization of Western Canada," *Transactions* (Royal Society of Canada, 1910), Appendix A, LVII.
9 Berger, *The Sense of Power,* pp. 26, 36, 41, 43.
10 Patterson, "The Canadian People," p. 135.
11 J.R. Conn, "Immigration," *Queen's Quarterly* 8, no. 2 (1900-01): 129.
12 Berger, *The Sense of Power,* p. 134.
13 *Ibid.,* p. 152.
14 Bryce, "The Canadianization of Western Canada," XLI.
15 Robert England, *The Colonization of Western Canada: A Study of Contemporary Land Settlement 1896-1934* (Toronto, 1936), p. 56.
16 Donald Smiley, *The Rowell/Sirois Report/Book I* (Toronto, 1963), p. 63.
17 James B. Hedges, *Building the Canadian West* (New York, 1939), p. 9; John Blue, *Alberta Past and Present: Historical and Biographical* (Chicago, 1924), 2:197.
18 R.B. Bennett, "The Northwest Provinces and their Relation to Confederation," *The Canadian Club* 9 (1911-12): 194.
19 W.A. Mackintosh, *The Economic Background of Dominion-Provincial Relations* (Toronto, 1964), p. 22.
20 *Ibid.,* p. 27.
21 R.H. Coats, "Canada" in *International Migrations: Interpretations,* ed. Walter F. Willcox (New York, 1931), 2:125.

22 England, *The Colonization of Western Canada*, p. 58.
23 Smiley, *The Rowell/Sirois Report/Book I*, p. 69.
24 Adapted from Coats, "Canada," p. 130.

Chapter 2: Canadian Immigration and the North-West

1 Cited in C.A. Magrath, *Canada's Growth and some Problems Affecting It* (Ottawa, 1910), p. 37.
2 Peter H. Bryce, *The Value to Canada of the Continental Immigrant* (Toronto, n.d.), p. 6.
3 Magrath, *Canada's Growth and some Problems Affecting It*, p. 38.
4 *Ibid.*, p. 41.
5 *Ibid.*, p. 43.
6 Hedges, *Building the Canadian West*, pp. 7-8.
7 *Ibid.*, p. 8.
8 James Lumsden, *Through Canada in Harvest Time: A Study of Life and Labour in the Golden West* (London, 1903), p. 164.
9 C.M. Studness, "Economic Opportunity and the Westward Migration of Canadians During the Late Nineteenth Century," *Canadian Journal of Economics and Political Science* 30, no. 4 (1964): 579.
10 John J. Deutsch et al., *The Canadian Economy: Selected Readings* (Toronto, 1961), p. 423.
11 John Blue, *Alberta Past and Present: Historical and Biographical* (Chicago, 1924), 1: 199-200.
12 Cited in Hedges, *Building the Canadian West*, p. 83.
13 *Ibid.*, pp. 85-86.
14 E.H. Oliver, "The Settlement of Saskatchewan to 1914," *Royal Society of Canada Transactions*, Series III, no. 20 (1926): 68.
15 Hedges, *Building the Canadian West*, p. 106.
16 E.B. Osborn, *Greater Canada, The Past, Present and Future of the Canadian North-West* (London, 1900), p. 130.
17 *Manitoba Daily Free Press*, 21 December 1889.
18 Adam Shortt and Arthur G. Doughty, eds., *Canada and Its Provinces* (Toronto, 1914), p. 171.
19 Oliver, "The Settlement of Saskatchewan to 1914," pp. 68-69.
20 Shortt and Doughty, *Canada and Its Provinces*, pp. 172-173.
21 *Ibid.*, p. 173.
22 *Ibid.*, pp. 173-174.
23 *Edmonton Bulletin*, 17 August 1899; Canada, House of Commons, *Debates*, 1891, 5225. Hereafter, *Commons Debates*.
24 *Commons Debates*, 1891, 5247.
25 *Ibid.*, 1893, 3420.
26 *Ibid.*, 1891, 5264.
27 *Ibid.*, 1892, 1908.
28 *Ibid.*, 1891, 5280.
29 *Ibid.*, 1891, 5228.
30 *Ibid.*, 1892, 1491.
31 *Ibid.*, 1892, 1474.
32 *House of Commons, Select Standing Committee on Agriculture and Colonization*, 1896, 220.
33 *Ibid.*, 221.

[34] David John Hall, "Clifford Sifton: Immigration and Settlement Policy 1896-1905," *The Settlement of the West,* ed. H. Palmer (Calgary, 1977), p. 64.

[35] David John Hall, "The Political Career of Clifford Sifton 1896-1905," (Ph.D. thesis, University of Toronto, 1973), p. 184.

[36] *Ibid.,* p. 180.

[37] *Ibid.,* pp. 180-182.

[38] Shortt and Doughty, p. 175 (footnote).

[39] See, for example, Mabel F. Timlin, "Canada's Immigration Policy, 1896-1910," *The Canadian Journal of Economics and Political Science* 26, no. 4 (November 1968): 518.

[40] Sifton, *Commons Debates,* July 27, 1899, 8654-5, cited in Hall, "The Political Career of Clifford Sifton, 1896-1905," p. 195.

[41] Cited in Hall, "Clifford Sifton: Immigration and Settlement Policy 1896-1905," p. 77.

[42] Hedges, *Building the Canadian West,* p. 11.

[43] Cited in Andrew Gregorovich, "The Ukrainians," *Many Cultures, Many Heritages,* ed. Norman Sheff (Toronto, 1975), pp. 505-507.

[44] William Darcovich and Paul Yuzyk, eds. *Statistical Compendium on the Ukrainians in Canada, 1891-1976* (Ottawa, 1980) pp. 513-14.

[45] W.T.R. Preston, *My Generation of Politics and Politicians* (Toronto, 1927), p. 215.

[46] Preston visited Amsterdam, Rotterdam, Antwerp, Brussels, Cologne, Dusseldorf, Basil, Vienna, Bremen, Hamburg, Odessa, Copenhagen, Gothenburg, Stockholm, Christiannia, Lemberg, Cracow, and Tarnapol, among others. *The Select Standing Committee on Agriculture and Colonization: The North Atlantic Trading Company* (cited hereafter as *SSCAC-NATC*) (6 Edward VII, Appendix no. 2, 1906), p. 323.

[47] *Ibid.,* p. 282.

[48] *Ibid.,* p. 281.

[49] *Ibid.,* p. 324.

[50] *Ibid.,* p. 344.

[51] *Ibid.,* p. 323.

[52] Preston, *My Generation of Politics and Politicians,* p. 257.

[53] *Idem.*

[54] Only three individuals were ever mentioned: J. Gluck, a "businessman" and later manager of the NATC; N. Kohan, "engaged in the steamship business" and later secretary of the company, and S. Carlesburg, a "steamship booking agent." All of them "apparently" operated from Amsterdam because Holland did not have restrictive emigration laws. *SSCAC-NATC,* pp. 289-290, 293.

[55] *Ibid.,* p. 285.

[56] *Ibid.,* p. 325. The NATC did make a deposit of £1000 to the government of Canada as a guarantee of good faith and security for the fulfilment of the agreement. *Commons Debates,* May 1 1906, 2331.

[57] *SSCAC-NATC,* p. 283.

[58] Preston, *My Generation of Politics and Politicians,* p. 260.

[59] *Idem.*

[60] The major steamship lines operating in Europe were as follows: The Norddeutscher Lloyd and Hamburg-America line, Bremen, Germany; Vereingte Osterreichische Schiffahrts — Aktiengeselleschaft, Trieste, Austria; Holland-America Line, Rotterdam, Holland; Red Star line, Antwerp, Belgium; the Russkii dobrovolnii flot, Libava, Russia; and the Cunard line, Trieste, Austria, Fiume, Hungary, and Liverpool, England. Julian Bachynsky, *Ukrainian Immigration in the United States of America* (Lviv, 1914), p. 16.

[61] *SSCAC-NATC,* p. 348.

[62] *Ibid.,* pp. 348-349.

[63] Bachynsky, *Ukrainian Immigration in the United States of America,* p. 16.

[64] *SSCAC-NATC*, p. 335.

[65] *Ibid.*, p. 331.

[66] *Ibid.*, p. 339.

[67] *A Session's Disclosures*, Conservative pamphlet (Ottawa, 1906), p. 26. In addition, the government paid the company $15,485.24 for advertising and "other purposes." When the contract was cancelled (November 3, 1906) the government had paid the company a total of $367,245.85. *Commons Debates,* December 10, 1907, 770.

[68] *Commons Debates*, April 20, 1906, 1808.

[69] *Ibid.,* 1816.

Chapter 3: The Seeds of Emigration

[1] Ivan Franko, *Tvory: Filosofski, ekonomichni ta istorychni* 19 (Kiev, 1956): 311.

[2] John-Paul Himka, "Western Ukraine on the Eve of Emigration" (unpublished paper, University of Alberta, 1977), p. 1.

[3] Himka, "Polish and Ukrainian Socialism: Galicia, 1860-1890" (unpublished manuscript, University of Alberta, 1977), p. 6.

[4] Franko, *Tvory: Filosofski, ekonomichni ta istorychni*, p. 319.

[5] *Idem.*

[6] *Idem.*

[7] Arthur May, *The Hapsburg Monarchy 1867-1914* (Cambridge, 1960), p. 173.

[8] Franko, *Tvory: Filosofski, ekonomichni ta istorychni*, p. 319.

[9] *Idem.*

[10] *Ibid.*, p. 312.

[11] W. Najdus, "Szkice z historii Galicji" 1 (Warsaw, 1958-60): 105, and D. Kvitkovsky, "Bukovyna li mynule i suchasne" (Paris, 1956), pp. 449-50, cited on a chart in Himka, "Western Ukraine on the Eve of Emigration," p. 6.

[12] Franko, *Tvory: Filosofski, ekonomichni ta istorychni*, p. 320.

[13] Himka, "Western Ukraine on the Eve of Emigration," p. 3.

[14] *Ibid.*, p. 2.

[15] *Ibid.*, p. 4.

[16] *Ibid.*, p. 3.

[17] *Idem.*

[18] Franko, *Tvory: Filosofski, ekonomichni ta istorychni*, p. 312.

[19] V. Kurylo et al., "Pivnichna Bukovyna, ii mynule i suchasne" (Uzhorod, 1969), p. 56, cited in Himka, "Western Ukraine on the Eve of Emigration," p. 22 (footnote).

[20] Franko, *Tvory Filosofski, ekonomichni ta istorychni*, p. 312.

[21] "Statistische Monstschrift" (Vienna, 1815), p. 136, cited in Himka, "Western Ukraine on the Eve of Emigration," p. 23 (footnote).

[22] An Austrian quoted in "The Future of Austria-Hungary," *Review of Reviews* 17 (1898):86.

[23] Marian Kukiel, "Dzieje Polski Porozbisrowej 1795-21" (London, 1961), pp. 412-15, cited in Ivan L. Rudnytsky, "The Ukrainians in Galicia Under Austrian Rule," *Austrian History Yearbook* 3 (1967):417.

[24] I.L. Rudnytsky, "The Ukrainians in Galicia Under Austrian Rule," *Austrian History Yearbook* (1967), p. 417.

[25] *Idem.;* Himka, "Western Ukraine on the Eve of Emigration," p. 22 (footnote).

[26] "Bevölkerung und Viehstrand von Galizien nach der Zächlung vom 31 December 1869" (Vienna, 1871), cited in John-Paul Himka, "Voluntary Artisan Associations and the Ukrainian National Movement in Galicia (The 1870s)" (unpublished paper, University of Alberta, 1977), p. 4.

[27] Kurylo et al., p. 56, cited in Himka, "Western Ukraine on the Eve of Emigration," p. 24 (footnote).

[28] Himka, "Western Ukraine on the Eve of Emigration," p. 24 (footnote).

[29] *Ibid.,* p. 9.

[30] *Idem.*

[31] *Ibid.,* p. 10.

[32] George M. Foster, "Peasant Society and the Image of Limited Good," *Peasant Society: A Reader,* eds. Jack M. Potter, May N. Diaz, and George M. Foster (Boston, 1967), p. 304.

[33] Wasyl Kutschabsky, "Die Westukraine im Kampfe mit Polen und dem Bolschewismus in den Jahren 1918-1923" (Berlin, 1934), p. 14, cited in Rudnytsky, "The Ukrainians in Galicia Under Austrian Rule," *Austrian History Yearbook,* p. 416.

[34] Dmytro Doroshenko, *A Survey of Ukrainian History* (Winnipeg, 1975), pp. 567-568.

[35] Michael Hrushevsky, *A History of Ukraine* (New Haven, 1970), p. 500.

[36] Himka, "Polish and Ukrainian Socialism: Galicia, 1860-1890," p. 15.

[37] Danylo Tanjackevyc, "Pys'mo narodovciv rus'Kych do redaktora politycnoji casopysi 'Rus jako protest i mermorijal" (Vienna, 1867), pp. 3, 5, 6, 15, cited in Rudnytsky, "The Ukrainians in Galicia Under Austrian Rule," *Austrian History Yearbook,* p. 411.

[38] Rudnytsky "The Ukrainians in Galician Under Austrial Rule," p. 411.

[39] *Ibid.,* p. 404.

[40] *Ausgleich* was a compromise between the Austrian Emperor and Hungarian nobility which established Hungary as a kingdom with autonomy in domestic affairs while leaving the rest of the Hapsburg territories as a loose federation nominally governed by a parliament in Vienna. Essentially, this constitutional agreement created Austria-Hungary.

[41] Himka, "Polish and Ukrainian Socialism: Galicia, 1860-1890," p. 13.

[42] Himka, "Western Ukraine on the Eve of Emigration," pp. 27-28 (footnote).

[43] Jozeb Buzek, "Stosunki zawodowe i socyslne ludnosci w Galicyi wedtug wyzania: narodowosci, na podstawie spisu ludnosci z 31 grudnia 1900 r." (Lviv, 1905), pp. 42-43, cited in Himka, "Polish and Ukrainian Socialism: Galicia, 1860-1890," p. 13.

[44] Orest T. Martynowych, "Village Radicals and Peasant Immigrants: The Social Roots of Factionalism Among Ukrainian Immigrants in Canada 1896-1918" (M.A. thesis, University of Manitoba, 1978), p. 13.

[45] Mykailo Lozyno'Kyi, "Sorok lit diial nosty Pros'vity" (Lviv, 1908), pp. 46-47, cited in John-Paul Himka, "Priests and Peasants: The Uniate Pastor and the Ukrainian National Movement in Austria 1867-1900" (unpublished paper, University of Alberta, 1977), p. 12.

[46] Himka, "Western Ukraine on the Eve of Emigration," p. 15.

[47] Himka, "Priests and Peasants," p. 12.

[48] Himka, "Voluntary Artisan Associations," p. 20.

[49] Himka, "Priests and Peasants," p. 6.

[50] P. Melnyk, "Pysmo z pid Drohobycha," *Batkivshchyna,* 1884, no. 31, p. 194, cited in Himka, "Western Ukraine on the Eve of Emigration," p. 21 (footnote).

[51] Himka, "Western Ukraine on the Eve of Emigration," p. 4.

[52] Shshyryi druh I, "Poriadky v. sknylovi," *Batkivshchyna,* 1890, no. 27, p. 235, cited in Himka, "Polish and Ukrainian Socialism: Galicia, 1860-1890," p. 323 (footnote).

[53] Himka, "Priests and Peasants," p. 8.

[54] Himka, "Western Ukraine on the Eve of Emigration," p. 16.

[55] Rudnytsky, "The Ukrainians in Galicia Under Austrian Rule," p. 418.

[56] Himka, "Polish and Ukrainian Socialism: Galicia, 1860-1890," pp. 120, 131, 134.

[57] *Ibid.,* p. 138.

58 *Ibid.*, p. 316.
59 W. Feldman, "Sprawa Ukrainska," in Stefan Kiemiewicz, p. 321, cited in *Ibid.*, p. 380.
60 Himka, "Polish and Ukrainian Socialism: Galicia, 1860-1890," p. 372.
61 *Ibid.*, p. 285.
62 *Ibid.*, p. 313.
63 Rudnytsky, "The Ukrainians in Galicia Under Austrian Rule," p. 423.

Chapter 4: Crossing the Rubicon

1 Pylyp Yasnovsky, *Pid ridnym i pid chuzhym nebom: spohady pionera* (Buenos Aires, 1961), pp. 104-23.
2 Emilio Willems, "Brazil," *The Positive Contribution by Immigrants* (New York, 1955), p. 120.
3 M.V., "Ukrainetz pro Kanadu Vrotsi 1895," *Preria Kanadskyi Almanakh* (Winnipeg, 1928), p. 20.
4 Sister Severina, "Emigration in Ukrainian Literature," *Memory Book* (New York, 1936), p. 409.
5 Willems, "Brazil," p. 121.
6 Wasyl Halich, *Ukrainians in the United States* (Chicago, 1931), p. 17.
7 Carl Wittke, "Immigration Policy Prior to World War I," *The Annuals of the American Academy* 252 (March, 1949): 10.
8 *Idem.*
9 Julian Bachynsky, *Ukrainska immigratsiia v ziednanykh derzhavok ameryky* (Lviv, 1914), p. 75.
10 *Ibid.*, p. 79.
11 *Ibid.*, pp. 79-80.
12 *Ibid.*, p. 79.
13 Bohdan P. Procko, "Pennsylvania: Focal Point of Ukrainian Immigration," *The Ethnic Experience in Pennsylvania*, ed. John E. Bodnar (Lewisburg, 1973), pp. 221-222.
14 Procko, "Soter Ortynsky: First Ruthenian Bishop in the United States, 1907-1916," *The Catholic Historical Review* 58, no. 4 (January, 1973): 514.
15 Roman S. Holiat, "Istoria Ukrainskoi presy v amerytsi," *Svoboda* (Jersey City, 1978), pp. 83-84.
16 *Ibid.*, p. 84.
17 *Ibid.*, p. 85.
18 Halich, *Ukrainians in the United States*, p. 18.
19 P.J. Lazarowich, "Ukrainian Pioneers in Western Canada," *Alberta Historical Review* 5, no. 4 (Autumn, 1957): 17.
20 M.H. Ponich, "Wasyl Eleniak, Father of Ukrainian Settlers in Canada," *Alberta Historical Review* 4, no. 3 (Summer, 1957): 17.
21 Paul Yuzyk, "The First Ukrainians in Manitoba," *Historical and Scientific Society of Manitoba*, Series III, no. 8, 1953, p. 10.
22 Yasnovsky, *Pid ridnym i pid chuzhym nebom: spohady pionera*, p. 124.
23 M.V., "Ukrainetz pro Kanadu Vrotsi 1895," p. 19.
24 V.J. Kaye, "Dr. Joseph Oleskiw's Visit to Canada, August-October 1895," *Revue de l'Université d'Ottawa* 33 (January-March, 1962):30.
25 Cited in M.V., "Ukrainetz pro Kanadu Vrotsi 1895," p. 22.
26 Orest Kyrylenko, *Ukraintsi v Amerytsi* (Vienna, 1916), p. 31.
27 Toma Tomashevsky, "Slovo Pionera," *Shistdesiat lit u Kanadi* (Toronto, 1951), p. 24.

[28] M.V., "Ukrainetz pro Kanadu Vrotsi 1895," p. 22; Rudnytsky, "The Ukrainians in Galicia Under Austrian Rule," p. 418.

[29] Franko, *Tvory: Filosofski, ekonomichni ta istorychni*, p. 315.

[30] Bachynsky, *Ukrainska immigratsiia v ziednanykh derzhavok ameryky*, p. 5.

[31] Franko, *Tvory: Filosofski, ekonomichni ta istorychni*, p. 322.

[32] *Idem.*

[33] *Ibid.*, p. 318.

[34] *Ibid.*, p. 321.

[35] Bachynsky, *Ukrainska immigratsiia v ziednanykh derzhavok ameryky*, p. 9.

[36] *Ibid.*, pp. 10-15.

[37] *Ibid.*, pp. 7-9.

[38] Petro Krawchuk, *Na Novii Zemli, Storinky z zhyttia, borotby i tvorchoii pretsi Kanadskykh ukraintziv* (Toronto, 1958), p. 80; Yuzyk, "The First Ukrainians in Manitoba," p. 32; Petro Svarich, *Spomyny 1877-1904* (Winnipeg, 1976), p. 72; Bachynsky, *Ukrainska immigratsiia v ziednanykh derzhavok ameryky*, pp. 5, 18.

Chapter 5: The Settlement Frontier

[1] B.L. Korchinski, "Ukrainian Pioneers," *From Dreams to Reality: A History of the Ukrainian Senior Citizens of Regina and District 1896-1976* (Winnipeg, 1977), p. 182.

[2] A. Akelinkh to L.M. Fortier, Public Archives of Canada, "Canadian Immigration; Immigration Branch Records," file 34214, 3 June 1897 (Hereafter cited as PAC (IB) with date).

[3] Svarich, *Spomyny*, p. 95.

[4] Yasnovsky, *Pid ridnym i pid chuzhym nebom: spohady pionera*, p. 131.

[5] *Ibid.*, pp. 131-132.

[6] *Ibid.*, p. 132.

[7] Svarich, *Spomyny*, p. 95.

[8] *Idem.*

[9] Dmytro Romanchych, cited in Harry Piniuta, trans., *Land of Pain, Land of Promise: First Person Accounts by Ukrainian Pioneers 1891-1914* (Saskatoon, 1978), p. 99.

[10] Maria Adamowska in *Ibid.*, p. 56.

[11] Svarich, *Spomyny*, p. 96.

[12] A. Akerlinkh to L.M. Fortier, PAC (IB), 3 June 1897.

[13] A. Akerlinkh to F. Pedley, *Ibid.*, 23 May 1898.

[14] A. Akerlinkh to L.M. Fortier, *Ibid.*, 3 June 1897.

[15] A. Akerlinkh to F. Pedley, *Ibid.*, 17 June 1898.

[16] A. Akerlinkh to F. Pedley, *Ibid.*, 24 December 1897.

[17] Yuzyk, "The First Ukrainians in Manitoba," p. 35.

[18] Immigration halls were located in Saskatoon, Lethbridge, Moose Jaw, Yorkton, Qu'Appelle, Regina, Rosthern, Prince Albert, Calgary, Strathcona, Craik, Davidson, Duck Lake, Lloydminster, Winnipeg, and Dauphin, and rented buildings or tent accommodation were provided at Macleod, Saltcoats, Edmonton, Olds, Battleford, Leduc, and other places. Shortt and Doughty, eds., *Canada and Its Provinces*, p. 175.

[19] Rev. Nestor Dmytriw in Piniuta, *Land of Pain, Land of Promise*, pp. 42-43.

[20] Svarich, *Spomyny*, p. 101.

[21] W.F. McCreary to J. Smart, PAC (IB), 13 May 1897.

[22] W.F. McCreary to J. Smart, *Ibid.*, 15 May 1897.

[23] W.F. McCreary to J. Smart, *Ibid.*, 28 May 1897.

24 A. Akerlinkh to F. Pedley, *Ibid.*, 8 July 1898.
25 Yuzyk, "The First Ukrainians in Manitoba," pp. 34-38.
26 Svarich, *Spomyny*, p. 103.
27 *Ibid.*, p. 105.
28 *Ibid.*, p. 108.
29 *Ibid.*, p. 113.
30 V. Kaye, *Early Ukrainian Settlements in Canada 1895-1900. Dr. Joseph Oleskiw's Role in the Settlement of the Canadian North-West* (Toronto, 1964), p. 174.
31 *Ibid.*, pp. 154-161.
32 *Ibid.*, p. 183.
33 *Ibid.*, p. 231.
34 J. Mouat to W.F. McCreary, PAC (IB), 10 May 1897.
35 Cited in Kaye, *Early Ukrainian Settlements in Canada*, p. 202.
36 *Ibid.*, p. 246.
37 *Ibid.*, p. 181.
38 *Ibid.*, pp. 212-214.
39 *Ibid.*, pp. 223-224.
40 *Ibid.*, p. 234.
41 *Ibid.*, p. 235.
42 *Ibid.*, p. 248.
43 F.W. McCreary to J. Smart, PAC (IB), 20 May 1898.
44 F.W. McCreary to J. Smart, *Ibid.*, 9 June 1897.
45 J.W. Speers to F.W. McCreary, *Ibid.*, 9 July 1897.
46 Kaye, *Early Ukrainian Settlements in Canada*, p. 296.
47 *Idem.*
48 A. Akerlinkh to W.F. McCreary, PAC (IB), 29 April 1898.
49 W.F. McCreary to J. Smart, *Ibid.*, 25 May 1898.
50 W.F. McCreary to J. Smart, *Ibid.*, 25 May 1898.
51 J.W. Speers to F.W. McCreary, *Ibid.*, 29 June 1898.
52 Kaye, *Early Ukrainian Settlements in Canada*, p. 317.
53 Yasnovsky, *Pid ridnym i pid chuzhym nebom: spohady pionera*, p. 152.
54 F.W. McCreary to J. Smart, PAC (IB), 14 May 1897.
55 John C. Lehr, "The Rural Settlement Behaviour of Ukrainian Pioneers in Western Canada, 1891-1914," *Western Canadian Research in Geography: The Lethbridge Papers*, ed. B. Barr (Vancouver, 1975), p. 51.
56 Svarich, *Spomyny*, p. 97.
57 *Ibid.*, p. 98.
58 *Idem.*
59 Lehr, "The Rural Settlement Behaviour of Ukrainian Pioneers in Western Canada," p. 60.
60 Kaye, *Early Ukrainian Settlements in Canada*, p. 163.
61 Svarich, *Spomyny*, p. 116.
62 *Ibid.*, p. 100.
63 Gregorovich, "The Ukrainians," p. 509.
64 Howard Angus Kennedy, *New Canada and the New Canadians (London, n.d.)*, p. 124.
65 Korchinski, "Ukrainian Pioneers," p. 180.
66 John C. Lehr, "Changing Ukrainian House Styles," *Alberta History* 23, no. 1 (1975):26.
67 *Ibid.*, p. 27.
68 Lehr, "Ukrainian Houses in Alberta," *Alberta History* 21, no. 4, (1973):11.
69 Adamowska in Piniuta, *Land of Pain, Land of Promise*, p. 60.
70 *Ibid.*, p. 76.

[71] Kennedy, *New Canada and the New Canadians,* p. 124.

[72] J. Patterson (Provincial Board of Health) to W.F. McCreary, PAC (IB), 11 June 1898.

[73] Lehr, "Changing Ukrainian House Styles," p. 28.

[74] Krawchuk, *Na Novii Zemli,* p. 87.

[75] Gimli Women's Institute, *Gimli Saga: The History of Gimli, Manitoba* (Gimli, 1975), p. 79.

[76] Romanchych in Piniuta, p. 106.

[77] Kaye, *Early Ukrainian Settlements in Canada,* p. 140.

[78] Aubrey Fullerton, "Our Homesteaders," *Canadian Magazine* 46, no. 3 (January, 1916):256.

[79] Tomashevsky, "Slovo Pionera," pp. 27-28.

[80] W.F. McCreary to J. Smart, PAC (IB), 2 July 1897.

[81] W.B. Scarth to J. Smart, *Ibid.,* 18 June 1898.

[82] W.F. McCreary to J. Smart, *Ibid.,* 21 June 1898.

[83] W.F. McCreary to J. Smart, *Ibid.,* 24 June 1898.

[84] W.F. McCreary to J. Smart, *Ibid.,* 4 July 1898.

[85] W.F. McCreary to J. Smart, *Ibid.,* 4 July 1898.

[86] J. Patterson to W.F. McCreary, *Ibid.,* 11 July 1898.

[87] J.W. Speers to W.F. McCreary, *Ibid.,* 11 May 1898.

[88] Kennedy, *New Canada and the New Canadians,* p. 127.

[89] Samuel Koenig, "Magical Beliefs and Practices among the Galician Ukrainians," *Folklore* 48 (March, 1937):79.

[90] *Ibid.,* p. 64.

[91] Martynowych, "Village Radicals and Peasant Immigrants," p. 84.

[92] Cited in *Ibid.,* p. 85.

[93] John Panchuk, *Bukovynian Settlements in Southern Manitoba (Gardenton Area)* (Battlecreek, 1971), p. 7.

Chapter 6: The Advisors

[1] Kaye, *Early Ukrainian Settlements in Canada,* p. 43.

[2] *Ibid., p. 44.*

[3] *Ibid., p. 386.*

[4] The paragraph is condensed from A. Makuch, "Synopsis of Tymko Hawryliuk" (unpublished paper, University of Alberta, 1980), pp. 2-3.

[5] M.V., "Ukrainetz pro Kanadu Vrotsi," p. 22.

[6] Makuch, p. 2.

[7] *Idem.*

[8] *Svoboda,* 8 October 1896.

[9] *Ibid.,* 10 August 1896.

[10] Kaye, *Early Ukrainian Settlements in Canada,* p. 381.

[11] *Svoboda,* 1 January 1897.

[12] *Ibid.,* 1 August 1895.

[13] *Ibid.,* 15 November 1893.

[14] *Ibid.,* 1 December 1893.

[15] *Ibid.,* 15 December 1893.

[16] *Ibid.,* 30 March 1894.

[17] *Ibid.,* 1 August 1894.

[18] *Ibid.,* 9 September 1897.

[19] *Ibid.,* 13 April 1899.

[20] *Ibid.,* 6 February 1895.

[21] *Ibid.,* 6 April 1894.

[22] *Ibid.,* 24 March 1898. See Chapter 9 for examples of the propensity to take arguments to court.

[23] *Ibid.,* 17 December 1896.

[24] *Ibid.,* 1 January 1897.

[25] Myroslav Stechishin, "Ukrainske Bratstvo v Kalifornii," *Kaliender Ukrainskoho Holusu* (Winnipeg, 1940), p. 112.

[26] *Svoboda,* 26 January 1899.

[27] *Ibid.,* 28 January 1897; 10 March 1898.

[28] T.A. Yastremsky, *Kanadiianizatsia: Political Development of Canadian Ukrainians During the Last 46 Years of Their Presence in Canada* (Winnipeg, 1946) p. 41.

[29] *Svoboda,* 16 November 1899.

[30] Yastremsky, *Kanadiianizatsia,* p. 41.

[31] *Svoboda,* 16 June 1898.

[32] *Ibid.,* 8 March 1900, cited in Orest T. Martynowych, "The Ukrainian Socialist Movement in Canada 1900-1918, Part I," *Journal of Ukrainian Graduate Studies* 1, no. 1 (Fall, 1976):35.

[33] *Svoboda,* 18 December 1898.

[34] *Ibid.,* 30 December 1897.

[35] *Ibid.,* 4 November 1897.

[36] *Ibid.,* 30 September 1897.

[37] *Ibid.,* 8 March 1898.

[38] *Ibid.,* 3 February 1899.

[39] *Ibid.,* 16 December 1897.

[40] *Ibid.,* 15 December 1898.

[41] *Ibid.,* 15 June 1899.

[42] *Ibid.,* 15 December 1898.

[43] *Ibid.,* 1 September 1898.

[44] Stechishin, "Ukrainske Bratstvo v Kalifornii," p. 119.

[45] Martynowych, "The Ukrainian Socialist Movement in Canada," p. 37.

[46] Stechishin, "Ukrainske Bratstvo v Kalifornii," p. 112.

[47] Cited in Orest T. Martynowych, "The Ukrainian Socialist and Working Class Movement in Manitoba" (unpublished paper, University of Manitoba, 1973), p. 5.

[48] *Svoboda,* 1 September 1898.

[49] Cited in Kaye, *Early Ukrainian Settlements in Canada,* pp. 113-114.

[50] *Svoboda,* 22 April 1897.

[51] *Ibid.,* 29 April 1897.

[52] *Ibid.,* 3 June 1897.

[53] *Ibid.,* 13 May 1897.

[54] *Ibid.,* 10 June 1897.

Chapter 7: Views from the Other Bridge

[1] Carl Berger, *The Sense of Power: Studies in the Ideals of Canadian Imperialism 1867-1914* (Toronto, 1973), p. 117.

[2] "Canada's Championships," *Canadian Magazine* 7 (October, 1896): 575-76.

[3] Terry L. Chapman, "Early Eugenics Movement in Western Canada," *Alberta History* 25, no. 4 (Autumn, 1977): 9.

[4] J.R. Conn, "Immigration," *Queen's Quarterly* 8, no. 2 (1900-01): 119.

[5] S.A. Thompson, "Possibilities of the Great North West," *Review of Reviews* 8, no. 5 (November, 1893): 10.

6 Cited in Robert Craig Brown and Ramsay Cook, *Canada 1896-1921: A Nation Transformed* (Toronto, 1974), p. 164.

7 *Commons Debates*, 1899, 6837.

8 *Ibid.*, 6842.

9 *Peterborough Daily Evening Review*, 5 April 1899.

10 *Halifax Herald*, 22 April 1899.

11 *Montreal Daily Star*, 6 May 1899.

12 *Ottawa Anglo-Saxon*, 9 June 1899.

13 *Idem.*

14 *Morden Chronicle*, 25 May 1899.

15 *Ottawa Anglo-Saxon*, 9 June 1899.

16 *Commons Debates*, 1891, 5227.

17 *Ibid.*, 5233.

18 *Peterborough Morning Times*, 21 March 1899.

19 *Edmonton Bulletin*, 10 April 1899.

20 *Commons Debates*, 1893, 3424.

21 *Idem.*

22 *Ibid.*, 1899, 8507.

23 *Edmonton Bulletin*, 8 June 1899.

24 Cited in Myrna Kostash, *All of Baba's Children: Between the Lines of Ukrainian-Canadian History* (Edmonton, 1977) pp. 34-35.

25 Oliver, "The Settlement of Saskatchewan to 1914," p. 77.

26 "Belleville Intelligencer," cited in *Halifax Herald*, 18 March 1899.

27 *Quebec Mercury*, 22 March 1899.

28 *Guelph Daily Herald*, 11 April 1899.

29 *Halifax Herald*, 18 March 1899.

30 *Ibid.*, 21 March 1899.

31 *Toronto Mail and Empire*, 10 April 1899.

32 Jones, "Immigrant Psychology," p. 206.

33 *Commons Debates*, 1898, 6845.

34 *Idem.*

35 *Ibid.*, 1899, 6862.

36 *Ibid.*, 1899, 6860.

37 *Ibid.*, 1901, 2940.

38 *Ibid.*, 1903, 6600.

39 *Ibid.*, 1903, 6883.

40 *Ibid.*, 1898, 6842; see also *Ibid.*, 1899, 8524 and *Ibid.*, 1901, 2936.

41 *Ibid.*, 1901, 2974.

42 *Ibid.*, 1901, 2956.

43 *Ibid.*, 1901, 2934.

44 *Ibid.*, 1899, 6837.

45 J.R. Conn, "Immigration," *Queen's Quarterly* 8, no. 2 (1900-01): 125.

46 *Ibid.*, p. 126.

47 *Idem.*

48 *Commons Debates*, 1898, 1074.

49 *Ibid.*, 1899, 6839.

50 *Ibid.*, 1901, 2941.

51 *Toronto Mail and Empire*, 1898, cited in Gregorovich, "The Ukrainians," p. 516.

52 *Dauphin Press*, 3 November 1899.

53 *Commons Debates*, 1901, 2943.

54 *Ibid.*, 1899, 6842; see also *Ibid.*, 1899, 8530.

55 Cited in Kaye, "Dr. Joseph Oleskiw's Visit to Canada," p. 43.

56 Cited in N. Kazymyra, "Political Activity of Ukrainians in Western Canada" (unpublished paper, 1976), p. 9.

[57] Canada, *Senate Debates*, 1903, 167.

[58] *Idem.*

[59] *Ibid.*, 1903, 269.

[60] *Commons Debates*, 1899, 6837.

[61] Conn, "Immigration," p. 123.

[62] *Commons Debates*, 1899, 6837.

[63] Cited in *Ibid.*, 1899, 6840.

[64] Cited in Andrij Makuch, "The Abolition of Bilingual Education in Manitoba 1916: The Ukrainians and the School Question" (unpublished paper, 1977), p. 8.

[65] Marilyn Barber, "Nationalism, Nativism and the Social Gospel: The Protestant Church Response to Foreign Immigrants in Western Canada 1897-1914," in *The Social Gospel in Canada,* ed. Richard Allen (Regina, 1968), p. 210.

[66] *Ibid.*, p. 209.

[67] Joanna Matejko, "Canada's Immigration Policy Towards Central and East Europeans in 1896-1847," in *Proceedings of the First Banff Conference on Central and East European Studies*, ed. T.M.S. Priestly (Edmonton, 1977), p. 60.

[68] Cited in Barber, "Nationalism, Nativism and the Social Gospel," p. 212.

Chapter 8: The Labouring Frontier

[1] Mykhailo Ivanchuk, *Istoria Ukrainskoho poselennia v okolytsi Gimli* (Winnipeg, 1975), p. 78.

[2] Yuzyk, "The First Ukrainians in Manitoba," p. 34.

[3] Romanchych in Piniuta, *Land of Pain, Land of Promise*, p. 106.

[4] Korchinski, "Ukrainian Pioneers," p. 180.

[5] Zonia Keywan and Martin Coles, *Greater Than Kings: Ukrainian Pioneer Settlement in Canada* (Montreal, 1977), p. 61.

[6] Romanchych in Piniuta, *Land of Pain, Land of Promise*, p. 106.

[7] Kennedy, *New Canada and the New Canadians*, p. 244.

[8] *Idem.*

[9] Myrna Kostash, *All of Baba's Children*, p. 198.

[10] Helen Potrebenko, *No Streets of Gold: A Social History of Ukrainians in Alberta* (Vancouver, 1977), p. 37.

[11] Svarich, *Spomyny*, p. 124.

[12] Tomashevsky, "Slovo Pionera," p. 29.

[13] Edmund Bradwin, *The Bunkhouse Man: A Study of Work and Pay in the Camps of Canada 1903-1914* (Toronto, 1972), p. 54.

[14] *Ibid.*, p. 56.

[15] *Ibid.*, p. 55.

[16] Yasnovsky, *Pid ridnym i pid chuzhym nebom: spohady pionera*, p. 146.

[17] *Idem.*

[18] Bradwin, *The Bunkhouse Man*, p. 171.

[19] *Ibid.*, p. 174.

[20] Yasnovsky, *Pid ridnym i pid chuzhym nebom: spohady pionera*, p. 147.

[21] *Idem.*

[22] Bradwin, *The Bunkhouse Man*, p. 179.

[23] Yasnovsky, *Pid ridnym i pid chuzhym nebom: spohady pionera*, p. 148.

[24] Yastremsky, *Kanadiianizatsia*, p. 148.

[25] *Ibid.*, p. 149.

[26] Bradwin, *The Bunkhouse Man*, p. 115.

[27] *Idem.*

[28] Potrebenko, *No Streets of Gold*, p. 56.

[29] M.H. Marunchak, *Petro Hawrysyshyn: Pioneer — budivnychyi Shashkevychivskoi dilnyii Point Douglas u Winnipegu* (Winnipeg, 1962), pp. 18-19.

[30] Potrebenko, *No Streets of Gold*, p. 38.

[31] Yastremsky, *Kanadiianizatsia*, p. 40.

[32] Bradwin, *The Bunkhouse Man*, p. 166.

[33] John M. Romaniuk in Piniuta, *Land of Pain, Land of Promise*, p. 141.

[34] *Ibid.*, p. 139.

[35] *Idem.*

[36] Martin Robin, *The Rush for Spoils: The Company Province 1871-1933* (Toronto, 1972), p. 17.

[37] Harold A. Innis, *Settlement and the Mining Frontier* (New York, 1974), p. 291 (footnote).

[38] Keywan and Coles, *Greater Than Kings*, p. 60.

[39] Svarich in Piniuta, *Land of Pain, Land of Promise*, p. 122.

[40] Innis, *Settlement and the Mining Frontier*, p. 291 (footnote).

[41] Svarich in Piniuta, *Land of Pain, Land of Promise*, p. 135.

[42] D.J. Bercuson, "Labour Radicalism and the Western Industrial Frontier 1897-1919," *Canadian Historical Review* (C.H.R.) 58, no. 2, (1977): 169.

[43] Kostash, *All of Baba's Children*, p. 201.

[44] Svarich in Piniuta, *Land of Pain, Land of Promise*, p. 135.

[45] Innis, *Settlement and the Mining Frontier*, p. 291 (footnote).

[46] *Ibid.*, p. 279 (footnote).

[47] Svarich in Piniuta, *Land of Pain, Land of Promise*, p. 144.

[48] Bercuson, "Labour Radicalism and the Western Industrial Frontier," p. 169.

[49] Compiled from Alan Artibise, *Winnipeg: A Social History of Urban Growth 1874-1914* (Montreal, 1975), p. 139.

[50] *Ibid.*, p. 142.

[51] *Ibid.*, p. 130.

[52] Svarich in Piniuta, *Land of Pain, Land of Promise*, p. 129.

[53] Paul Voisey, "The Urbanization of the Canadian Prairie 1871-1916," *Social History* 8 no. 15 (May, 1975): 85.

[54] Artibise, *Winnipeg*, p. 140.

[55] Jean Morrison, "Ethnicity and Violence: The Lakehead Freight Handlers Before World War I," *Essays in Canadian Working Class History*, ed. Gregory S. Kealey and Peter Warrian (Toronto, 1976), p. 149.

[56] Artibise, *Winnipeg*, p. 160.

[57] *Ibid.*, p. 161.

[58] *Ibid.*, p. 165.

[59] Svarich in Piniuta, *Land of Pain, Land of Promise*, p. 130.

[60] *Idem.*

[61] *Ibid.*, p. 132.

[62] *Idem.*

[63] *Idem.*

[64] *Idem.*

[65] Paul Phillips, *The British Columbia Mining Frontier 1880-1920* 21, Series I (Ottawa, 1974): 5.

[66] *Idem.*

[67] A. Ross McCormack, *Reformers, Rebels and Revolutionaries: The Western Canadian Radical Movement 1899-1919* (Toronto, 1977), p. 39.

[68] D.J. Bercuson, *Confrontation at Winnipeg: Labour, Industrial Relations and the General Strike* (Montreal, 1974), pp. 9-10.

[69] *Ibid.*, p. 10.

Chapter 9: The Social and Institutional Frontier

[1] *Svoboda*, 10 September 1897.
[2] Rev. A. Roborecky, "A Short Historical Summary of the Ukrainian Catholics in Canada," *Catholic Church Historical Association (C.C.H.A.) Report* (1949), p. 32.
[3] Gregorovich, "The Ukrainians," p. 528.
[4] *Svoboda*, 10 August 1899.
[5] Roborecky, "A Short Historical Summary," p. 32.
[6] Panchuk, *Bukovynian Settlements in Southern Manitoba*, p. 12.
[7] *Ibid.*, p. 10.
[8] G.N. Emery, "Methodist Missions Among the Ukrainians," *Alberta Historical Review* 19, no. 2 (Spring, 1971): 10.
[9] Roborecky, "A Short Historical Summary," p. 32.
[10] I.M. Romaniuk, "Pochatcky nebilivskykh rodyn v Kanadi," *Kaliendar Ukrainskoho Holosu* (1942), p. 83.
[11] G.W. Simpson, "Father Delaere, Pioneer Missionary and Founder of Churches," *Saskatchewan History* 3, no. 1 (Winter, 1950): 9.
[12] M. Kumka, "Litopys Kanadiiskykh Ukraintsiv," *Kaliendar Ukrainskoho Holosu* (1938), p. 151.
[13] *Svoboda*, 20 January 1898.
[14] *Ibid.*, 16 December 1897; 4 August 1898; 8 June 1899.
[15] *Ibid.*, 6 April 1899.
[16] *Ibid.*, 14 August 1899.
[17] Cited in Myra Dubczak, "The Organizational Life of the First Ukrainian Immigration to the United States and Canada" (unpublished paper, 1974), p. 41.
[18] Bohdan P. Procko, "The Establishment of the Ruthenian Church in the United States, 1884–1907," *Pennsylvania History*, no. 42 (1975): pp. 140, 142.
[19] *Idem.*
[20] Paul Yuzyk, "Religious Life" (unpublished paper, 1976), p. 7.
[21] Basilian Fathers, *Monder uchora i sohodni* (Mundare, 1969), p. 29.
[22] *Ibid.*, p. 26.
[23] Maria Adamovsky, "Beginning in Canada," *Ukrainian Voice Almanac* (Winnipeg, 1937), p. 100.
[24] Mykailo Stasyn, "Moi spohady za sorok lit zhyttia v Kanadi," *Kaliender Ukrainskoho Holosu* (1938), pp. 82–83.
[25] *Svoboda*, 10 May 1897.
[26] Yuzyk, "Religious Life," pp. 6–7.
[27] Simpson, "Father Delaere," p. 8.
[28] A. Luhovy, "The Ukrainian Catholic Immigrants in Canada," *Migration News* 11 (September–October, 1962): 2.
[29] *Svoboda*, 5 July 1900.
[30] Yastremsky, *Kanadiianizatsia*, p. 30.
[31] Kumka, "Litopys Kanadiiskykh Ukraintsiv," p. 151.
[32] *Svoboda*, 3 February 1899.
[33] Emery, "Methodist Missions Among the Ukrainians," p. 12.
[34] Basilian Fathers, *Monder uchora i sohodni*, p. 30.
[35] Simpson, "Father Delaere," pp. 8–10; Roborecky, "A Short Historical Summary," p. 34.
[36] *Svoboda*, 30 June 1898.
[37] *Ibid.*, 24 February 1898.
[38] Panchuk, *Bukovynian Settlements in Southern Manitoba*, p. 9.
[39] *Ibid.*, p. 14.

[40] Yuzyk, "Religious Life," p. 9.

[41] *Svoboda,* 30 June 1898.

[42] *Svoboda,* 27 January 1898; 1 September 1898.

[43] Orest T. Martynowych, "Ukrainian Catholic Clericalism in Western Canada 1900-1932: Disintegration and Reconsolidation" (unpublished paper, University of Manitoba, 1974), p. 13.

[44] Kumka, "Litopys Kanadiiskykh Ukraintsiv," p. 151.

[45] Yuzyk. "Religious Life," p. 10.

[46] A. Makuch, "The Formation of the Ukrainian Orthodox Church in Canada: The Clash of Transplanted Ideologies" (unpublished paper, University of Alberta, 1977), p. 5.

[47] H. Domashovets, *Narysistorri Ukrainskoi ievanhelsko-batyskoi tseryvhy* (Toronto, 1967), p. 402.

[48] *Ibid.,* pp. 403-411.

[49] *Ibid.,* p. 403; see also J.E. Harris, *The Baptist Union of Western Canada: A Centennial History 1873-1973* (Saint John, n.d.).

[50] Emery, "Methodist Missions Among the Ukrainians," p. 12.

[51] *Svoboda,* 21 April 1898.

[52] Manoly R. Lupul, "The Ukrainians and Public Education" (unpublished paper, University of Alberta, 1976), p. 3.

[53] Kaye, *Early Ukrainian Settlements,* p. 221.

[54] Cited in Robert Fletcher, "The Language Problem in Manitoba Schools," *Historical and Scientific Society of Manitoba,* Series 3, no. 6 (1951): p. 53.

[55] *Idem.*

[56] Cited in Skelton, "Language Issue in Canada," p. 456.

[57] Cited in A.A. Herriot, "School Inspectors of the Early Days in Manitoba," *Historical and Scientific Society of Manitoba,* Series 3, no. 4 (1949): p. 28.

[58] A. Makuch, "The Abolition of Bilingual Education in Manitoba 1916: The Ukrainians and the School Question" (unpublished paper, University of Alberta, 1977), pp. 4-5.

[59] *Svoboda,* 4 August 1898.

[60] O. Woychenko and F. Swiripa, "Community Organizations and Private Education" (unpublished paper, University of Alberta, 1976), p. 2.

[61] *Svoboda,* 19 January 1899.

[62] *Svoboda,* 3 March 1898.

[63] Yastremsky, *Kanadiianizatsia,* p. 58.

[64] *Svoboda,* 6 November 1899.

[65] *Ibid.,* 7 December 1899.

Chapter 10: Canadian Immigration Policy after 1905

[1] Morris Zaslow, *The Opening of the Canadian North 1870-1914* (Toronto, 1971), p. 188.

[2] J.A. Lower, *Canada, An Outline History* (Toronto, 1966), p. 144.

[3] "Immigration," *Roundtable* 18, no. 3 (1928): 90.

[4] Zaslow, *The Opening of the Canadian North,* p. 182.

[5] Gilbert A. Stelter, *The Northern Ontario Mining Frontier 1880-1920* 10, Series I (Ottawa, 1974) p. 5.

[6] Zaslow, *The Opening of the Canadian North,* p. 191.

[7] R.H. Coats, "Immigration Program of Canada," in *Population Problems in the United States and Canada,* ed. Louis I. Dublin (Boston, 1926), p. 178.

[8] *Idem.*

[9] Innis, *Settlement and the Mining Frontier*, p. 372.

[10] Donald H. Avery, "Canadian Immigration Policy and the Alien Question 1896-1919: The Anglo-Canadian Perspective" (Ph.D. thesis, University of Western Ontario, 1973), p. 202.

[11] Donald H. Avery, "Continental European Immigrant Workers in Canada 1896-1919: From Stalwart Peasant to Radical Proletariat," *Canadian Review of Sociology and Anthropology* 12, no. I (1975): 56.

[12] William Waddell, "The Honorable Frank Oliver" (M.A. thesis, University of Alberta, 1950), p. 23.

[13] William Waddell, "Frank Oliver and the Bulletin," *Alberta Historical Review* 10, no. 3 (1952): 7.

[14] *Commons Debates,* 1906, 1954.

[15] *Ibid.,* 1907, 6162.

[16] *Idem.*

[17] *Ibid.,* 1907, 6165-6.

[18] Cited in Donald H. Avery, "Canadian Immigration Policy and the Foreign Navvy, 1896-1914," *Canadian Historical Association Papers* (1972), pp. 137-38.

[19] *Ibid.,* p. 139.

[20] *Commons Debates,* 1907, 6165-6.

[21] Avery, "Canadian Immigration Policy and the Foreign Navvy," p. 140.

[22] Avery, "Canadian Immigration Policy and the Alien Question," p. 209.

[23] *Idem.*

[24] *Commons Debates,* 1908, 6688.

[25] Avery, "Canadian Immigration Policy and the Alien Question," p. 213.

[26] *Idem.*

[27] Compiled from Ivan J. Tesla, "The Ukrainian-Canadians in 1971," in *The Jubilee Collection of the Ukrainian Free Academy of Sciences in Canada*, ed. A. Baran, O.W. Gerus, J. Rozumnyj (Winnipeg, 1976), p. 502.

[28] Compiled from *Idem.*

[29] *Commons Debates,* 1911, 615; *Ibid.,* 1914, 1612.

[30] Avery, "Canadian Immigration Policy and the Alien Question," p. 19.

[31] Compiled from Tesla, "The Ukrainian-Canadians in 1971," p. 502.

[32] Compiled from *Idem.*

[33] Wsevolod W. Isajiw, "Occupational and Economic Development" (unpublished paper, 1976), p. 12.

[34] Compiled from *Canada, Sessional Papers,* "Nationality, Sex, Occupation and Destination of Immigrant Arrivals at Ocean Ports for Fiscal Years 1906-1914 inclusive" (Hereafter *Sessional Papers*).

[35] Compiled from *Ibid.*

[36] Cited in M.H. Marunchak, *The Ukrainian Canadians: A History* (Winnipeg, 1970), p. 67.

[37] Cited in *Idem.*

[38] Compiled from *Sessional Papers.*

[39] Marunchak, *The Ukrainian Canadians,* p. 89.

[40] Avery, "Canadian Immigration Policy and the Alien Question," pp. 243 and 246.

[41] *Ibid.,* p. 256.

[42] Marunchak, *The Ukrainian Canadians,* p. 216.

[43] Avery, "Canadian Immigration Policy and the Alien Question," p. 52.

[44] *Sessional Papers.*

[45] Marunchak, *The Ukrainian Canadians,* p. 218.

46 Donald H. Avery, "Immigrant Workers and Labour Radicalism in Canada 1900-1920: A Case Study of the Rocky Mountain Coal Mining Industry" (unpublished paper, University of Western Ontario, 1975), p. 7.
47 Cited in Orest T. Martynowych, "The Ukrainian Socialist Movement in Canada 1900-1918," J.U.G.S. 2, no. 1 (1977), Part I, p. 29.
48 Avery, "Canadian Immigration Policy and the Alien Question," p. 263.
49 Avery, "Continental European Immigrant Workers in Canada," p. 57.

Chapter 11: Labour and the Socialist Perspective

1 The socialists were the first to use the term Ukrainian widely to describe their nationality.
2 Stuart Marshall Jamieson, *Times of Trouble: Labour Unrest and Industrial Conflict in Canada 1900-66* (Ottawa, 1966), pp. 62-72.
3 P. Krawchuk, "Ukrainians in Winnipeg: The First Century," *Ukrainian Canadian* (May, 1974), p. 2.
4 George Fisher Chipman, "Winnipeg the Melting Pot," *Canadian Magazine* 33 (September 1909): 19.
5 Edmund S. Kirby, Manager of the War Eagle Consolidated Mining and Development Company, Rossland, B.C., cited in Martin Robin, *Radical Politics and Canadian Labour 1880-1930* (Kingston, 1971), p. 44.
6 *Cotton's Weekly*, 22 May 1913.
7 Petro Krawchuk, *Ukraintsi v Istoria Viniphea* (Toronto, 1951), p. 51.
8 Krawchuk, "Ukrainians in Winnipeg," p. 3.
9 Jamieson, *Times of Trouble*, p. 79.
10 Morrison, "Ethnicity and Violence," p. 154.
11 *Ibid.*, pp. 154-55.
12 Jamieson, *Times of Trouble*, p. 80.
13 Joyce L. Kornbluh, *Rebel Voices: An I.W.W. Anthology* (Ann Arbor, 1972), p. 3.
14 McCormack, *Reformers, Rebels and Revolutionaries*, p. 101.
15 *Ibid.*, p. 109.
16 Donald H. Avery, *Dangerous Foreigners: European Immigrant Workers and Labour Radicalism in Canada 1896-1922* (Toronto, 1979), p. 55.
17 Jamieson, *Times of Trouble*, p. 146.
18 Potrebenko, *No Streets of Gold*, p. 93.
19 McCormack, *Reformers, Rebels and Revolutionaries*, p. 116.
20 *Ibid.*, p. 111.
21 Bercuson, "Labour Radicalism and the Western Industrial Frontier," p. 167.
22 Jamieson, *Times of Trouble*, p. 127; Avery, *Dangerous Foreigners*, p. 56.
23 See Victor R. Greene, *The Slavic Community on Strike: Immigrant Labour In Pennsylvania Anthracite* (Notre Dame, 1968).
24 Avery, *Dangerous Foreigners*, p. 56.
25 See Jamieson, *Times of Trouble*, pp. 127-132.
26 *Robotchyi Narod*, 18 December 1912.
27 *Robotchyi Narod*, 16 October 1912, cited in Martynowych, "The Ukrainian Socialist and Working Class Movement in Manitoba," p. 2.
28 *Robotchyi Narod*, 15 October 1913, cited in *Idem*.
29 For a fuller treatment of this group see Chapter 12.
30 Nadia O.M. Kazymyra, "The Defiant Pavlo Krat and the Early Socialist Movement in Canada," *Canadian Ethnic Studies* 10, No. 2 (1978): 52.

[31] *Ibid.,* p. 42.

[32] McCormack, *Reformers, Rebels and Revolutionaries,* p. 51.

[33] *Ibid.,* p. 65.

[34] *Ibid.,* p. 66.

[35] Cited in Krawchuk, "Ukrainians in Winnipeg," pp. 32-33.

[36] Cited in McCormack, *Reformers, Rebels and Revolutionaries,* p. 68.

[37] See Martynowych, "The Ukrainian Socialist Movement in Canada," Part I, p. 40 for details.

[38] Martynowych, "The Ukrainian Socialist and Working Class Movement in Manitoba," p. 7; see Chapter 12 for fuller treatment.

[39] Cited in Marunchak, *The Ukrainian Canadians,* p. 266.

[40] Martynowych, "The Ukrainian Socialist Movement in Canada," Part I, p. 42.

[41] Marunchak, *The Ukrainian Canadians,* p. 225.

[42] A. Ross McCormack, "Radical Politics in Winnipeg 1899-1915," *Historical Society of Manitoba Transactions* 3, no. 29 (1972-73): 91.

[43] Martynowych, "The Ukrainian Socialist and Working Class Movement in Manitoba," p. 8.

[44] "Robitnchyi Kalendar," cited in Martynowych, "The Ukrainian Socialist Movement in Canada, 1900-1918," Part I, p. 43.

[45] Kazymyra, "The Defiant Pavlo Krat," pp. 43-44.

[46] See Martynowych, "The Ukrainian Socialist Movement in Canada 1900-1918," Part II, p. 24 for details.

[47] Kazymyra, "The Defiant Pavlo Krat," p. 46.

[48] Martynowych, "The Ukrainian Socialist and Working Class Movement in Manitoba 1900-1918," p. 12.

[49] Kazymyra, "The Defiant Pavlo Krat," p. 46.

[50] Martynowych, "The Ukrainian Socialist and Working Class Movement in Manitoba," p. 12. For a fuller discussion of this aspect see Kazymyra, "The Defiant Pavlo Krat," pp. 47-48.

[51] *Chervony Prapor,* 28 November 1907, cited in Krawchuk, "The Ukrainians in Winnipeg," p. 34.

[52] Martynowych, "The Ukrainian Socialist Movement in Canada," Part II, p. 30.

Chapter 12: Politics and the Issue of Education

[1] "Presbyterian Record," July, 1910, cited in Marilyn Barber, "Canadianization Through the Schools of the Prairie Provinces Before World War I: The Attitudes and Aims of the English-Speaking Majority," *Ethnic Canadians: Culture and Education,* ed. Martin L. Kovacs (Regina, 1978), p. 282.

[2] "Presbyterian Record," January, 1910, cited in *Idem.*

[3] J.S. Woodsworth, *Strangers Within Our Gates* (Toronto, 1972), p. 112.

[4] See Frances Swyripa, *Ukrainian-Canadians: A Survey of Their Portrayal in English Language Works* (Alberta, 1978), pp. 12-20.

[5] "Annual Report of the Missionary Society of the Methodist Church, 1909-1910," cited in Barber, "Canadianization Through the Schools of the Prairie Provinces Before World War I," pp. 222-23.

[6] *The Missionary Outlook,* June, 1918.

[7] Marilyn Barber, "Introduction" to Woodsworth, *Strangers Within Our Gates,* xvii.

[8] See Martynowych, "Village Radicals and Peasant Immigrants," pp. 178-198.

[9] Barber, "Canadianization Through the Schools of the Prairie Provinces Before World War I," p. 283.

[10] Francis W. Grey, "Education and Nationality," *University Magazine* 12, no. 1 (February, 1913): 108; also see C.B. Sissons, "Illiteracy in the West," *University Magazine* 2, no. 3 (October, 1913).

[11] Woodsworth, *Strangers Within Our Gates*, p. 234.

[12] *Report of the Department of Education for 1909* (Manitoba), p. 31.

[13] O.D. Skelton, "The Language Issue in Canada," *Queen's Quarterly* 24, no. 3 (January, 1917): 453.

[14] M.P. Toombs, "A Saskatchewan Experiment in Teacher Education 1907-1917," *Saskatchewan History* 18, no. 1 (1968): 5.

[15] Sissons, "Illiteracy in the West," *University Magazine,* p. 450.

[16] *Report of the Department of Education for 1909* (Manitoba), p. 115.

[17] *Ibid.,* 1908, p. 79.

[18] Skelton, "The Language Issue in Canada," p. 440.

[19] Savella Curnisky, "How to Teach a Ukrainian," in *Ethnic Canadians: Culture and Education,* ed. Martin L. Kovacs, p. 366.

[20] John H. Syrnick, "Community Builders: Early Ukrainian Teachers," *Historical and Scientific Society of Manitoba Transactions,* Series III, no. 21 (1964-65), p. 29.

[21] See Lupul, "The Ukrainians and Public Education," p. 5; Cornelius J. Jaenen, "The Manitoba School Question: An Ethnic Interpretation," in Kovacs, p. 326.

[22] M.R. Lupul, *The Roman Catholic Church and the North-West School Question: A Study in Church-State Relations in Western Canada* (Toronto, 1974), p. 159.

[23] Makuch, "The Abolition of Bilingual Education," pp. 6-7.

[24] J. Skwarok, *The Ukrainian Settlers in Canada and Their Schools 1891-1921* (Toronto, 1959), p. 61; Lupul, "The Ukrainians and Public Education," p. 4.

[25] Skwarok, *The Ukrainian Settlers in Canada and Their Schools,* p. 61; Orest Zerebko, *Ukrayianski Uchetelski Seminariyi v Kanadi* (Lviv, 1914), pp. 158-162.

[26] Marunchak, *The Ukrainian Canadians,* p. 121.

[27] Syrnick, "Community Builders," p. 33.

[28] *Ibid.,* p. 30.

[29] *Idem.*

[30] Marunchak, *The Ukrainian Canadians,* pp. 118-119.

[31] *Idem.*

[32] *Ibid.,* p. 144.

[33] *Ukrainskyi Holos,* 14 March 1910.

[34] C.B. Sissons, *Bilingual Schools in Canada* (Toronto, 1917), pp. 116-119.

[35] *Idem.;* see also Sissons, "Illiteracy in the West."

[36] *Manitoba Free Press,* 3 November 1911.

[37] *Ibid.,* 16 July 1913.

[38] *Idem.*

[39] W.J. Mihaychuk, "Ruthenian Teachers' Convention," *Western School Journal* 10 (1915): 278.

[40] *Ibid.,* p. 270.

[41] Skelton, "The Language Issue in Canada," p. 440.

[42] Cornelius J. Jaenen, "Ruthenian Schools in Western Canada 1897-1919," *Paedogogica Historica* 10, no. 3 (1970): 522.

[43] *Liberal Handbook* (Winnipeg, 1914), p. 16.

[44] See Barber, "Canadianization Through the Schools of the Prairie Provinces Before World War I," pp. 291-292.

[45] Fletcher, "The Language Problem in Manitoba Schools," p. 53.

[46] *Ukrainskyi Holos,* pp. 8, 15, 22, and 29, March 1916, provides the complete text; Martynowych, "Village Radicals and Peasant Immigrants," p. 212; Lupul, "The Ukrainians and Public Education," p. 6.

[47] Martynowych, "Village Radicals and Peasant Immigrants," p. 212; C.K. New-combe, *Special Report on Bilingual Schools in Manitoba* (Winnipeg, 1916).

[48] Martynowych, "Village Radicals and Peasant Immigrants," p. 212.

[49] *Ukrainskyi Holos*, 13 October 1913.

[50] Donald Creighton, *Canada's First Century* (Toronto, 1970), p. 114.

[51] See Raymond Huel, "The Public School as a Guardian of Anglo-Saxon Traditions: The Saskatchewan Experience 1913-1918," in Kovacs, p. 296.

[52] J.W. Brennan, "Wooing the Foreign Vote: Saskatchewan Politics and the Immigrant 1905-1919" (paper presented at the Canadian Historical Association Annual Meeting, 1978), pp. 5-8.

[53] Marunchak, *The Ukrainian Canadians*, p. 141.

[54] Skwarok, *The Ukrainian Settlers in Canada and Their Schools*, p. 111.

[55] Cited in Lupul, "The Ukrainians and Public Education," p. 12, and Jaenen, "Ruthenian Schools in Western Canada," p. 529.

[56] Lupul, "The Ukrainians and Public Education," p. 12.

[57] R.A. Wilson, "The Educational Survey of Saskatchewan," *Queen's Quarterly* 26, no. 3 (January 1919), p. 323.

[58] Huel, "The Public School as a Guardian of Anglo-Saxon Traditions," p. 298.

[59] H.W. Foght, *A Survey of Education in the Province of Saskatchewan* (Regina, 1918), pp. 59-62.

[60] Lupul, "The Ukrainians and Public Education," p. 13.

[61] Jaenen, "Ruthenian Schools in Western Canada," p. 533.

[62] Cited in Martynowych, "Village Radicals and Peasant Immigrants," p. 217.

[63] See *Vegreville Observer*, 3 March 1909 (Biography of Svarich)

[64] *Idem.*

[65] *Idem.*; Lupul, "The Ukrainians and Public Education," p. 19.

[66] *Vegreville Observer*, 3 March 1909.

[67] See Lupul, "The Ukrainians and Public Education," p. 19 for details.

[68] *Vegreville Observer*, 1 February 1912.

[69] Lupul, "The Ukrainians and Public Education," p. 19.

[70] *Ibid.*, pp. 19-20.

[71] *Vegreville Observer*, 19 January 1913.

[72] *Ibid.*, 2 April 1913 (See Svarich's letter).

[73] *Ibid.*, 27 August 1913.

[74] Martynowych, "Village Radicals and Peasant Immigrants," p. 230.

[75] *Idem.*

[76] *Vegreville Observer*, 25 June 1913.

[77] *Novyny*, 23 September 1913.

[78] See Lupul, "The Ukrainians and Public Education," p. 23 for further details.

[79] "The Great Ruthenian Revolt" is based on R. Fletcher's account in *Annual Report of the Department of Education for 1913* (Alberta).

[80] See editorials in *Novyny*, 11, 15, 22, 25 July 1913.

[81] See *Manitoba Free Press*, 11, 18, 19, 27 September 1913.

[82] J.W. Chalmers, "Strangers in Our Gates," *Alberta History* 16, no. 1 (Winter, 1968): 20.

[83] Lupul, "The Ukrainians and Public Education," p. 20.

[84] See A.J. Hunter, "The Educational Problem in the West," *The Presbyterian*, 13 February 1908.

[85] J.T.M. Anderson, "Canadianization," *Western School Journal* 14 (1919): 215.

[86] Hunter, "The Educational Problem in the West."

Chapter 13: Consolidating the Religious Question

[1] Paul Yuzyk, "Ukrainian Greek Orthodox Church of Canada 1918-1951," (Ph.D. thesis, University of Minnesota, 1958), p. 90.

[2] *Ibid.,* p. 92.

[3] See Chapter 9.

[4] See A.J. Hunter, "Our Missionary Work In Western Canada," *The Missionary Messenger* 2 (1915): pp. 200-02; J.A. Cormie, "The Problem of The Church In the West," *The Presbyterian*, 27 May 1905; A.J. Hunter, "The Crisis of the Independent Greek Church," *The Presbyterian*, 25 July 1912.

[5] Yuzyk, "Ukrainian Greek Orthodox Church of Canada," p. 97.

[6] Cited in Martynowych, "Village Radicals and Peasant Immigrants," p. 142.

[7] *Idem.;* Also A. Sheptytsky, *Address on the Ruthenian Question to Their Lordships the Archbishops and Bishops of Canada* (Winnipeg, 1977), p. 11.

[8] George Thomas Daly, *Catholic Problems in Western Canada* (Toronto, 1921), p. 77.

[9] *Ibid.,* p. 86.

[10] Bohdan Kazymyra, "Metropolitan Andrew Sheptytsky and the Ukrainians in Canada," *CCHA Report* (1959) p. 78.

[11] Simpson, "Father Delaere," p. 1.

[12] See R.P.A. Delaere, *Memoire Sur les Tentatives de Schisme et D'Heresie Au Milieu Des Ruthenes de l'Ouest Canadien* (Quebec, 1908).

[13] Simpson, "Father Delaere," p. 11; *Svoboda*, 3 December 1908.

[14] Marunchak, *The Ukrainian Canadians*, p. 108.

[15] Kazymyra, "Metropolitan Andrew Sheptytsky and the Ukrainians in Canada," pp. 79-80.

[16] Sheptytsky, *Address on the Ruthenian Question,* p. 12.

[17] *Ibid.,* p. 15.

[18] *Ibid.,* p. 21.

[19] *Idem.*

[20] For details see Procko, "Soter Ortynsky: First Ruthenian Bishop in the United States, 1907-1916," *The Catholic Historical Review* 58, no. 4 (January, 1973).

[21] Sheptytsky, *Address on the Ruthenian Question,* p. 24.

[22] A. Lukovy, "The Ukrainian Catholic Immigrants in Canada," *Migration News* 11 (September-October, 1962), p. 3.

[23] *Kanadysky Rusyn,* 26 April 1913, cited in Martynowych, "Village Radicals and Peasant Immigrants," p. 153.

[24] Marunchak, *The Ukrainian Canadians,* p. 111.

[25] Hunter, "The Crisis of the Independent Greek Church," p. 31.

[26] Cited in Marunchak, *The Ukrainian Canadians,* p. 111.

[27] See Odarka S. Trosky, *The Ukrainian Greek Orthodox Church in Canada* (Winnipeg 1968), p. 7; also Yuzyk, "Ukrainian Greek Orthodox Church of Canada," p. 97.

[28] *Robotchyi Narod*, 8 February 1914.

[29] *Ukrainskyi Holos*, 2 November 1910.

[30] *Ukrainskyi Holos*, 2 November 1910.

[31] *Ibid.,* 25 December 1912.

[32] *Ibid.,* 13 August 1913.

[33] *Idem.*

[34] Yuzyk, "Ukrainian Greek Orthodox Church of Canada," p. 115.

[35] *Ukrainskyi Holos*, 15 November 1913.

[36] *Ibid.,* 27 May 1914.

[37] *Kanadysky Rusyn*, 17 May 1911.

[38] *Ibid.,* 5 July 1913.

[39] *Ibid.,* 1 August 1914.

[40] Yuzyk, "Ukrainian Greek Orthodox Church of Canada," p. 118.

[41] *Ukrainskyi Holos,* 1 August 1917.

[42] *Ibid.,* 3 October 1917.

[43] *Kanadyskyi Farmer,* 25 January 1918.

[44] See Yuzyk, "Ukrainian Greek Orthodox Church of Canada," pp. 128-29; Trosky, *The Ukrainian Greek Orthodox Church in Canada,* p. 12.

[45] Yuzyk, "Ukrainian Greek Orthodox Church of Canada," pp. 129-30; *Kanadyskyi Farmer,* 7 June 1918.

[46] *Kanadyskyi Farmer,* 2 November 1917.

[47] The National Priest was Father Kusy. See Trosky, *The Ukrainian Greek Orthodox Church in Canada,* p. 13.

[48] *Kanadyskyi Farmer,* 12 April 1918.

[49] Yuzyk, "Ukrainian Greek Orthodox Church of Canada," pp. 145-46.

Conclusion

[1] Compiled from Ivan Tesla, *Ukrainian Population in Canada,* p. 502.

[2] I am indebted to Orest Martynowych's brilliant thesis, "Village Radicals and Peasant Immigrants," for the clear delineation of these groups.

[3] See, for example, W.R. Petryshyn, ed. *Changing Realities: Social Trends Among Ukrainian Canadians* (Edmonton, 1980).

SELECTED
BIBLIOGRAPHY

Although space limitations prevent an exhaustive bibliography, the following is a fairly comprehensive index of the material (both published and unpublished) that was profitably consulted in preparing this work.

As the footnotes indicate, aside from what is listed below a wide variety of government records and publications was utilized, the most important of which were the Department of Interior Immigration Branch Files, the House of Commons Debates, Senate Debates, and Sessional Papers. Manuscript collections at the Public Archives of Canada that were consulted include those of Sir Wilfrid Laurier, Sir Clifford Sifton, and James Shaver Woodsworth. Another major source of information was the newspapers of the time (including the ethnic press), which were extensively surveyed.

1. Articles

Adamowska, Maria, "Beginnings in Canada," *Ukrainian Voice* (Calendar), Winnipeg, 1937.

Ananevych, Josafat, "Ukrainians in Brazil," *Provodinnia* (Calendar), Philadelphia, 1946.

Anderson, J.J.M., "The School and the Newer Citizen of Canada," *Proceedings of the National Conference on Character Education,* Winnipeg, October 20-22, 1919.

Andrusiak, J. "The Ukrainian Movement in Galicia," *The Slavonic Review* Part 1, Vol. 45, no. 40, July 1935; Part 2, Vol. 45, no. 41, October, 1935.

Angus, H.F., "The Future of Immigration into Canada," *Canadian Journal of Economics and Political Science* 12, no. 3, August, 1946.

Anon., "Austria's Whirlpool of Nationalities," *The Contemporary Review* 96, no. 5, November, 1909.

——————, "Canada," *The Round Table* 9, no. 1, December, 1918.

——————, "The Cry of Ukraine," *Review of Reviews* 52, no. 4, April, 1916.

——————, "The Education of the Citizen," *The Round Table* 7, no. 3, June, 1917.

——————, "Golden Anniversary of Ukrainian Publishing in Canada," *The Ukrainian Review* 5, no. 1, 1958.

——————, "The Migration of the Races," *The Round Table* 11, no. 2, January, 1921.

——————, "The Realm of the Hapsburgs: Will it Hold Together?" *Review of Reviews* 27, no. 3, March, 1903.

——————, "Who are the Ruthenians?" *Review of Reviews* 53, no. 1, January, 1916.

Ardan, Ivan, "The Ruthenians in America," *Charities* 13, 1904-5.

Artibise, A.F.J. "An Urban Environment: The Progress of Growth in Winnipeg 1874-1914," *Canadian Historical Association (CHA) Papers*, 1972.

——————, "Divided City: The Immigrant in Winnipeg Society 1874-1924," in *The Canadian City: Essays in Urban History*, ed. Stelter and Artibise, Ottawa, 1977.

Avery, Donald, "Continental European Immigrant Workers in Canada 1896-1919: from 'stalwart peasant to radical proletariat'," *The Canadian Review of Sociology and Anthropology* 12, no. 1, February, 1975.

——————, "Immigrant Workers and Labour Radicalism in Canada 1900-20: A Case Study of the Rocky Mountain Coal Mining Industry," unpublished paper, 1975.

——————, "Canadian Immigration Policy and the Foreign Navvy 1896-1914," *Canadian Historical Association, Historical Papers*, 1972.

——————, "The Immigrant Industrial Worker in Canada 1896-1919: The Vertical Mosaic as an Historical Reality," in *Identities*, ed. W. Isajiw, Vol. 5, 1977.

Bailey, F.G., "The Peasant View of the Bad Life," in *Peasants and Peasant Societies: Selected Readings*, ed. Teodor Shanin, Middlesex, 1971.

——————, "Life in Eastern Galicia," *Fortnightly Review* 104, 98, July, 1915.

Balch, Emily Green, "Slav Emigration at its Source," *Charities and the Commons*, January, 1906.

Baron, D., "Canada's First Ukrainian," *Country Guide* 13, September, 1955.

Bercuson, D.J., "Labour Radicalism and the Western Industrial Frontier 1897-1919," *Canadian Historical Review* 58, no. 2, 1977.

Betten, Neil, "The Origins of Ethnic Radicalism in Northern Minnesota 1900-20," *International Migration Review* 4, no. 2, 1970.

Bicha, Karel Denis, "The Plains Farmer and the Prairie Province Frontier 1897-1914," *Proceedings of the American Philosophical Society* 109, no. 6, December 1965.

Bilinsky, Yaroslav, "Mykhailo Drahomanov, Ivan Franko and the Relations between the Dnieper Ukraine And Galicia in the Last Quarter of the 19th Century," *The Annals of the Ukrainian Academy* 3, nos. 1 and 2, 1959.

Black, N.F. "Western Canada's Greatest Problem: The Transformation of Aliens into Citizens," *The Western School Journal* 9, 1914.

Bodnar, John, "Immigration and Modernization: the Case of Slavic Peasants in Industrial America," *Journal of Social History* 10, 1976.

Bodrug, Ivan, "Why the Ruthenians are Poor," *Home Mission Pioneer* 4, 1907.

Brown, R.C., "For the Purposes of the Dominion: A Background Paper on the History of Federal Public Lands Policy to 1930," in *Canadian Public Land Use In Perspective,* ed, J.G. Nelson, R.C. Scace, R. Kouri, Ottawa, 1973.

Bryce, G., "The Canadianization of Western Canada," *Royal Society of Canada Transactions,* Presidential Address, 1910.

Canuck, Janey, "Communing with Ruthenians," *The Canadian Magazine* 40, no. 5, March, 1913.

Carmichael, J.A. "Work Among the Ruthenians," *The Presbyterian Record*, September, 1911.

——————, "Ruthenian Ministers in the West," *The Presbyterian Record,* February, 1911.

Carrothers, W.A., "The Immigration Problems in Canada," *Queen's Quarterly* 36, no. 3, 1929.

Chalmers, J.W., "Strangers in Our Midst," *Alberta Historical Review* 45, no. 1, 1968.

Chmedar, Johann, "The Austrian Emigration 1900-1914," in *Dislocation and Emigration: the Social Background of American Immigration,* ed. Donald Fleming, Bernard Bailyn, Cambridge, Mass., 1974.

Coats, R.H., "The Immigration Program of Canada," in *Population Problems in the United States and Canada*, ed. Louis I. Dublin, Boston, 1926.

Conn, J.R., "Immigration," *Queen's Quarterly* 8, no. 2, 1900-01.

Corbett, D.C., "Immigration and Economic Development," *Canadian Journal of Economics and Political Science* 17, no. 3, August, 1951.

Dafoe, John W., "Western Canada: Its Resources and Possibilities," *The American Monthly Review of Reviews* 35, 1907.

Dalyk, M., "Memoirs of a Pioneer," *Ukrainian Voice* (Calendar), 1942.

Dasko, D., "Attitudes Toward Ukrainians in Canada Between 1896 and 1914: A Content Analysis of Three Canadian Newspapers," unpublished paper, University of Toronto Department of Sociology.

Davie, Menie Murier, "In Ruthenia," *Living Age* 87, November, 1890.

d'Easum, Basil C., "A Galician Wedding: A North-West Incident," *Canadian Magazine,* May, 1899.

Dobrwolski, Kazimierz, "Peasant Traditional Culture," in *Peasants and Peasant Societies,* ed. Teodor Shanin, London, 1971.

Doroshenko, V., "The Life of Mykhailo Drahomanov," in *Mykhailo Drahomanov: A Symposium and Selected Writings*, ed. I.L. Rudnytsky, New York, 1952.

Dubczak, Myra, "The Organizational Life of the First Ukrainian Immigration to the United States and Canada," unpublished paper, 1974.

Eleniak, W.V., "Ottawa Honours Wasyl Eleniak," *Opinion*, January-February, 1947.

Emery, G.N. "The Methodist Church and 'European Foreigners' of Winnipeg: The All People's Mission, 1889-1914," *Historical and Scientific Society of Manitoba Transactions,* 1971-72.

_____, "Methodist Missions Among Ukrainians," *Alberta Historical Review* 19, no. 2, 1971.

England, Robert, "Continental Migration," *Queen's Quarterly* 36, no. 4, 1929.

Farion, Anna, "My Memoirs," *Ukrainian Voice* (Calendar), 1942.

Fitzpatrick, A., "Neglected Citizen in the Camps," *Canadian Magazine* 25, May, 1905.

_____, "Outnavvying the Navvies," *Canadian Magazine* 47, no. 1, May, 1916.

_____, "Education on the Frontier," *Queen's Quarterly* 21, July, 1913.

Fletcher, Robert, "The Language Problem in Manitoba Schools," *Historical and Scientific Society of Manitoba,* Series III, no. 6, 1951.

Foraneus, "Some Thoughts on the Ruthenian Question in the United States and Canada," *A.E.R.* 52, January, 1915.

_____, "The Ruthenian Question Again," *A.E.R.* 52, June, 1915.

Foster, George M., "Interpersonal Relations in a Peasant Society," *Human Organization* 19, no. 4, 1960-61.

_____, "Introduction: Peasant Character and Personality," in *Peasant Society: A Reader*, ed. Jack M. Potter, May N. Diaz, and George M. Foster, Boston, 1967.

_____, "What is a Peasant?" in *Peasant Society: A Reader*, Boston, 1967.

_____, "Peasant Society and the Image of Limited Good," in *Peasant Society: A Reader*, Boston, 1967.

Friedmann, F.G., "The World of 'La Miseria'," in *Peasant Society: A Reader*, Boston, 1967.

Greene, Victor, "A Study in Slavs, Strikes, and Unions: The Anthracite Strike of 1897," *Pennsylvania History* 31, 1964.

Gregorovich, Andrew, "The Ukrainians," in *Many Cultures, Many Heritages*, ed. Norman Sheffe, Toronto, 1975.

Gunn-Walberg, Kenneth W., "Non-Anglo-Saxon Work by the Methodist and Presbyterian Churches in Canada: Cultural Determinants and Praxis," in *Proceedings of the First Banff Conference on Central and East European Studies*, ed. T.M.S. Priestly, Edmonton, 1977.

Gwillim, J.C., "A Glimpse of the Canadian West," *Queen's Quarterly* 18, no. 1, 1910.

Halich, Wasyl, "Ukrainian Farmers in the United States," *Agricultural History* 10, no. 1, January, 1936.

Hall, D.J., "Clifford Sifton: Immigration and Settlement Policy, 1896-1905," in *The Settlement of the West*, ed. H. Palmer, Calgary, 1977.

Hardy, J.H., "The Ruthenians in Alberta," *Onward*, November 1, 1913.

Hart, Thomas, "The Educational System of Manitoba," *Queen's Quarterly* 12, no. 3, January, 1905.

Heaps, F., "Ukrainians in Canada," *The Canadian Magazine* 53, May, 1919.

Herriot, A.A., "School Inspectors of the Early Days in Manitoba," *Historical and Scientific Society of Manitoba*, Series III, no. 4, 1949.

Himka, John-Paul, "Voluntary Artisan Associations and the Ukrainian National Movement in Galicia (the 1870s)," unpublished paper, University of Alberta, 1977.

_____, "Polish and Ukrainian Socialism: Galicia, 1860-1890," unpublished paper, University of Alberta, 1977.

_____, "Priests and Peasants: the Uniate Pastor and the Ukrainian National Movement in Austria, 1867-1900," unpublished paper, (n.d.).

Hobsbawn, E.J., "Peasants and Politics," *Journal of Peasant Studies 1,* no. 1, 1973.

Hunter, Alexander J., "A View on Ukrainian Canadians," *Historical and Scientific Society of Manitoba,* Series III, no. 10, 1955.

Hurd, Archibald, "Foreign Invasion of Canada," *Fortnightly Review* 78, December, 1902.

Huts, A., "Memoirs of a Manitoba Pioneer," *Ukrainian Voice* (Calendar), 1940.

Ignatiuk, G.T., "Ukrainian Settlements in the Canadian West," in *Proceedings at Seminar Development of Agriculture on the Prairies,* Regina, 1975.

Ivanchuk, Ivan V., "Memories of Svoboda in Canada," in *Svoboda Jubilee Almanac 1893-1953,* ed. L. Myshuha and A. Dragan, Jersey City, 1953.

Jaenen, Cornelius J., "Ruthenian Schools in Western Canada, 1897-1919," *Paedagogica Historica* 10, 1970.

Jean, J., "S. E. Mgr. Adélard Langevin, Archevêque de St. Boniface et les Ukrainiens," *La Société Canadienne d'Histoire de L'Eglise Catholic,* Rapport, 1944-45.

Kaye, V.J., "Immigrant Psychology: Reactions Caused by Changes of Environment," *Revue de L'Université d'Ottawa* 28, no. 2, 1958.

_____, "Dr. Joseph Oleskiw's Visit to Canada, August-October 1895," *Revue de L'Université d'Ottawa* 32, January-March, 1962.

_____, "Golden Jubilee of Participation of Ukrainians in Political Life in Canada," *The Ukrainian Quarterly* 12, no. 2, 1963.

Kazymyra, Bohdan, "Metropolitan Andrew Sheptyckyj and the Ukrainians in Canada," *Canadian Catholic Historical Association (CCHA) Report,* 1957.

Khomyak, Rev. R., "Preparations For the First Bishop For Ukrainian Catholics of Canada," *Kalendar, Holos Spasytelia,* 1939.

Koenig, Samuel, "Cosmogonic Beliefs of the Hutuls," *Folklore* 47, no. 4, 1936.

_____, "Beliefs and Practices Relating to Birth and Childhood Among the Galician Ukrainians," *Folklore* 50, no. 3, 1939.

_____, "Geographic and Ethnic Characteristics of Galicia," *Journal of Central European Affairs* 1, no. 1, April, 1941.

_____, "Marriage and the Family among the Galician Ukrainians," in *Studies in the Science of Society,* ed. George P. Murdock, Freeport, 1969.

_____, "Magical Beliefs and Practices Among the Galician Ukrainians," *Folklore* 48, March, 1937.

_____, "Supernatural Beliefs Among Galician Ukrainians,"

Folklore 49, 1937-38.

_____ "Beliefs Regarding the Soul and the Future World Among the Galician Ukrainians," *Folklore* 49, June, 1938.

Korchinski, B.L., "Ukrainian Pioneers," in *From Dreams to Reality: A History of The Ukrainian Senior Citizens of Regina and District 1896-1976,* Winnipeg, 1977.

Kostash, Myrna, "All of Baba's Children: Between the Lines of Ukrainian-Canadian History," *Journal of Ukrainian Graduate Studies,* Fall, 1978.

Lazarowich, P.J., "Ukrainian Pioneers in Western Canada," *Alberta Historical Review* 5, no. 4, 1957.

Lehr, John C., "The Government and the Immigrant: Perspectives on Ukrainian Block Settlement in the Canadian West," *Canadian Ethnic Studies* 9, no. 2, 1977.

_____, "The Rural Settlement Behaviour of Ukrainian Pioneers in Western Canada, 1891-1914," in *Western Canadian Research in Geography: The Lethbridge Papers,* ed. B. Barr, Vancouver, 1975.

_____, "Ukrainian Houses in Alberta," *Alberta History* 21, no. 4, 1973.

_____, "Changing Ukrainian House Styles," *Alberta History* 23, no. 1, 1975.

Lloyd, J.A.T., "Teuton versus Slav," *Fortnightly Review* 593, May 1, 1916.

Lobay, Danylo, "Ukrainian Press in Canada," in *Svoboda Jubilee Almanac, 1893-1953,* ed. L. Myshuha and A. Dragan, Jersey City, 1953.

Lewis, Oscar, "Some of My Best Friends are Peasants," *Human Organization* 19, 1960-61.

Lukovy, A., "The Ukrainian Catholic Immigrants in Canada," *Migration News* 11, September-October, 1962.

Lumby, J.R., "The Stranger Within Our Gates," *Proceedings of the Fifty-first Annual Convention of Ontario Educational Association,* April 9-11, Toronto, 1912.

Makuch, Andrij, "The Abolition of Bilingual Education in Manitoba 1916: The Ukrainians and the School Question," unpublished paper, 1977.

_____, "The Formation of the Ukrainian Orthodox Church in Canada: The Clash of Transplanted Ideologies," unpublished paper, 1977.

_____, "Over Three Generations of Assimilation: Ukrainians and Identity in Canada," unpublished paper, 1978.

Marchin, Andrew A., "Early Emigration from Hungary to Canada," *The Slavonic and East European Review* 13, no. 37, 1934.

Martynowych, Orest T., "The Ukrainian Socialist and Working Class Movement in Manitoba," unpublished paper, 1973.

_____, "Ukrainian Catholic Clericalism in Western Canada, 1900-32: Disintegration and Reconsolidation," unpublished paper, 1974.

Matejko, Joanna, "Canada's Immigration Policy Towards Central and East Europeans in 1896-1947," in *Proceedings of the First Banff Conference on Central and East European Studies,* ed. T.M.S. Priestly, Edmonton, 1977.

McBriarty, A., "The History of the Redemptorists in Western Canada," *CCHA Report*, 1946-47.

McCormack, A.R., "Puttee and the Liberal Party: 1899-1904," *CHR*, no. 2, 1970.

_____, "Radical Politics in Winnipeg: 1899-1915," *Historical and Scientific Society of Manitoba Transactions,* Series III, no. 29, 1972-73.

Morton, W.L., "The Historical Phenomenon of Minorities: The Canadian Experience," 14th International Congress of Historical Sciences, San Francisco, August 22-29, 1975.

Navalkowski, Anna, "Shandro School," *Alberta Historical Review* 18, 1970.

Norrie, K.H., "The Rate of Settlement on the Canadian Prairies, 1870-1911," *Journal of Economic History* 35, 1975.

Oleksevych, Sofron, "Short History of My Life," *Ukrainian Voice* (Calendar), 1940.

Oliver, E.H., "The Settlement of Saskatchewan to 1914," *Royal Society of Canada Transactions,* Series III, 20, 1926.

Park, Robert E., "Human Migration and the Marginal Man," *The American Journal of Sociology* 33, no. 6, May, 1928.

Peterson, J., "Ethnic and Class Politics in Manitoba," *Canadian Provincial Politics*, ed. Martin Robin, Scarborough, 1972.

Pike, W.H., "The Flame: A Story of the Church's Ukrainian Work in Alberta," unpublished manuscript, 1968, United Church Archives.

Ponich, M.H., "Wasyl Eleniak, Father of Ukrainian Settlers in Canada," *Alberta Historical Review* 4, no. 3, 1957.

Procko, Bohdan P., "Pennsylvania: Focal Point of Ukrainian Immigration," in *The Ethnic Experience in Pennsylvania,* ed. John E. Bodnar, Lewisburg, 1973.

_____, "The Establishment of the Ruthenian Church in the United States, 1884-1907," *Pennsylvania History* 42, 1975.

_____, "Soter Ortynsky: First Ruthenian Bishop in the United States, 1907-1916," *The Catholic Historical Review* 58, no. 4, January, 1973.

Rea, J.E., "The Roots of Prairie Society," in *Prairie Perspectives*, ed. David P. Gagon, no. 4, 1970.

Roborecky, Rev. Andrew, "A Short Historical Summary of the Ukrainian Catholics in Canada," *CCHA Report*, 1947.

Romaniuk, Ivan M., "Memoirs," *Ukrainian Voice* (Calendar), 1942.

Rossman, Alexander, "A Journey in Ruthenia," *The Contemporary Review* 136, no. 5, November, 1929.

Royick, Alexander, "Ukrainian Settlements in Alberta," *Canadian Slavonic Papers* 10, no. 3, 1968.

Rudnytsky, I.L., "The Ukrainians in Galicia Under Austrian Rule," *Austrian History Yearbook,* 1967.

Ryus, Yurko, "My Work in Canada," *Ukrainian Voice* (Calendar), 1940.

Sabourin, Abbé J., "L'Apostolat chez les Ruthènes au Manitoba: Est — il Prudent de s'y Engager?" Quebec, 1911.

Scott, W.L., "The Catholic Ukrainian Canadians," *Dublin Review*, no. 5, 1938.

Shortt, A., "Some Observations on the Great North-West," *Queen's Quarterly* 2, no. 3, January, 1895.

Sifton, Clifford, "The Immigrants Canada Wants," *Maclean's Magazine,* 1 April 1922.

——————, "The Needs of the North-West," *The Canadian Magazine* 20, no. 5, March, 1903.

——————, "Immigration," *The Canadian Club* 19, 1921-22.

Simpson, G.W., "Father Delaere, Pioneer Missionary and Founder of Churches," *Saskatchewan History* 3, no. 1, 1950.

Sissons, C.B., "Illiteracy in the West," *University Magazine* 12, no. 3, October, 1913.

Skelton, O.D., "The Language Issue in Canada," *Queen's Quarterly* 24, no. 3, January, 1917.

Stashyn, Mykhailo, "Memoirs of My Forty Years in Canada," *Ukrainian Voice* (Calendar), 1938.

Stechishin, M., "Ukrainian Commune in California," *Ukrainian Voice* (Calendar), 1940.

Svarich, Petro, "For Cooperatives," *Ukrainian Voice* (Calendar), 1916.

——————, "Ukrainians and their Progress in the West During Thirty Years," *The Vegreville Observer,* 18 March 1931.

Swystun, V., "Our Lives in Canada," *Ukrainian Voice* (Calendar), 1915.

Syrnick, J., "This Bogey of the Tower of Babel," *Ukrainian Voice*, March, 1964.

——————, "Community Builders: Early Ukrainian Teachers," *Historical and Scientific Society of Manitoba Transactions*, Series 161, no. 2, 1964-65.

Tait, Lyn, "Attitudes Toward East European Immigrants as Projected in the Canadian Parliamentary Debates, 1895–1939" in *Proceedings of the First Banff Conference on Central and East European Studies,* ed. T.M.S. Priestly, Edmonton, 1977.

Timlin, Mabel F., "Economic Theory and Immigration Policy," *Canadian Journal of Economics and Political Science* 16, no. 3, August, 1950.

_____, "Canada's Immigration Policy, 1896–1910," *The Canadian Journal of Economics and Political Science* 26, no. 4, November, 1960.

Toombs, M.P., "A Saskatchewan Experiment in Teacher Training, 1907–17: The Foreign School for Teachers for Foreign Speaking Communities," *Saskatchewan History* 17, no. 1, 1964.

Tomashevsky, Toma, "Word of A Pioneer," *Sixty Years in Canada,* Toronto, 1951.

Waddell, W.S., "Frank Oliver and the Bulletin," *Alberta Historical Review* 5, no. 3, 1952.

Wangenheim, Elizabeth, "The Ukrainians: A Case Study of the Third Force," in *Nationalism in Canada,* ed. P. Russell, Toronto, 1966.

Warman, C., "An Empire Opener," unpublished manuscript, Public Archives of Canada, 1904.

Weinstein, H.R., "Land Hunger and Nationalism in the Ukraine, 1905–17," *Journal of Economic History* 2, May, 1942.

Wilson, R.A., "The Educational Survey of Saskatchewan," *Queen's Quarterly* 26, no. 3, January, 1919.

Witcutt, W.P., "Mortuary Beliefs and Practices Among the Galician Ukrainians," *Folklore* 57, no. 2, June, 1946.

Wittke, Carl, "Immigration Policy Prior to World War I," *The Annals of the American Academy* 262, March, 1949.

'Winnipeg Free Press', "The Ruthenians" printed in 'Notes and Comments', *Canadian Slavonic Papers* 10, no. 1, 1968.

Woodsworth, J.S., "The Immigration Problem in Canada," *University Magazine* 16, February, 1917.

_____, "Ukrainian Rural Communities: Report by the Bureau of Social Research," Winnipeg, 1917.

_____, "Social Conditions in Rural Communities in the Prairie Provinces," 1917, Public Archives of Canada, *Woodsworth Papers,* MG 27, 111, C7, Vol. 19.

_____, "Some Aspects of Immigration," *University Magazine* 13, no. 2, April, 1914.

Woywitka, Anne B., "Recollections of a Union Man," *Alberta Historical Review* 23, no. 4, 1975.

Yuzyk, Paul, "The First Ukrainians in Manitoba," *Historical and Scientific Society of Manitoba,* Series III, no. 8, 1953.

2. Books

Abbott, Edith, *Historical Aspects of the Immigration Problem*, Chicago, 1926.

Allen, W.E.D., *The Ukraine: A History*, Cambridge, 1940.

Ames, Hebert, *Our Western Heritage and How it is Being Squandered By the Laurier Government*, Montreal, 1908.

Anon., *Manitoba and the North-West Territories: Assiniboia, Alberta and Saskatchewan*, New York, 1899.

Artibise, Alan, *Winnipeg: A Social History of Urban Growth 1874-1914*, Montreal, 1975.

Bachynsky, Julian, *Ukrainian Immigration in the United States of America*, Lviv, 1914.

Balch, Emily Greene, *Our Slavic Fellow Citizens*, New York, 1910.

Basilian, Frs., *Mundare, Yesterday and Today*, Mundare, 1969.

Berger, Carl, *The Sense of Power: Studies in the Ideals of Canadian Imperialism 1867-1914*, Toronto, 1973.

Biletsky, L., *Ukrainian Pioneers in Canada, 1981-1951*, Winnipeg, 1951.

Blue, John, *Alberta Past and Present: Historical and Biographical*, Vol. 1, Chicago, 1924.

Bodnar, John E., ed. *The Ethnic Experience in Pennsylvania*, Lewisburg, 1973.

Borovyk, Mykhailo, *The Ukrainian-Canadian Press and its Significant Role in the Ukrainian Minority in Canada*, Munich, 1977.

Bozyk, P., *History of Ukrainian Emigration to Canada from 1890 to 1930*, 1930.

Bradwin, Edmund, *The Bunkhouse Man: A Study of Work and Pay in the Camps of Canada, 1903-1914*, Toronto, 1972.

Budka, Nykyta, *Pastoral Letter: The Need for Organization*, Winnipeg, 1913.

Burko, Vasyleva, *Vasyl's History*, Prudentohill, 1963.

Bychynsky, Z., *History of Canada*, Winnipeg, 1928.

Chyz, Yaroslaw J., *The Ukrainian Immigrants in the United States*, Scranton, 1940.

Citroen, H.A., *European Emigration Overseas Past and Future*, The Hague, 1951.

Connor, Ralph, *The Foreigner*, Toronto, 1909.

Conservative Party, *A Session's Disclosures: Some Transactions of the Laurier Administration Exposed in the Session of 1906*, Ottawa, 1906.

Corbett, David C., *Canada's Immigration Policy: A Critique*, Toronto, 1957.

Dafoe, John W., *Clifford Sifton in Relation to his Times*, Toronto, 1931.

Daly, George Thomas, *Catholic Problems in Western Canada*, Toronto, 1921.

Darcovich, William, *Ukrainians in Canada: The Struggle to Retain their Identity*, Ottawa, 1967.

Davidson, G.A., *Ukrainians in Canada: A Study in Canadian Immigration*, Montreal, 1947.

Dawson, C.A., *Group Settlement: Ethnic Communities in Western Canada*, Toronto, 1936.

Dmytriw, Rev. Nestor, *Traveller's Memoirs*, Vol. 1, Winnipeg, 1972.

Ehrlich, Richard L., ed., *Immigrants in Industrial America, 1850-1920*, Charlottesville, 1977.

England, Robert, *The Central European Immigrant in Canada*, Toronto, 1929.

_____, *The Colonization of Western Canada: A Study of Contemporary Land Settlement, 1896-1934*, Toronto, 1936.

Fitzpatrick, Alfred, *Handbook for New Canadians*, Toronto, 1925.

Fowke, V.C., *The National Policy and the Wheat Economy*, Toronto, 1957.

Franko, Ivan, *Tvory* (Works), Vol. 19, Kiev, 1956.

Gerus, O.W., et al., eds., *The Jubilee Collection of the Ukrainian Free Academy of Sciences in Canada*, Winnipeg, 1976.

Gimli Women's Institute, *Gimli Saga: The History of Gimli, Manitoba*, Gimli, 1975.

Greene, Victor R., *The Slavic Community on Strike: Immigrant Labor in Pennsylvania Anthracite*, Notre Dame, 1968.

Gregorovich, Andrew, *Chronology of Ukrainian Canadian History*, Toronto, 1974.

Halich, Wasyl, *Ukrainians in the United States*, New York, 1970.

Hedges, James B. *Building the Canadian West: The Land and Colonization Policies of the Canadian Pacific Railway*, New York, 1939.

Hobart, C.W., *Persistence and Change: A Study of Ukrainians in Alberta*, Edmonton, 1966.

Honcharenko, A., *Memoirs*, Edmonton, 1965.

Humeniuk, Peter, *Hardships and Progress of Ukrainian Pioneers: Memoirs from Stuartburn Colony And Other Points*, Steinbach, n.d.

Hunchak, N.J., *Canadians of Ukrainian Origin: Population*, Winnipeg, 1945.

Innis, Harold A., *Settlement and the Mining Frontier*, Toronto, 1936.

_____, *Industrialism and Settlement in Western Canada*, Cambridge, 1928.

_____, *A History of the Canadian Pacific Railway*, London, 1923.

Isajiw, W.W., ed., *Identities: the Impact of Ethnicity on Canadian Society*, Toronto, 1977.

_____, ed., *Ukrainians in American and Canadian Society*, Jersey City, 1976.

Ivanchuk, Mykhailo, *History of Ukrainian Settlement in the Gimli Area*, Winnipeg, 1975.

Kachor, A., *Role of "Prosvita" in the Economic Development of Western Ukraine*, Winnipeg, 1960.

Karmansky, Petro, *Among Kin in South America*, Kiev, 1922.

Kaye, Vladimir J., *Dictionary of Ukrainian Canadian Biography: Pioneer Settlers of Manitoba, 1891-1900*, Toronto, 1975.

_____, *Early Ukrainian Settlements in Canada 1895-1900: Dr. Josef Oleskiw's Role in the Settlement of the Canadian Northwest*, Toronto, 1964.

Kazymyra, Bohdan, *Achievements of Metropolitan A. Sheptytskyj*, Toronto, 1958.

_____, *First Basilian in Canada*, Toronto, 1961.

Keywan, Zonia, and Martin Coles, *Greater Than Kings: Ukrainian Pioneer Settlement in Canada*, Montreal, 1977.

Kobzey, Toma, *On the Thorny Way and Crossroads: Memoirs of Fifty Years in Canada*, Vols. 1 and 2, Scranton, 1972.

Kostash, Myrna, *All of Baba's Children*, Edmonton, 1977.

Kovacs, Martin L., ed., *Ethnic Canadians: Culture and Education*, Regina, 1978.

Koziak, Brother Methodius, *Ukrainian in Saskatchewan Schools*, Toronto, 1976.

Krat, Pavlo, *Ukrainian Antiquity*, Toronto, 1950.

_____, *After the Sunrise*, Toronto, 1918.

_____, *When Will It Be Better*, Winnipeg, 1921.

Krawchuk, Peter, *On New Lands: Pages from the Life, Struggles and Creative Work of Ukrainian Canadians*, Toronto, 1958.

Kyrlenko, Orest, *Ukrainians in America*, Vienna, 1916.

Levitsky, K., *History of the Political Ideas of the Galician Ukrainians from 1848 to 1914*, 2 vols., Lviv, 1929.

Luhovy, O., *Homeless Children of the Steppe*, Edmonton, 1946.

Lumsden, James, *Through Canada in Harvest Time: A Study of Life and Labour in The Golden West*, London, 1903.

Mackintosh, W.A., *Prairie Settlement: The Geographical Setting*, Toronto, 1934.

Magrath, C.A., *Canada's Growth and some Problems Affecting It*, Ottawa, 1910.

Manning, Clarence, *Outline of Ukrainian History*, Winnipeg, 1964.

Marunchak, M.H., *The Ukrainian Canadians: A History*, Winnipeg, 1970.

_____, ed., *Two Documents of the Ukrainian Catholic Church, 1911-1976,* Winnipeg, 1977.

May, Arthur, *The Hapsburg Monarchy, 1867-1914,* Cambridge, 1960.

McCormack, A. Ross, *Reformers, Rebels and Revolutionaries: The Western Canadian Radical Movement, 1899-1919,* Toronto, 1977.

Narizhnyi, Symon, *Ukrainian Emigration: Cultural Work of the Ukrainian Emigration Between the Wars,* Prague, 1942.

Nimchuk, Ivan, *Beginnings of Organizational Life of Canadian Ukrainians,* Edmonton, 1952.

_____, *Ukrainians in British Columbia,* Edmonton, 1953.

Palmer, H., ed., *The Settlement of the West,* Calgary, 1977.

Paluk, W., *Canadian Cossacks: Essays, Articles and Stories on Ukrainian-Canadian Life,* Winnipeg, 1943.

Panchuk, John, *Bukovynian Settlements in Southern Manitoba (Gardenton Area),* Battle Creek, 1971.

Piniuta, Harry, *Land of Pain, Land of Promise: First Person Accounts by Ukrainian Pioneers, 1891-1914,* Saskatoon, 1978.

Potrebenko, Helen, *No Streets of Gold: A Social History of Ukrainians in Alberta,* Vancouver, 1977.

Preston, W.T.R., *My Generation of Politics and Politicians,* Toronto, 1927.

Regehr, T.D., *The Canadian Northern Railway: Pioneer Road of the Northern Prairies, 1895-1918,* Toronto, 1976.

Robin, Martin, *The Rush for the Spoils: The Company Province, 1871-1933,* Toronto, 1972.

Rountree, G.M., *The Railway Worker: A Study of Employment and Unemployment Problems of the Canadian Railways,* Toronto, 1936.

Rudnytsky, I.L. ed., *Mykhailo Drahomanov: A Symposium and Selected Writings,* New York, 1952.

Scott, W.L., *The Ukrainians, Our Most Pressing Problem,* Toronto, 1931.

Shanin, Teodor, *Peasants and Peasant Societies: Selected Readings,* Middlesex, 1971.

Sheptytsky, A., *For Canadian Ruthenians,* Zhovkva, 1911.

Sherbinin, M.A., *The Galician Dwelling in Canada and their Origin,* Winnipeg, 1906.

Shortt, Adam and Arthur G. Doughty, eds., *Canada and Its Provinces,* Toronto, 1914.

Skwarok, J., *The Ukrainian Settlers in Canada and their Schools with Reference to Government, French Canadian and Ukrainian Missionary Influences, 1891-1921,* Toronto, 1959.

Stechishin, Julian, *History of Ukrainian Settlements in Canada,* Toronto, 1975.

_____, *Twenty-five Years of the P. Mohyla Ukrainian Institute in Saskatoon,* Winnipeg, 1945.

Stevens, G.R., *Canadian National Railways,* Toronto, 1963.

Svarich, Petro, *Memoirs, 1877-1904,* Winnipeg, 1976.

Swyripa, Frances, *Ukrainian Canadians: A Survey of their Portrayal in English-Language Works,* Edmonton, 1978.

Tesla, Ivan, *Ukrainian Population in Canada,* Toronto, 1968.

Trosky, Odarka, *The Ukrainian Greek Orthodox Church in Canada,* Winnipeg, 1968.

Ukrainian Pioneers Association of Alberta, *Ukrainians in Alberta,* Edmonton, 1975.

Vucinich, Wayne S., ed., *The Peasant in Nineteenth Century Russia,* Stanford, 1968.

Willcox, Walter F., *International Migrations,* Vol. 1, New York, 1969.

Woycenko, O., *The Annals of Ukrainian Life in Canada,* 4 vols., Winnipeg, 1961-69.

Yasnovsky, Pylyp, *Under Native and Foreign Sky: Pioneer Memoirs,* Buenos Aires, 1961.

Yastremsky, T.A., *Political Development of Canadian Ukrainians During the Last 46 Years of their Presence in Canada,* Winnipeg, 1946.

Yuzyk, Paul, *The Ukrainians in Manitoba: A Social History,* Toronto, 1953.

3. Theses

Anderson, Alan Betts, "Assimilation in the Block Settlements of North-Central Saskatchewan," Ph.D., University of Saskatchewan, 1972.

Avery, Donald H., "Canadian Immigration Policy and the Alien Question, 1896-1919: The Anglo-Canadian Perspective," Ph.D., University of Western Ontario, 1973.

Bilash, B.N., "Bilingual Public Schools in Manitoba, 1897-1916," M.Ed., University of Manitoba, 1960.

Breen, David H., "The Canadian West and the Ranching Frontier, 1875-1922," Ph.D., University of Alberta, 1972.

Byrne, T., "The Ukrainian Community in North Central Alberta," M.A., University of Alberta, 1937.

Cameron, John D., "The Law Relating to Immigration to Canada, 1872-1914," Ph.D., University of Toronto, 1945.

Chisick, Ernie, "The Development of Winnipeg's Socialist Movement, 1900-1915," M.A., University of Manitoba, 1972.

Corbett, D.C., "A Study of Factors Governing Canada's Absorption of Immigrants, 1867-1914," M.A., University of Toronto, 1949.

Dubinski, W., "History of Ukrainians in the Sudbury Basin," M.A., University of Western Ontario, 1962.

Emery, George, "Methodism on the Canadian Prairies, 1896-1914," Ph.D., University of British Columbia, 1970.

Hall, David John, "The Political Career of Clifford Sifton, 1896-1905," Ph.D., University of Toronto, 1973.

Golden, H., "Western Canadian Immigration: The Operation of Laws of Naturalization and Canadianization," Ph.D., Harvard University, 1928.

Ivens, William, "Canadian Immigration," M.A., University of Manitoba, 1909.

Lehr, John Campbell, "Ukrainian Rural Settlement in the Prairie Provinces, 1891-1914," Ph.D., University of Manitoba, 1978.

Lishchynsky, Andrew, "Msgr. Nicetus Budka and the Ukrainian Immigrants in Canada, 1912-1919," M.A., University of Ottawa, 1955.

Martynowych, Orest, "Village Radicals and Peasant Immigrants: The Social Roots of Factionalism Among Ukrainians in Canada, 1896-1918," M.A., University of Manitoba, 1978.

Mitchner, E. Alyn, "William Pearce and Federal Government Activity in Western Canada, 1882-1904," Ph.D., University of Alberta, 1971.

Morrison, Jean, "Community and Conflict: A Study of the Working Class and its Relationship at the Canadian Lakehead, 1903-1913," M.A., Lakehead University, 1974.

Owram, Douglas Robb, "The Great North West: The Canadian Expansionist Movement and the Image of the West in the Nineteenth Century," Ph.D., University of Toronto, 1976.

Palmer, H., "Responses to Foreign Immigration: Nativism and Ethnic Tolerance in Alberta, 1880-1920," M.A., University of Alberta, 1971.

Stevens, R.C., "Western Canadian Immigration in Sir Clifford Sifton's Time," M.A., University of Western Ontario, 1963.

Udod, Hryhory, "Julian W. Stechishin: His Life and Work," M.A., University of Saskatchewan, 1974.

Yuzyk, P., "The History of the Ukrainian Orthodox Church in Canada," Ph.D., University of Minnesota, 1958.

_____, "The History of the Ukrainian Catholic (Uniate) Church in Canada," M.A., University of Saskatchewan, 1948.

INDEX